KV-177-001

FRANCIS WARNER'S POETRY
A CRITICAL ASSESSMENT

By the same author

Francis Warner and Tradition

FRANCIS WARNER'S POETRY:
A Critical Assessment

Glyn Pursglove

COLIN SMYTHE
Gerrards Cross, 1988

Copyright © 1988 by Glyn Pursglove

All rights reserved

First published in 1988 by Colin Smythe Limited,
Gerrards Cross, Buckinghamshire

British Library Cataloguing in Publication Data

Pursglove, Glyn, 1947–
Francis Warner's poetry: a critical
assessment.
1. Poetry in England. Warner, Francis.
Critical studies
I. Title
821'.914

ISBN 0-86140-271-5

Distributed in North America by Dufour Editions Inc.
P.O. Box 449, Chester Springs, PA 19425

Produced in Great Britain
Phototypeset by Textflow Services Ltd., Belfast
and printed and bound by Billing & Sons Ltd., Worcester

For
Three Graces:
Parvin, Valeh, Lalle.

Contents

Preface

In the following study I have attempted to provide a guide to the body of work contained in Francis Warner's *Collected Poems, 1960-1984*, and in his two verse plays *Moving Reflections* (1983) and *Living Creation* (1985).

Francis Warner's work is marked by its independence of contemporary literary fashions. It has an integrity of personal vision, and it responds to patterns of literary history larger and more embracing than those of the last twenty-five years. Unlike most (though not of course all) of his contemporaries, Warner is a poet whose work is 'traditional' in the sense explored by T.S. Eliot in his famous essay on 'Tradition and the Individual Talent'. Warner's work, that is to say, is written out of a fully developed historical sense, that sense which, to quote Eliot, 'compels a man to write not merely with his own generation in his bones, but with a feeling that the whole of the literature of his own country has a simultaneous existence and composes a simultaneous order'. A parallel historical sense is required of us as readers. Given such a sense, observes Eliot, 'we shall often find that not only the best, but the most individual parts of [a poet's] work may be those in which the dead poets, his ancestors, assert their immortality most vigorously'. It is a reading based on such premises that I have sought to offer here—an assessment of Warner's poetry which starts from Eliot's assertion that 'no poet, no artist of any art, has his complete meaning alone. His significance, his appreciation is the appreciation of his relation to the dead poets and artists'.

Certain dead poets and artists assert their immortality with particular vigour in Warner's work. Shakespeare is perhaps too natural and inevitable a case to need much discussion here. Warner has not been afraid to conduct a kind of 'dialogue' with Shakespeare in works such as his *Experimental Sonnets*. This is not hubris; rather it is a recognition that since such a presence cannot be evaded it had better be

ix

recognized and handled creatively, rather than allowed merely to overshadow. Marlowe is a less inevitable, but thoroughly vigorous presence. Warner's creative imagination has frequently drawn upon *Dr. Faustus*, locating and articulating itself by reference to Marlowe's masterpiece. The following chapters illustrate and analyse some such cases. Faustus' career was of 'four and twenty years' lived 'in all voluptuousness'; twenty-four years lived between the conflicting awarenesses of Hell and Heaven, damnation and salvation, years emblematic both of the grandeur and the trivial absurdity of human endeavour. Warner's *Collected Poems* are the poems of twenty-four years (1960-84); their prefatory poem has twenty-four lines. The tensions and polarities that characterize the poems are those of Marlowe's play; the abiding awareness is of both human splendour and human insignificance. Marlowe's work is a tragedy of damnation, and though the play is a recurrent and informing presence in Warner's work, we must not imagine that Marlowe's view of things is merely reiterated in the twentieth-century poet. One will find few traces of Warner's Christian neo-Platonism in Marlowe. Marlowe, after all, is but one of the dead poets whose voices are to be heard afresh in Warner's work. Marlowe's presence is balanced by that of Ficino and Spenser, above all by that of Virgil. Virgil's Fourth Eclogue, with its celebration of social and individual harmony, and its prophecy of renewal, asserts itself repeatedly in the texture of Warner's imagination. In the plays renewal asserts itself in the midst of destruction—though without any simple or cosy assumption that the two forces can always be readily distinguished. In the lyrical poems love stands in antithesis to the lustful and the loveless. Love, in all of Warner's work, is the medium of renewal.

I have chosen to let each of the following chapters stand as a more or less independent study of the work(s) with which it deals. I have not overburdened these studies with cross-references, or with lengthy comparisons and contrasts between works. Nor, of course, have I sought to identify or comment upon all the ways in which Warner's work is the product of the kind of historical sense outlined above. To have done so would have been to risk making the poems and plays sound pedantic. That would do them a great disservice. My aim has not been to provide an exhaustive study of sources and influences, but to offer some guidelines which might act as an invitation to the reader to explore some of the most rewarding and individual poetry of the last quarter-century.

For their advice and knowledge I owe debts of gratitude to my colleagues Katie Jones, Johanna Proctor and Mark Love-ridge. For their help thanks are due to Chris Smith and Sheila Gordon-Rae and, above all, to my wife, who by her patience and wisdom has made this, as so much else, possible.

CHAPTER 1

Lyrics

In a very perceptive review of Francis Warner's *Collected Poems*[1] William Oxley drew attention to an interaction which is at the heart of Warner's work. That work is, on the one hand, 'academic' and thoroughly traditional; on the other, the voice of the poems is very individual, and above all lyrical. Oxley's judgement was that 'there is nothing in this volume that does not sing, nothing that does not define a poem as "song"', and he spoke of the poet as 'an academic insider who sings with a lark-like freedom'. In Warner's shorter poems the reader is frequently made aware both of the poet's consciousness of his predecessors, and of his own innate ability to 'sing'. At times the 'academic' predominates, or since that phrasing may be taken as necessarily derogatory, let us say that the individual poem is thoroughly conditioned by its predecessors, and the reader's pleasure in it will in part depend upon his awareness of its relationship to the tradition. Take, for example, 'My Patient Pen', which first appeared in *Early Poems* in 1964:

> My patient pen, help me in this,
> Shape out these thoughts that break my bliss
> In brine, make words to woo her heart;
> Be courtier for her angry kiss:
> Do this for me; I have no art.

> For all my skills in rhyme are numb,
> These tears have paralysed all dumb;
> She rates them insubstantial, vain,
> Having no faith in times to come:
> My silent pen, win her again.

> But what are words when faith is fled?
> And what is truth when trust is dead?
> Is there an art to recreate
> Such joy, when cruel words are said?
> Unkernel tenderness from hate.

1

And do not write your lines in ink,
Nor in this salt that makes me blink,
But use my blood; yes, take my all,
My eyesight, if it make her think
And know my heart is at her call.

Blood, sight and heartbreak, pain and fear,
My pen, say nothing is too dear,
Although she mock with curt retort.
What can I do to make her care?
The cry of every bird that's caught.

The sparrow snared by laughing boys,
The fledgeling caged for children's toys,
The eagle trapped in hunter's net,
The shrike, that smaller birds destroys,
Each seeks compassion in regret.

The nodding mole warm underground,
The nested finch and kennelled hound,
The tusky boar strawed in his sty,
Each seeks for hope where fear is found,
Each needs such love; and so do I.

Tell her, brave pen, although she say
Her path must weave another way,
Tell her no other way's for me;
In frost at night or mist by day
My harbour, my life-breath is she.

Come, gentle pen, help me in this,
Shape out these thoughts that break my bliss
In brine, call up your finest art;
Be courier for her angry kiss
And medicine my murdered heart.

The poem is shaped, but not limited, by its relationship to the poetry of Wyatt. One of Wyatt's lyrics in the Devonshire Manuscript is an address to his pen, though with the opposite purpose to that expressed in Warner's poem—which might be regarded as a kind of variation on a theme provided by Wyatt. Wyatt instructs his pen to write no more, to abandon pursuit of the lady; Warner invites his pen to accomplish what he has been unable to, to supplement his own 'baffled' art. Each is a response to a similar situation, but

the quasi-dramatic dialogue of writer and pen works towards
different conclusions. The relationship between the poems
has its formal aspect too, and comparison of the two is
instructive. Here is Wyatt's address to his pen:

> My pen, take payn a lytyll space
> To folow that whyche dothe me chace,
> And hath in holde my hart so sore;
> But when thow hast thys browght to passe,
> My pen, I prithe, wryght nomore!
>
> Remember, oft thow hast me eaysyd,
> And all my payne full well apeaysyd,
> But now I know, unknowen before,
> Ffor where I trust I am dysceavyd:
> And yet my pen, thow canst no more.
>
> A tyme thow haddyst as other have
> To wryght whyche way my hope to crave;
> That tyme is past: withdrawe therffore!
> Syns we do lose that other save,
> As good leve off and wryght no more.
>
> Yn worthe to use another waye,
> Not as we wold but as we maye;
> For ons my losse ys past restore,
> And my desyre ys my decaye,
> My pen, yet wryght a lytyll more.
>
> To love in vayn who ever shall,
> Off worldlye payn yt passythe all,
> As in lyke case I fynd. Wherfore
> To hold so fast and yet to ffall?
> Alas, my pen, now wryght no more!
>
> Syns thow hast taken payn thys space
> To folow that whyche dothe me chace,
> And hathe in hold my heart so sore,
> Now hast thow browght my minde to passe:
> My pen, I prithe, wryght no more![2]

Warner's poem, it will be noted, is in basically the same
stanza-form as Wyatt's—iambic octosyllabics rhyming
aabab. (Two other poems of Wyatt's in the same stanza form
are also strong presences in the background of Warner's
poem—'Suffryng in sorrow in hope to attayn' and 'My lute

awake! perfourme the last'. In the second of these the
address to the lute replaces that to the pen, but again reaches
a conclusion which elects future silence). Wyatt's three
poems in this stanza, like the one quoted in full above, all
involve the repetition of the *b* rhyme from the first stanza,
and the partial repetition of that stanza's final line as a kind of
refrain, in following stanzas. Warner does not imitate this
feature. Wyatt's poems have another formal feature in
common, the re-employment in the final stanza of both the
rhymes of the first stanza and much of that stanza's phrasing.
One example has been given already. Another is provided by
the first and last stanzas of 'My lute awake!':

> My lute awake! perfourme the last
> Labor that thou and I shall wast,
> > And end that I have now begon;
> For when this song is sung and past,
> > My lute be still, for I have done . . .

> Now cesse, my lute, this is the last
> Labour that thou and I shall wast,
> > And ended is that we begon;
> Now is this song boeth sung and past:
> > My lute be still, for I have done.[3]

In Warner's final stanza the same technique is employed, but
again with an individual variation. Warner uses the same
rhyme words as were used in the first stanza, but changes
their order, inverting the two *b* rhymes. In doing so he is able
both to achieve that near repetition of phrasing which we saw
in the examples from Wyatt, and to effect the concluding
change in tone which is also characteristic of his Renaissance
exemplars. Warner's final line, with its emphatic alliteration
and dramatic adjective, has an emotional intensity not
present in the poem's opening stanza.

'My patient pen' is, of course, indebted to Wyatt and his
tradition in more than matters of form. Its stance—the
unsuccessful lover seeking means to win his lady, reflecting
on the possibilities of art and on the nature of his feelings—is
one that we are thoroughly familiar with from courtly love
and Renaissance poetry. There is much in the diction which

locates Warner's poem in this tradition. The pen is a 'courtier' (and later, the poet hopes, a 'courier'); the lover speaks of the 'bliss' he has lost; he is sick, and only her kiss can 'medicine' his heart. Warner enquires 'what is truth when trust is dead?' much as Wyatt had earlier enquired 'what vaileth trouth?' or, by it 'to take payn?'[4] Here are tears of salt. Wyatt addresses himself to

> ye salt teares againe my will eche nyght
> That are with me when fayn I would be alone.[5]

The 'murdered heart' of Warner's lover-poet is close kin to that of Wyatt in a poem from *Tottel's Miscellany* which carries the title 'The lover blameth his love for renting of the letter he sent her'. It opens thus;

> Suffised not, madame, that you did teare
> My wofull hart, but thus also to rent
> The weping paper that to you I sent,
> Wherof eche letter was written with a teare.[6]

Perhaps she found it, to borrow words from Warner's poem, 'insubstantial, vain'? The poetic situations, indeed, are very similar, even if Warner's lover-poet instructs his pen to write, not with tears, but with his blood! Yet for all such similarities it would be wrong to think of Warner's poem as a mere pastiche. Wyatt himself would have understood what was happening as an example of the doctrine of imitation in action. Such a doctrine stands, of course, at the very heart of the most characteristic achievements of Renaissance poetry. That the poets of the Renaissance should themselves become the objects of imitation is entirely fitting. Such a relationship does, though, run counter to the most dominant trends of modernist art. In a brilliant series of essays[7] Guy Davenport has shown how the modernist movement can be characterized by what one might call its refusal of the Renaissance, its avoidance of the classical patterns which typify the Renaissance. Davenport finds the key to modernism in the archaic, the pre-classical:

If we say, as we can, that the archaic is one of the great inventions of the twentieth century, we mean that as the first European renaissance looked back to Hellenistic Rome for a range of models and symbols, the twentieth century has looked back to a deeper past in which it has imagined it sees the very beginnings of civilization. The Laocoön was Michelangelo's touchstone; the red-stone *Kouros* from Sounion was Picasso's. What is most modern in our time frequently turns out to be the most archaic. The sculpture of Brancusi belongs to the art of the Cyclades in the ninth century B.C. Corbusier's buildings in their cubist phase look like the white clay houses of Anatolia and Malta. Plato and Aristotle somehow mislaid the tetrahedron from among Pythagoras's basic geometric figures. Recovered by R. Buckminster Fuller, the tetrahedron turns out to be the basic building block of the universe . . . We can now see how Pound proceeded to study and imitate the earliest Greek poetry, the earliest Italian, the earliest Chinese. Pound culminated his long career by translating the Chinese *Book of Odes*, the first poems of which are archaic folksongs collected by Confucius . . . One definition of *modern* is a renaissance of the archaic (as *the* Renaissance was a reaching back to Hellenism, to Rome, to a ripened civilization rather than to the green springtime of that same civilization).[8]

It is in his preference for the models of the Renaissance, and through them those of classical poetry, that Warner's position outside the mainstream of modernism is determined. Of course Renaissance poetry has not been without its influence on twentieth-century poetry. One thinks of Ivor Gurney's lyrics which grow unmistakably out of Elizabethan song; or of A.D. Hope's creative manipulation of the forms and tones of seventeenth-century love poetry. Donne, of course, has had his imitators, but it is the line that runs through Spenser, Blake and Yeats which is most important in Warner's work.

The Spenserian stanza, the pseudo-Ovidian epyllion, the song, the sonnet and the sonnet sequence are the forms which Warner's poetry most typically employs—all of them quintessentially Renaissance forms. It is no coincidence that one of his collections should have been named *Madrigals*. His most characteristic subjects are the high poetic common-places of the Renaissance—love and death. The Renaissance's conception of one of poetry's chief purposes as the praise of the worthy is extensively reflected in his poetry. If

that poetry has a single dominant philosophy it is the
Christian neo-Platonism of the Renaissance.

One of the poems in Warner's first collection, *Early Poems*
of 1964, considers the poet's unknown future and in doing so
recognizes only two certainties, the 'Two Things' of its title:

> I do not know the way my life will go,
> Or whether hopes speak true;
> Whether old age will be the after-glow
> Of spirit blazing through
> This cabinet of clay
> That final day:
>
> Or whether, forced by threadbare circumstance,
> I'll stunt these inmost thoughts
> In midnight sweat of mercenary glance —
> The scrawled reports
> On volumes new
> For rushed review.
>
> Whether the armies and the kingcups fall,
> Or nests and daisies perish from this land,
> Whether the owls or politicians call,
> Demand my hand,
> I know that I
> Must love, and die.

A simultaneous awareness of these 'two things' marks the
best of Warner's lyrics, a sense of the mutability of things,
once again akin to one of the dominant notes of Renaissance
poetry. It is the initial premise of one 'Lyric':

> Cliffs and forest pass away,
> Towers and palaces decay,
> Soon we too will end our day
> In dust.
>
> Brief the rose upon its stem,
> Briefer still the snowflakes' den,
> Briefest, sick desires of men
> Soon past.

The same awareness is at the heart of another poignant
'Lyric', elegant and grave in its simplicity:

Time passes,
Youth flies away;
The greenest grasses
Soon are hay.

That bunch of straw
Is last year's nest,
And woodworms gnaw
The lavender chest.

Her eyes were brown,
Her lips were soft,
Her cheeks like down
The dew has washed.

We laughed and played
And loved our fill:
Till dusk we stayed
On Madingley Hill.

An acorn grows;
Is felled at last.
The west wind blows,
And the hill stands fast.

The prose introduction to the original printing of *Early Poems* (it is not reproduced in the *Collected Poems*) sees both love and poetry as apprehensions of the eternal in the experience of mutability:

Perhaps the difference between verse and poetry is not unlike that between liking and love. One becomes the other when the commonplace captures the transcendental: and though the emotion takes precedence, the art does have this advantage—it captures for ever the brief moment at which the here-and-now became transfigured.[9]

In the dialogue of 'Venus and the Poet', though, confidence in the power of either love or poetry to defy chance and time seems more than a little strained:

He   Must a circumstantial blow
         Murder what was born to grow
         While the passing wintry days
         Echo 'All decays, betrays . . .'?
         Love and poetry sustain
         Small defence against the rain.

She   Come, leave mutability,
Lie me down beneath this tree;
Surging spring laughs doubts to flight,
Strength increases with delight
Till, where Absence long has lain,
My lover reaps his ripened grain.

It is in the embrace of Venus herself that the consciousness of mutability might be escaped. *Perennia*, reprinted in *Early Poems*, carries as its epigraph some sentences from Edgar Wind's *Pagan Mysteries in the Renaissance*:

Only by looking towards the Beyond as the true goal of ecstasy can man become balanced in the present. Balance depends on ecstasy.

In looking beyond, in those moments 'when the commonplace captures the transcendental', and in song-like affirmation of them, resides the poet's response to mutability's destructive powers. The initial recognition is of the limitations of the 'worldly man's' capacity to discover meaning in the world he occupies:

When the wild
Rose is snapped,
And the child
Caught and trapped,
When the hare
Is crushed in the road,
A mental snare
Starts to corrode.

Love is beyond
The worldly man.
Marriage bond
Of Pot and Pan
Is a pale
Mockery
Lifelong stale
Lechery.

'Love is beyond / The worldly man'. It is 'towards the Beyond' that that man must look who would escape mutability's corrosive snares. Love and poetry are, in Warner's work, linked facets of any such escape:

> By the toccata of this autumn's wane,
> By all this headstrong girasole of leaf,
> By the bare winter truth none will remain
> When the fanged frost has split the frozen sheaf,
> By this fen's ploughed vernacular of weeds,
> I bring you permanence, as all recedes.

We know that in few fleeting years mankind will be
>   no more,
The barrel of humanity run dry, the grain crushed on
>   a granite floor,
We know that in man's evolution lies his fatal flaw.

> Yet, in this empire of necessity,
> Of ravaged autumn preluding the spring,
> Of mock heroic man's effrontery
> Cradling extinction, permanence can sing:
> Season outlives the species, yet is evanescent too;
> Only perception of this fact and human love are true.

The 'truth' perceived is close to the Spenserian sense of a world 'eterne in mutabilitie'[10] and it is in human love that the truth can be known, that the 'beyond' can be encountered.

The experience of that love which is 'beyond the worldly man' is the subject of some of Warner's finest love-lyrics, celebrations of those moments lived in the 'universe of light'.[11] Only in the presence of the beloved does the world have meaning:

> There is no splendour in the sun
> While you are absent from my arms,
> And though I search till day is done
> Remission in oblivion,
> Watching the busy crowd go past,
> Driving the brain, callousing palms,
> No high philosophy rings true
> Nor can contentment come, till you
> Bring peace of mind, and rest at last.

The world transformed here by love is an urban one, a world where 'the busy crowd' goes past. Elsewhere the poet's response to the natural world is also seen to be dependent on the transforming power of love:

> Within a moment's meeting
> Life is pure again,
> The heather springs its greeting,
> Eyes sparkle with new rain,
>
> The trees and hedgerows glisten
> And pulses race delight,
> Our ears as quick to listen
> As frosty stars at night.[12]

A consequence of the realization that

> Love is imaginative sympathy
> Pure in unlimited intensity[13]

is a 'sympathy' that extends beyond the relationship of the two lovers themselves. That relationship takes on full significance as part of the natural world—'eyes sparkle with new rain' and ears are 'as quick to listen / As frosty stars at night'. In human and natural terms the arrival of love is renewal; it is spring and dawn:

> Your spring despoiled my common winter sense
> And peace and joy took up their residence.[14]
>
> Gentle lady, in your face
> Dances every human grace
> And the sunshine of your eyes
> Breaks the dawn in Paradise—
> If you will not share this song
> A living moment's lost, and gone.[15]

Light, music, dawn, spring—these are Warner's most frequent symbols in his attempt to articulate poetically what he calls

> The highest aspiration that we know:
> The love of God reflected here below.[16]

Such symbols recur in numerous lyrics, and in the later sequences of Warner's love poetry, and become the positive values against which disappointment and bitterness are measured in those poems. Underpinning, and inseparable from, those positive values is a warm sensuality. If 'the love of God' is 'reflected' here below then it is assuredly reflected in human bodies. Part of Warner's 'balance' is located in the perception expressed memorably by Donne:

> Loves mysteries in soules doe grow,
> But yet the body is his booke.[17]

Perhaps nowhere in Warner's lyrical poems does that perception find more beautiful expression than in the following 'Lyric':

> Sweetheart lie still, that's not the sun
> Touching the sky, dawn's not begun;
> Sweetheart lie still, no night is passed
> While we are tight like oysters clasped.
>
> Darling, no daylight streaks the wall
> Over our bodies, no birds call:
> Ghosts of lovers unborn and dead
> Shroud tomorrow from this bed.
>
> Freshest bread needs freshest leaven,
> Saplings will spring up anew;
> Born we are in rain from heaven,
> Rise again in morning dew.

Images of physical intimacy are joined with the poet's characteristic symbols of renewal, cosmic and personal, in an aubade which, like so many of the poems discussed in this chapter, has behind its own distinctively lyrical notes a clear model in earlier poetry. The denial here of morning's arrival echoes the similar denial in a particularly beautiful lyric of the English Renaissance which first appeared in full in John Dowland's *A Pilgrim's Solace* (1612):

> Sweet, stay awhile; why will you rise?
> The light you see comes from your eyes.
> The day breaks not, it is my heart,
> To think that you and I must part.
> O stay, or else my joys must die
> And perish in their infancy.
>
> Dear, let me die in this fair breast,
> Far sweeter than the Phoenix' nest.
> Love raise desire by his sweet charms
> Within this circle of thine arms;
> And let thy blissful kisses cherish
> Mine infant joys that else must perish.[18]

In *Madrigals* in particular Warner's love-poetry is marked by its rich celebration of the sensuous. In 'Womanhood' the joy of the sensuous is again united with the kind of imagery considered above. The redeeming power of love is apprehended in a moment of sensuous innocence:

> Womanhood washed and warm
> Delays before her image in the glass
> Held by her form;
> Deaf to the storm
> That rifts and stabs the full clouds as they pass;
> Only aware of wonder in the air
> Feeling her breasts unbounded and her body bare.
>
> Come, my spring dawn, with sunbreak in your eyes,
> Bud freshly blown, flower that no frosts destroy,
> Beauty incarnate in her own surprise
> And made a woman in a night of joy,
>
> Division yields to dewfall when we play,
> Discords resolve on music of your kiss;
> Your petals turn and open to my day
> And all the storms of life are lost in this.

Elsewhere the same invitation to love and renewal finds room for a wit which does not forget the poet's familiarity with the literary tradition. 'Song' may, in that sense, be 'academic', but the obvious allusion to Donne's Elegy 'To His Mistris Going to Bed' does not disguise the erotic force of the poem; the allusion serves, rather, to suggest that the poet-lover remains in control of his erotic anticipation, rather than becoming a slave of it:

> Lift your hair from the water
>   And lie and let it lap
> Till bubbles rise round nipples
>   To wanton with the tap.
> What modesty's offended
>   When beauty's hid from view?
> What artistry more splendid
>   Than you?

> If cleanliness of body
>   Shows purity of mind,
> Come, let this soap excite you
>   Before, between, behind;
> Let dalliance have leisure
>   And luxury caress
> Till elemental pleasure
>   Possess.
>
> Come to me naked darling,
>   Spread pillows on the bed:
> I break this rarest perfume
>   To bless new maidenhead.
> Come warm, refreshed and trembling
>   With joy that dares delight
> To fathom through dissembling
>   Tonight.

(The same Elegy of Donne is alluded to, to very different effect, in the second stanza of the poem 'For Koinonia':

> I see a dream around you,
> You slip half in, half out.
> I reach to help surround you
> Above, between, about,
> With threads of golden lacework
> Woven in snowflake stars
> Until the dream grows tangible
> And you heal my face of scars.)

The wit and sense of ceremony which characterize the 'Song' discussed above serve to control and order feeling in a way that gives the poem a poise absent from the related 'When You are Mine'; certainly not without poise is the exquisite 'Still Life', a miniature of epigrammatic concision:

> Afternoon sun; she lies upon the bed
> Breast down: ripe apple plucked by ecstasy.

The Donnean allusion in 'Song', the 'image in the glass' in 'Womanhood', and the very title of 'Still Life', all operate to establish the tone of their respective poems; each establishes the woman's body as an object of aesthetic contemplation as

well as the focus of desire. The poet becomes observer as well
as erotic participant, and the poems hold the two impulses in
precise balance. 'The Walled Garden' adapts a deeply traditional motif to achieve a related effect:

> Careful! Now salt is spilt across the board.
> But what's the tracery these grains inscribe?
> Look where the sky's resplendent overlord
> Strokes the walled-garden sunbather his bride.
> See how she lies: her hands beneath her head
> One knee half-raised to part the warming beams
> Sultry and young, a breeder gently bred,
> The distillation of ripe nature's means.
> Come, stare no more. No prying eyes may graze
> On innocence that has not learned to cloy.
> Cursed be the man whose moral-surfeit brays
> Sully the living moments of her joy!
> These grains of salt: and memory is stung—
> And this the most disturbing picture sung.

Here the poet's observation is not made as prelude or
postlude to his own erotic involvement. He is much more
nearly a voyeur; the memory thus disturbs. Some distance is
achieved by the very fact that the episode is presented as a
memory; such distance is further emphasized by the second
quatrain's use of the characteristic vocabulary of Shakespeare's *Sonnets* (e.g. 'a breeder gently bred', 'distillation . . .
ripe nature'). Here, though, the detachment thus achieved
does not exist, as it did in the poems discussed above, as a
counterweight to the erotic involvement of the poet. 'The
Walled Garden', indeed, is a poem of exclusion rather than
invitation or involvement. The attempt to make of the
sunbathing woman an object of pure aesthetic contemplation
does not succeed. Observation rouses desire, the eyes inescapably seem to be 'prying', and they seek to 'graze' rather than
to 'gaze'. The figure of a woman (though not, of course, a
nude) in an enclosed garden is a familiar literary motif of the
Middle Ages. It is as such a figure that Palamon and Arcite
first see Emilye in *The Knight's Tale*. In the lyrics of the
Middle Ages the Virgin Mary is a 'close garden of grace',[19] a
title deriving ultimately from *The Song of Songs*: 'A garden

inclosed is my sister, my spouse'.[20] The distance between
The Song of Songs and a modern sunbather secretly observed
is a measure of the poet's recognition of his own incipient
voyeurism here. He cannot continue to gaze without the risk
that he, like the moralist, will 'sully' the girl's innocence.
That she does not know he is there robs his contemplation of
its innocence. Innocence, as poems such as 'Lift your hair
from the water' have suggested, is only possible to mutuality.
In mutual love, indeed, lies the possibility of lost innocence's
restoration.

'Love's Counterpoint' is dated 20th June 1984, and
succeeds the poet's own 'Epithalamium' of the previous
summer. It records the temporary parting of poet and bride,
but not with the kind of anguish characteristic of some of the
earlier love-poems about separation or absence. Separation
here is not exclusion; it is transcended by love. Here the
transforming power of love is not dependent upon physical
proximity. The poem, consequently, has a quality of more
certain, if less rhetorical, assurance than is possessed by any
of its predecessors. Less immediately excited than some
other poems, it speaks of a greater emotional stability. The
title of the poem takes us back to the musical imagery of the
earlier love poems, and perhaps we should place greatest
weight on the word 'counterpoint'. It is in its emphasis on
full mutuality, on the poet and beloved as figures in a
pattern, figures who have only a limited and partial meaning
distinct from that structure, that 'Love's Counterpoint'
strikes one as a kind of perfected refinement of the earlier
love-poems:

> The cliffs divide our song.
> Subject and counter-subject prick their art
>   Like a bee on a girl's breast
>   Shocking and strong,
> We wait astonished, hoping for the best.
> Yet do not grieve for newly-weds apart:
> Tears wash the cheeks but cannot change the heart.

> Ah yes, it's true
> Absence is gilded by first light's fresh hue
> When thoughts of you
> Awake my darkness and make all things new,
> And reuniting is our morning's due.
> Closed eyes can see, even absence makes us one:
> So pauses hold the notes resolved to unison.

(The sustained musical imagery will perhaps awake in the reader the memory that, in the words of the Oxford English Dictionary, 'Clef' was often 'in spelling formerly confused with the various forms of Cliff'). The poem's central motif is the triumph of union over separation, of unison over division. This motif is expressively enacted by the disposition of the poem's rhymes. In the first stanza the rhyme scheme is as follows: *abcacbb*. In the first five lines the 'song' is, indeed, divided. There are no consecutive rhymes. Only in the sixth and seventh lines do we first meet consecutively rhyming lines. They arrive, that is, at exactly that point in the poem at which the poet first affirms that he shares a love superior to the powers of division:

> Yet do not grieve for newly-weds apart:
> Tears wash the cheeks but cannot change the heart.

In the second stanza only two rhyme sounds are employed: *aaaaabb*. The five identical rhymes of the first five lines are poetic emblems of the lovers undivided by their distance; physically apart their hearts are not 'changed', their emotions continue to rhyme. The poem is another dawn, another renewal, like those of earlier poems, but felt and articulated with a greater certainty—with confidence enough, indeed, for the gentle wordplay of 'morning's due'. In the knowledge that 'closed eyes can see' is the assurance of a point of rest, a certainty that the notes are 'resolved to unison'. It is not a poem that Wyatt could have written, and it is not the poem of a poet limited by Renaissance models; nor is it one that could have been written by a poet ignorant of such models.

CHAPTER 2

Pastoral, Elegy and Epithalamium

Francis Warner's work has been marked by the controlled eclecticism with which he has drawn on a great variety of poetic traditions. His dramatic writing has found room both for the modified surrealism and cubism of the (predominantly) prose plays of the *Requiem* sequence and for the relatively conservative blank verse of *Moving Reflections* and *Living Creation*. In his poems he has worked in forms and metres of romance origin (the sonnet, for example) and of classical derivation (such as the pastoral elegy, the epithalamium, the epyllion, sapphics); he has employed native English forms (like the ballad) and exotic forms such as the calypso, the blues and the rubaiyat. This second chapter considers some of the ways in which Warner's work has been conditioned by the models of classical poetry, especially as re-interpreted by the Renaissance.

Plainsong was written in 1962; its epigraph quotes words ('Reapt ere half ripe, finisht ere half begunne') from lines by the Elizabethan poet Thomas Edwards upon the recently dead Sir Philip Sidney:

> And thou Arcadian Knight, earthes second Sunne
> Reapt ere half ripe, finisht ere half begunne.[1]

This epigraph locates *Plainsong* firmly within the tradition of the pastoral elegy that runs from Theocritus and Virgil to Mathew Arnold and beyond. The first Idyll of Theocritus was perhaps responsible for defining the outlines of the genre; its evolution at the hands of such as Bion (in the *Lament for Adonis*) and Moschus (in the *Lament for Bion*—if it is his) makes a fascinating study.[2] In English the tradition is the informing presence behind such poems as Spenser's *Astrophel*, Browne's Eclogue on Thomas Manwood in *The Shepheard's Pipe*, Milton's *Lycidas*, Shelley's *Adonais* or

18

Arnold's *Thyrsis*. Warner makes no attempt to conceal his poem's relationship to such a tradition; indeed, the acknowledgement of that relationship is an essential element in the poem's frame of reference. The occasion for *Plainsong* was the death of

> two warm and living friends
> Wasting in mud and loam: suddenly snuffed
> On reaching manhood.

In an interview published in 1986 Warner explained that 'two of the undergraduates I had been teaching committed suicide within months of each other'.[3] In describing the two as 'wasting in mud and loam' Warner sets up important echoes. The passage remembers, for example, lines from the first Idyll of Theocritus:

> So down the stream
> Went Daphnis: closed the waters o'er a head
> Dear to the Nine.

Theocritus' lines were surely in Milton's mind when he wrote of how 'the remorseless deep / Clos'd o're the head' of Lycidas, and he lay 'sunk . . . beneath the watry floor'.[4] The learned poet cannot forget such lines. To attempt to do so would be the merest *faux-naiveté*. Yet he cannot, either, allow himself to be trapped by such memories; to let that happen would be to settle for academic pastiche. *Plainsong* confronts the dilemma:

> I must not pose, colour or decorate
> And clothe an ugly fact: lament Adonis,
> Or mourn on Lycidas's golden urn.
> As memory grows distortion will encroach,
> And the brute impact of shattering moment on soul
> Borne in the heart alone, but labelled sorrow,
> Will fade: yet while it cuts into my brain
> I'll make a map of torment; bend the verse
> And wrest from it an iron ore of truth
> Stripped of accretions made from imitations:
> Lift up that flap of the brain and journey in
> To grip the bit and bridle of the heart.

The very declaration, of course, has about it a kind of self-contradictoriness. It is like the speaker's insistence in 'A Nocturnall upon S. Lucies Day' (by a repeated use of the first person singular pronoun, and by a rigorous process of self-analysis) that 'I' do not exist; the very declaration constitutes disproof of that which is declared. The poet of *Plainsong* cannot ignore the elegiac tradition—the very declaration that he will not employ it in any straightforward fashion already sets up a relationship between his poem and the tradition:

> I've said I'll strike no attitude—and yet
> Saying that may itself be one more pose
> No truer than those first ones stripped away:
> Or do I like, enjoy the sound of grief
> And say I say I mourn? Away, mind-spider!
> This creeping ivy's curst. I doubt my doubts,
> And meanings have no meaning when intellect
> Battens on raw emotion: one more way
> Creation tries to hide, to shift the burden,
> Seeking a screen in arguments on terms,
> Fleeing the core and crawling round the skin
> Wide of the bitter heritage within.

The ivy is doubtless that of the poet's home—the poem is dated from 'Alpha Cottage, Trumpington'; it is also, of course, the labyrinthine self-reflexivity of the poet's mind. We should not, though, forget that it is also one of the symbolic evergreens of pastoral elegy appearing, for example, in the opening lines of *Lycidas*. Unable to ignore the tradition, refusing to be confined by it, the poet can at least determine to

> bend the verse
> And wrest from it an iron ore of truth.[5]

Plainsong presents, consequently, a distorted image of the materials of pastoral elegy. Its use of centre-rhyme, in those parts of the poem which are in twelve-line stanzas, lends to its formality a matching obliquity. Milton can look back to a time of pastoral content when he and King shared the pleasures of the 'homely slighted Shepherds trade', and register the destruction of those pleasures in King's death:

> Together both, ere the high Lawns appear'd
> Under the opening eye-lids of the morn,
> We drove a field, and both together heard
> What time the Gray-fly winds her sultry horn,
> Batt'ning our flocks with the fresh dews of night,
> Oft till the Star that rose, at Ev'ning, bright
> Toward Heav'ns descent had slop'd his westering wheel.
> Mean while the Rural ditties were not mute,
> Temper'd to th'Oaten Flute,
> Rough *Satyrs* danc'd, and *Fauns* with clov'n heel,
> From the glad sound would not be absent long,
> And old *Damætas* lov'd to hear our song.
> But O the heavy change, now thou art gon,
> Now thou art gon, and never must return![6]

Refusing the diction of the pastoral elegy, *Plainsong* confronts a similar experience in language which registers in more naturalistic fashion the poet's immediate situation:

> Then, all was fresh. Imagination clothed
> Each fact of nature in its simplest joy.
> No irons had been heated for the soul;
> No snare or mesh had sprung and trapped the pulse
> Each single creature woke inside my heart.
> Now evening blows and sleet begins to fall
> And I must force corroding images
> Away, lest grief becomes a luxury.
> Daylight has nearly gone, yet clear outside
> A cart-track runs; a course that I must take.
> The window's dark. A dead leaf taps the glass.
> I'll drag myself alone into the night.[7]

It is of the very nature of the pastoral elegy in its traditional form that it should register the poet's psychological movement from a sense of loss to his final awareness of the possibilities of renewal and continuity. In *Lycidas* the movement is from 'forc'd fingers rude' and 'berries harsh and crude' to the recognition that '*Lycidas* your sorrow is not dead', and to the almost eager anticipation of the closing lines:

> At last he rose, and twitch'd his Mantle blew:
> Tomorrow to fresh Woods, and Pastures new.

Freshness is restored to the poet's apprehension of the world. Josephine Miles writes of *Lycidas* that it ends with a speaker able to take up 'life on earth again . . . in the light of hope beyond earth, tomorrow, fresh, and new'.[8] Though the terms of reference employed are very different, it is a similar movement towards renewed freshness which shapes *Plainsong*.

Plainsong falls into three distinct phases—as, indeed, does *Lycidas*; we might borrow the terminology of Bonamy Dobrée and Herbert Read, and regard *Plainsong* as a 'symphonic poem' in three movements.[9] Each phase of *Plainsong* is brought to a conclusion by one of the lyrics interpolated within the poem—the transitions being thus marked by lyrics rather as they are between the separate acts in a number of Warner's plays. The first phase therefore occupies lines 1-123; the second runs from line 124 to line 257 and the final phase from line 258-289.

The first phase of *Plainsong* is concerned with the poet's sense of his own impotence in the face of loss. The difficulties and contradictions of the attempt at elegy we have seen already; elegiac art itself seems trivial and pointless, a measure only of human insufficiency:

> Sorrow humiliates, is hard to bear
> Because the mightiest structures of the mind
> Prove groundless; vanish in a puff of smoke;
> And puny man retaliates in grief
> Throwing his weightiest words in the empty air;
> A whistling ant on an orange.

His impotence is reflected, it appears, by nature. He sits alone, listening to 'that creaking movement' of a tree blown by a cold wind. Dated March 1962, the poem exists at the very moment of the spring equinox:

> Tomorrow will be spring,
> Yet grey-white clouds are piling in the sky
> Like down: the snow is staying late this year,
> And dusk soon falls. No proof has come of spring,
> No swarming crowds of peewits in the fields:
> Only this hollow deadness in my chest.

Spring's renewal appears to be denied. In his hollowness, in his loss of responsiveness to the natural world, lies the temptation to let 'grief become a luxury'. He identifies, very precisely, what it is he has lost:

> Then all was fresh. Imagination clothed
> Each fact of nature in its simplest joy.
> No irons had been heated for the soul;
> No snare or mesh had sprung and trapped the pulse
> Each single creature woke inside my heart.

The sense of present lifelessness contrasts with his experience only a few nights ago, when

> the dawn
> Had scarcely touched the sky. Faint, earliest light
> Tipped the trees white and froze each hedge and bush
> With needle-blue of frosted handiwork . . .
> Slowly full day had spread across the sky
> Freeing the water from the chilled spring-well.

Now, though, with 'no proof . . . of spring', the poet's own poetic springs are frozen; his condition might be described, in Coleridgian terms, as one of 'dejection'.[10] The poet of *Plainsong*, like Coleridge in 'Dejection: An Ode', finds his 'genial spirits fail'. In 'Dejection' Coleridge writes out of the temporary loss of his 'shaping spirit of Imagination'; he has, finally, to dismiss excessive self-analysis:

> Hence, viper thoughts, that coil around my mind,
> Reality's dark dream!

In *Plainsong* Warner's opening lines pick up a key word from Coleridge:

> A viper's cored within this apple-world.

Warner's language as he records his sense of what he has lost seems similarly indebted to Coleridge. To say that formerly 'Imagination clothed / Each fact of nature in its simplest joy' is, inescapably, to evoke memories of Coleridge's poem:

> O Lady! we receive but what we give
> And in our life alone does Nature live:
> Ours is her wedding garment, ours her shroud! . . .
>
> Joy, Lady! is the spirit and the power,
> Which wedding Nature to us gives in dower
> A new Earth and new Heaven.[11]

Trapped in the webs spun by his own 'mind-spider' the poet of this opening movement of *Plainsong* has lost the twin and interdependent faculties of Imagination and Joy. In the resolve to escape from 'word-spun distractions' and 'anatomies of grief' the first phase of *Plainsong* comes to a close; the resolve is to go out into the night. Symbolically, the poet chooses to confront darkness, rather than seek to avoid it. All the intellectual consolations he has so far been able to construct for himself are dismissed as 'mere tricks', as 'surface crusts spanning the torn abyss'. Now, in turning from mental conflict to physical assault upon the 'dark extreme', he seeks purgation of the 'bitterness of doubt':

> Cold lashes strike my face. The track is hard
> And slippery; storm wind cuts through my hair
> In rifts, while far away dim city lights
> Beckon me on like fishing-lamps at sea.
> Storms in my mind should cease while icy gusts
> Hold well at bay all but immediate thoughts—
> Dark hollows full of weeds, my sodden hair,
> This bitter rain and massacre of wind:
> Music of elements that scours the soul
> And makes the muscles pull their proper strength.
> This blast will clear my brain and fight the growth
> Of weird embellishments that breed despair.

The lyric which closes this first phase of *Plainsong* presents the writer's inner darkness in the larger, enfolding outer darkness. He is drawn on to the distant lights of the city, his own feverish mind—an 'image echoing-chamber'—casting 'shadows that camp-fire the night'.

The journey begun at the end of this first movement of the poem occupies the whole of its second movement. Leaving his cottage at Trumpington, the poet approaches and enters

Cambridge. There is no comfort to be found there. It is the 'landscape of suffering worse' than the poet's own. The door of a College Chapel offers him some temporary physical protection—there is no suggestion here that the church might offer him another kind of support. He hears an anthem sung. The 'mind-spider' of the first phase of the poem finds an echo in both the architecture and the movement of the choral music:

> From the far end
> Boyish vitality soars to the roof
> Worrying out each sleeping spider's web.
> The climbing words sink down into my ears
> Like silkworms, calling, 'He that shall endure
> To the end . . . ' A leech has slipped down on my sleeve
> And thirds descending end the anthem's tale.

The spiders' webs of his own brain cannot be wholly unravelled by such consolations as the overheard choir has to offer. He remains, for the moment, outside. The words of the anthem come from Christ's eschatological discourse on the occasion of the destruction of the Temple.[12] They have an obvious relevance to the poet's own time of trial, as well as to the apocalyptic imagery of *Plainsong's* conclusion. The city and the chapel offer no point of enduring rest. Driven on alike by inner turmoil and by the 'dragon of night' the poet approaches the fens. Release has yet to be attained; more has yet to be endured before any salvation can be found that might liberate the poet from 'the coffin-leaded laws / That rule this meaningless and cancered globe'. Human markings—like the 'railway-crossing'—are dwarfed and insignificant against the primitive fens. Nearby are the Gog Magog Hills, legendary burial place of two Celtic giants

> who shake their hill
> With sleepless tossing and dream-stifled fears
> And trudge the peat beyond the dyke in storms.

The fens themselves have a primeval energy that stands before and beyond human intellect. For the poet they offer

the possibility of renewal. Such possibilities have their centre
in a spot familiar to him:

> I know a lonely inn where two streams meet
> To make a river, where a goat is tied;
> A ferry moors; and broken window-frames
> Offer their thin resistance to the storm:
> Unsheltered coltsfoot shiver on the bank,
> And bindweed claws and chokes the fishy reeds.
> Now that the wind has held its breath, I'll make
> My way there; try to find pure solitude,
> That silent space of quiet that enfolds
> The vacuum kingdom of the realm within;
> Far from all cry of crippling appetites
> That race exhausted blood about the veins.

As the storm-wind subsides, so the poet's inner turmoil
lessens in intensity. In the 'pure solitude' of the lonely inn
the poet anticipates the opportunity to think of 'past summer
days' spent there, with their catalogue of natural life observed in exact and faithful detail. The remembered observations of the stickleback, weaving, hovering, and flicking its
fin, or

> The vole that held a twig between his teeth
> Keeping it dry aloft, as on he swam
> Steered by his heirloom tail

are records of that earlier time when 'all was fresh', when
'each fact of nature' was 'clothed in its simplest joy' for a
living imagination. The observation was not that of the
objective scientist. It was itself an act of sympathy, the very
obverse of that alienation with which the poem began:

> So often I have knelt to watch a plant
> Or insect, or a tiny animal,
> Zoo-beast or meadow-grazer, fish or fly,
> And known I felt with every living growth
> That feels.

The poet's arrival at the lonely inn actually leads him into an
experience of a very different kind, a difference registered in
the change to ballad measure, and to third-person narrative,

in lines 201-224. The lonely inn of the poem is the Fish and
Duck at Little Thetford, where the Ouse joins the Cam, as
Warner has explained in his later prose account of the poem's
genesis. Arriving at the then desolate inn he discovered that
'there in the middle of a downstairs room in the derelict
building was a woman mourning the death of her son, aged
18-20, who was laid out beside her'.[13] The circumstances and
identity of the mourner and mourned have remained unknown to the writer. The encounter with this strange and
unexplained pair, recounted in forceful ballad language,
marks an important transition in the poet's mental state. In
the encounter is a different response to death, to death by
drowning. The mother's silent ritual has about it a resigned
acceptance which has hitherto eluded the poet. He climbs
into the ferry-boat moored at the inn. Without oars he
abandons himself to the movement of the waters:

> This speeding, wheaten, clay-gold river speeds,
> Carries me on.

He can still interrogate the fate of men in general and himself
in particular. The images employed here (especially the
'whirlwind' of the lyric's first line) locate his questionings
both in the context of the Old Testament prophets[14] and as a
stage in a growing recognition of humanity as no more than
part of a larger elemental pattern:

> The thoughts of love in a whirlwind
> Cry out from the antique shore
> To strike the nerve of the heart of man for evermore.

> The cries of the frozen sparrow
> Pinched in spears of snow
> Waste in the winding winds where the arctic mirrors
> blow.

> Half through our life, half through our dark,
> Gusts on the flickering fen—
> The madness of wind and storm scatters the breath of
> men.

What dawn brings, in the third movement of the poem, is
a vision of a coming purgation, a paradoxically 'midnight

bull', an apocalypse of destruction and new creation. Individual human death and sorrow are placed and measured against, and as part of, a 'universe / In chaos', and a 'holocaust of joy / And hatred, fear, pride, laughter, pain'. The imagery and diction of this final phase of the poem are heavily indebted to a source first pointed out by Suheil Bushrui, the philosophical poems of Empedocles,[15] also an important influence on *Perennia*. There survive some one hundred and fifty fragments of Empedocles' two poems, *On Nature* and *Katharmoi* (or *Purifications*). One of the most sustained analyses of Empedocles' thought is that by D. O'Brien.[16] His opening pages contain a summary which will serve as a background for our consideration of this final phase of *Plainsong*:

> Empedocles' world is made of four elements, earth, air, fire, and water. These are ruled by two forces, Love and Strife. Love is the cause of happiness and unity. Strife is the cause of separation and misery.
>
> These two forces rule in turn. Strife makes the elements many, and so long as the elements are many they are moving. Love makes the elements into a single whole, the Sphere. In the Sphere the elements are at rest. The period of unity and rest under Love lasts for as long as the period of plurality and movement under Strife.
>
> During the period of plurality and movement the elements are first increasingly separated by Strife and then, as soon as they have been fully separated into four distinct wholes, they begin to be increasingly united by Love. In this way the elements pass through varying stages of separation and of combination. In one of these is the world in which we are living now.[17]

A consequence of this theory of cosmic cycle is a belief that Becoming and Annihilation are illusions, rather than realities, no more than incomplete human perceptions of natural processes. To Empedocles words such as 'birth' and 'death' (though he himself uses them) are misleading linguistic habits:

> Of no one of all the things that perish is there any birth, nor any end in baneful death. There is only a mingling and a separation of what has been mingled. But 'birth' is the name men use for this.[18]
>
> Fools—for they have no far-reaching thoughts—who fancy that

that which formerly was not can come into being or that anything can perish and be utterly destroyed. For coming into being from that which in no way is is inconceivable, and it is impossible and unheard-of that that which is should be destroyed.[19]

What O'Brien calls the 'storm of the elements' in Empedocles' cosmogony is what *Plainsong* anticipates in its vision of the 'midnight bull', which has all the power, the simultaneously destructive energy and procreative fertility, of the bull which is the storm-god of Sumerian mythology and was probably its prototype:

> The midnight bull
> Mighty, primeval, bursting from the sky
> To butt this worthless bubble globe aside
> Trampling the fair and circus of mankind
> Like clover in a field: thirsting for death
> His horns rip up the heavens and cyclones swoop
> Wresting up trees and rocks, swamping the land
> Beneath a sheet of sea. Towers tottering
> Bend and crash.

In Empedocles 'all the elements are equal'.[20] In *Plainsong*:

> All things boast equal terms
> Beneath the unchaining elements.

What is promised beyond and through the poem's apocalyptic storm of the elements is fittingly Empedoclean. In the cosmic cycle 'the first mortal objects to be created from the four elements are the Sun, the Earth, the Sky and the Sea, the parts of which are inwardly harmonious'.[21] For the 'wanderer' of *Plainsong*;

> A mighty view of sun, season, earth, sea, and sky
> Bound in one chain of perfect love, joyous that man must die,
> Sends out a silent, ageless oath: that the new will be undefiled,
> And all the archaic world unknown in the joy of their new-born child.

Plainsong's consolations are perhaps more hypothetical and tentative than present and realized. The renewing storm is as yet no more than a 'speck in the north'. If the closing vision has much about it that is Empedoclean, it also implies possibilities beyond the austere dignity of such consolations as are offered by that scheme of things—possibilities which Warner was to explore in later poems and plays. The 'chain of perfect love' anticipates important passages in *Killing Time* and *Meeting Ends*, for example.[22] The closing motif of the 'new-born child' has inescapably Christian implications; it also, of course, returns us to the pastoral world, to Virgil's Fourth Eclogue. *Plainsong* is not contained by the generic possibilities of classical pastoral. Yet it begins and ends there. The poem engages with its material in ways which are fully conditioned by a well-developed sense of the traditional but which are not, finally, to be defined in terms of 'accretions made from imitations'.

The pastoral, in a different form, shapes 'The Passionate Goatherd' and 'Jet Pastoral'. Both belong in the tradition of the pastoral invitation to love. 'The Passionate Goatherd' proclaims its immediate ancestry most obviously:

> Come love with me and be my life
> And be my mistress and my wife
> And in your lover you will find
> Outrageous joy in humankind.
>
> Your bridal gown will be the dawn
> When first light tips the golden corn,
> Before those rougher beams of day
> Have pushed the insects from their hay.
>
> Your veil, to whisper down your cheeks,
> Be spider-spun five-hundred weeks;
> The shoes that clasp your milk-white toes
> Those shells where mermaids find repose,
>
> And breezes round you as you walk
> Will pull each lip to hear it talk;
> Fresh grass about you as you dance
> Peep sideways up with sparkling glance.
>
> Your bridegroom's ring, be Constant Love;
> The daisy-chain Content, your glove;
> And running streams on every side
> Will ripple sunshine down my bride.

If in this dowry there is art
To race your blood and beat your heart,
Come live with me in sweet delight:
And love me, sweet, this very night.

Warner's poem clearly belongs to the long line of poems
prompted by Christopher Marlowe's lyric 'Come live with
me, and be my love'. Perhaps it also reaches back behind
Marlowe to what was presumably one of *his* sources, Catullus
5:

> Vivamus, mea Lesbia, atque amemus,
> rumoresque senum seueriorum
> omnes unius aestimemus assis!
> soles occidere et redire possunt:
> nobis cum semel occidit breuis lux,
> nox est perpetua una dormienda.[23]

Marlowe's lyric first appeared in *The Passionate Pilgrim* in
1599, and was included in the following year in *Englands
Helicon*. The version in *The Passionate Pilgrim* is four stanzas
long; some seventeenth-century versions contain as many as
seven stanzas. The version in *Englands Helicon* is perhaps the
most familiar, however, and it is to its six stanzas that the six
stanzas of Warner's poem seem most obviously to make
reference:

THE PASSIONATE SHEEPHEARDE TO HIS LOVE

> Come live with mee, and be my love,
> And we will all the pleasures prove,
> That Vallies, groves, hills and fieldes,
> Woods, or steepie mountaine yeeldes.

> And wee will sit upon the Rocks,
> Seeing the Sheepheards feede theyr flocks,
> By shallow Rivers, to whose falls,
> Melodious byrds sing Madrigalls.

> And I will make thee beds of Roses,
> And a thousand fragrant poesies,
> A cap of flowers, and a kirtle,
> Imbroydred all with leaves of Mirtle.

> A gowne made of the finest wooll,
> Which from our pretty Lambes we pull,
> Fayre lined slippers for the cold:
> With buckles of the purest gold.
>
> A belt of straw, and Ivie buds,
> With Corall clasps and Amber studs,
> And if these pleasures may thee move,
> Come live with mee, and be my love.
>
> The Sheepheards Swaines shall daunce & sing,
> For thy delight each May-morning,
> If these delights thy minde may move;
> Then live with mee, and be my love.[24]

Englands Helicon itself contains an anonymous variation on
Marlowe's original—'Another of the Same Nature, Made
since'—varying the original invitational format slightly:

> Come live with mee, and be my deere,
> And we will revell all the yeere.[25]

Englands Helicon also includes Ralegh's reply—in the persona of the nymph—to Marlowe's poem. Other imitations of
Marlowe's lyric were not slow to appear. Donne, in 'The
Baite', makes the offered temptations primarily piscatorial,
while retaining Marlowe's opening line and stanza pattern.
Herrick abandons the Marlovian stanza (but not the metre or
the rhyming couplets) in his invitation 'To Phillis to love,
and live with him':

> Live, live with me, and thou shalt see
> The pleasures Ile prepare for thee: . . .
> The soft sweet Mosse shall be thy bed,
> With crawling Woodbine over-spread:
> By which the silver-shedding streames
> Shall gently melt thee into dreames.
> Thy clothing next shall be a Gowne
> Made of the Fleeces purest Downe . . .
> Thou sha't have Ribbands, Roses, Rings,
> Gloves, Garters, Stockings, Shooes, and Strings
> Of winning Colours, that shall move
> Others to Lust, but me to Love.
> These (nay) and more, thine own shal be,
> If thou wilt love, and live with me.[26]

Though Charles Cotton's father was a good friend of Robert Herrick, it was presumably to a different 'Phillis' that Cotton addressed *his* 'Invitation to Phillis':

> Come live with mee and be my Love
> And thou shalt all the pleasures prove
> The mountaines' towring tops can show,
> Inhabiting the vales below . . .
> Thy Summer's Bower shall overlooke,
> The subtill windings of the Brooke
> For thy delight which onely springs,
> And cutts her way with Turtle's Wings.
> The Pavement of thy Roomes shall shine,
> With the Bruis'd treasures of the Mine . . .
> These, and more Pleasures shalt thou proove;
> Then Live with mee, and be my Love.[27]

There were a great many other seventeenth-century imitations and variations. The poem's influence did not, however, end there. Its shadow is clearly to be discerned behind poems of radically different tones and purposes in later periods. It surely stands, for example, behind Clare's harrowing 'Invitation to Eternity', a reversal of Marlowe's pastoral delights:

> Wilt thou go with me, sweet maid,
> Say, maiden, wilt thou go with me
> Through the valley depths of shade,
> Of night and dark obscurity,
> Where the path hath lost its way,
> Where the sun forgets the day,—
> Where there's nor light nor life to see,
> Sweet maiden, wilt thou go with me?
>
> Where stones will turn to flooding streams,
> Where plains will rise like ocean waves,
> Where life will fade like visioned dreams
> And mountains darken into caves,
> Say, maiden, wilt thou go with me
> Through this sad non-identity,
> Where parents live and are forgot,
> And sisters live and know us not.[28]

In our own century Marlowe's poem has served C. Day Lewis as a base on which to build an ironic invitation to another kind of pleasureless non-pastoral:

Come, live with me and be my love,
And we will all the pleasures prove
Of peace and plenty, bed and board,
That chance employment may afford.

I'll handle dainties on the docks
And thou shalt read of summer frocks:
At evening by the sour canals
We'll hope to hear some madrigals.

Care on thy maiden brow shall put
A wreath of wrinkles, and thy foot
Be shod with pain: not silken dress
But toil shall tire thy loveliness.[29]

Warner's 'Passionate Goatherd' belongs more innocently (insofar as an imitation can be innocent) in the Marlovian line, in the Renaissance poetic traditions of the Invitation to Love and the Catalogue of Delights. The 'bridal gown' of dawn, and the veil 'spider-spun five-hundred weeks' remind one of the delights of Drayton's 'Nimphidia' or Herrick's 'Oberon's Palace'. The lady's 'milk-white toes' reflect the attractions of Herrick's Electra:

> More white then are the whitest Creames,
> Or Moone-light tinselling the streames.[30]

It is a very seventeenth-century conceit that the grass should be eager to see the poet's lady:

> Fresh grass about you as you dance
> [will] Peep sideways up with sparkling glance.

The grass here behaves, if a little more modestly, in just the fashion of those plants in the garden where the Amanda of Nathaniel Hookes takes her walks:

> And now what monarch would not gard'ner be?
> My fair Amanda's stately gait to see!
> How her feet tempt! how soft and light she treads!
> Fearing to wake the flowers from their beds;
> Yet from their sweet, green pillows everywhere,
> They start and gaze about to see my Fair.
> Look at yon flower yonder! how it grows
> Sensibly! how it opes its leaves and blows!

> Puts its best Easter clothes on, neat and gay!
> Amanda's presence makes it holiday!
> Look how on tiptoe that fair lily stands
> To look on thee; and court thy whiter hands
> To gather it! I saw in yonder crowd
> That tulip bed of whom Dame Flora's proud
> A stout dwarf flower did enlarge its stalk,
> And shoot an inch to see Amanda walk![31]

Marlowe's passionate shepherd appears not to have marriage in mind; Warner's equally passionate goatherd does, and this conditions the diction of the poem. The distinction governs Warner's rephrasing of Marlowe's opening line—surprising the reader with the appearance of 'love' instead of the expected 'live' as the second word, and then completing a near inversion by replacing 'love' by 'life' at the end of the line and creating the rhyme with 'wife'. The invitation to marriage sets up the particular list of delights to be offered—bridal gown and veil, ring and gloves. The whole, fittingly, is a 'dowry' in Warner's final stanza, instead of the less specific 'delights' of Marlowe's last stanza. Again, though, the word thus displaced teasingly reappears in Warner's penultimate line:

> Come live with me in sweet delight.

'Jet Pastoral', as its title implies, finds in ultra-modern technology, and its human possibilities, a realm of experience and imagery closely akin to the ancient genre of the pastoral. One function of the pastoral is to present us with images of a world of physical and emotional perfection which exists always as human aspiration and possibility but never, it seems, as realized fact. The pastoral poem offers images of harmony and tranquillity, images which 'correspond to, and serve to awaken, the paradigmatic order of the archetypal world'.[32] In doing so it may be an important force in the 'restoration' of the soul, to borrow the language of Psalm twenty-three. The pastoral may also, of course, offer us a fresh perspective on the actual by means of its presentation of the ideal. 'Jet Pastoral' finds in soaring flight a peculiarly modern version of pastoral transcendence. The poet enters a

realm of 'golden, cloudless blue', 'a world beyond the West'
where 'long earth-shadows' are 'lost for ever'. Here is a
'pastoral' land of 'fleecy beds', where 'sheep's wool yawns to
pander eternity', where, indeed, are 'angels picking but-
tercups' and old man's beard is, in ecstatic simultaneity,
both flower and reminder of God. Flight into this pastoral
world makes possible, or perhaps compels, a re-assessment
of earth itself. Wonder is renewed, the world is freshly
discovered and possessed. The joy is communicated in playful image and allusion, the long lines rhythmically buoyant:

> Sunlight plays ducks and drakes with the waves on Santa
>   Barbara bay,
> The sailing boats balloon the wind in mock Armada play;
> The palms crowd like late-flowering dowagers huddled
>   within their coats
> And over all the green-rich hills life like a giant gloats
> Birdsong content and motionless, relaxed beyond all
>   care—
> Lord of the edge of the fecund earth, enticed by Eden's
>   air:
> Even so Cabrillo must have felt sighting this haven mile,
> Storm-tossed Odysseus himself, lost on Calypso's isle.

In the heightened sensitivity of this flight the poet's apprehension of the world itself takes on an erotic quality:

> Now the Pacific lies ahead
>   One half the globe is ours,
> Gentle Japan unfolds her head
> Welcoming as a bridal bed
>   To down-descending powers.

The 'bridal bed' is a fitting metaphor for that sense of
absolute mutuality which is central to the pastoral vision.
The poet and his lady anticipate

> Another continent beyond
> The guessing side of thought

as the aeroplane has taken the poet to 'a world beyond the
West'. It is a continent in which poet and lover, undazzled by
the sun like true 'eagles' brood', will 'like willow-pattern

birds . . . share / Music untold, untaught'. The landscape here finds its image, not in a Grecian urn, but a Chinese plate; in both, though, in the 'pastoral' of art it is no paradox that the sweetest melodies should be unheard, the finest music untold. Even in separation the inhabitants of that 'continent' can hear

> The linking willow-song once more,
> The ancient willow-song's profound
> Flight-haunting poignance wafted to the ground.

The sky, in its 'splendour of art', is here the modern poet's Arcady. In the acknowledgements to the collection *Poetry of Francis Warner* published in 1970, the poet thanked that volume's dedicatee Margaret Kelley, agent for a series of lecture tours in America, as one 'whose encouragement has sustained an English pastoral poet catapulted into the jet set'.[33] 'Jet Pastoral' suggests that these two areas may have rather more in common than is superficially apparent.

In the 'Epithalamium' of 1983 Warner takes up another classical form. Theocritus, again, has claims to be regarded, in his eighteenth Idyll, as the first important Greek writer of an epithalamium. In Latin there are familiar and important compositions by, amongst others, Statius, Claudian and Catullus. The epithalamium was an especially popular genre in the Renaissance, both in Latin (*e.g.* Pontanus, Johannus Secundus, Jean Bonnefons) and in the vernacular (*e.g.* Tasso, Ronsard, Herrick). Perhaps the two earliest original poems in the genre in English are those by Sidney and Spenser. Both have their relevance to the consideration of Warner's 'Epithalamium'. The song of the Shepherd Dicus, for the marriage of Thyrsis and Kala, which appears amongst the Third Eclogues of the *Arcadia*, establishes the frequently pastoral nature of epithalamic imagery. Spenser's *Epithalamion* was, of course, written on the occasion of his own marriage; it provides the most obvious precedent for Warner's composition of an epithalamium for *his* own marriage. Spenser's is one of the greatest formal lyrics in the language, and Warner's is a modest poem in comparison.

There are a few verbal echoes. Warner's poem opens in celebration of 'this girl all in white'; Spenser's bride makes her first appearance 'clad all in white'. Modern scholarship has elucidated the intricate numerological and structural patterns which make Spenser's *Epithalamion* so perfect a 'monument'.[34] In fact, as Alistair Fowler has pointed out, number symbolism is a particularly regular feature in epithalamia.[35] It is entirely fitting, then, that the Envoy of Warner's poem should direct us to the numerological pattern that it, too, contains:

> One rhyming verse for each day of the week
> With sixteen quatrain lines for daylight's hours,
> Then twenty-four lines follow to complete
> Night's clockface while the bridal dark is ours.

The first two lines here are readily explicable in terms of the simple symbolism of temporal numbers, affirmations of the temporal cycles against which the Envoy locates this day of marriage. Seven is also, of course, the number of creation. When Pico della Mirandola produced his *Heptaplus*, a work dealing with the creation, he divided it into seven books, each subdivided into seven chapters. He explains that this structure corresponds to the seven days of creation and that the reader is brought, in every seventh chapter, to the contemplation of Christ and to the peace and happiness made possible by Christ's victory.[36] It is therefore wholly apt and significant that the seventh stanza of Warner's 'Epithalamium' should contain the poem's most ringing affirmation of marriage's redemptive role in human life:

> Later today we'll be scattered away,
> But something is altered for good:
> Here death is defeated by life-giving love,
> And light conquers dark, as it should.

Spenser's *Epithalamion* marks off the sixteen hours of summer daylight (it was written for a June wedding) by changing the wording of the refrain after the first sixteen of its twenty-four stanzas. In the first sixteen stanzas the refrain is phrased positively—'the woods may answer', 'the woods shall answer' and so on. From the seventeenth stanza onwards the refrain is phrased negatively—'the woods no more us answer, nor our echo ring!', for example. In confirmation, the seventeenth stanza opens:

> Now cease, ye damsels, your delights forepast;
> Enough it is that all the day was yours:
> Now day is done, and night is nighing fast.

In Warner's 'Epithalamium' for another summer wedding (the poem is dated 2nd July, 1983) the sixteen daylight hours are marked off by the changes in metre and stanza form which are made after the first sixteen lines of the poem. Again, in confirmation, these first sixteen lines deal with the events of the daytime. Only after the transition at line seventeen do we hear of 'the whole night' (V) and the flowers that 'will delight my girl tonight' (VI). In Warner's poem the remaining eight hours are represented by three eight-line stanzas, so that 'twenty-four lines follow to complete / Night's clockface'. The total number of lines, prior to the 'Envoy', is thus forty. The total, as we should by now expect, is no accident. As Douglas Brooks observes '40 is a nuptial number with important harmonic and generative properties'.[37] Forty is numerologically significant since 'as an elevation of four it is wholeness and totality'.[38] The manner in which this line total is achieved is also significant. The night-time hours are represented in eight-line stanzas, and the number eight was another number especially associated with marriage in the epithalamic tradition.[39] Renaissance epithalamia make particularly frequent use of eight-line stanzas—e.g. Jonson's 'Glad time is at his point arrived' which closes his wedding masque *Hymenaei*, the same poet's 'Epithalamion' for Mr. Hierome Weston and Lady Francis Stuart, Chapman's 'Parcarum Epithalamion' from *Andromeda Liberata*, or Henry Peacham's 'All fears are fled' and Thomas Heywood's 'Now the glad and cheerful day', both for the marriage of Princess Elizabeth in 1613. Other poets were careful to ensure that their marriage poem was made up of eight stanzas—e.g. Donne's 'Hail! Bishop Valentine, whose day this is' and 'The sunbeams in the East are spread', or his friend Henry Goodere's 'Which of you Muses please'. If we include the Envoy then Warner's 'Epithalamium' also has eight stanzas. The disposition of the first forty lines, the main body of the poem, has at least one further numerological significance which should not be overlooked. Again Alistair Fowler's account of the numerological traditions which underlie the patterns of the Renaissance epithalamia is helpful. Fowler points out that division in the ratio 1:2 is a common feature of such Renaissance poems:

> denoting as it does the octave proportion, this ratio would be the obvious spatial correlate to a sentiment of harmonious concord. Moreover, there was an appropriate psychological implication. According to Pico, the diapason was the proportion between the rational and concupiscible faculties in a well-ordered soul. These considerations made the ratio particularly suitable for nuptial songs.

The simplest case is exemplified by Dekker's *Patient Grissil* song, whose 2 stanzas, of very unequal length in spite of their identical refrains, consist of 8 and 4 lines.[40]

Warner's (and Spenser's) division of the hours into sixteen of daylight and eight of darkness obviously mimics this epithalamic ratio. So too does the transition from four-line to eight-line stanzas. That the poem should be brought to a close by a stanza of nine lines has its numerological fitness too. Nine, traditionally, was the number of 'completion, fulfilment'.[41] Martianus Capellanus explains it thus:

> The ennead is . . . perfect and is called more than perfect, since it is perfected from the multiplication of the perfect triad . . . It marks the end of the first numerical sequence . . . The number nine is also the last element of harmony: a tone is produced according to the ratio of eight to nine.[42]

Warner's 'Epithalamium', it can be seen, has some fair complexity of structural patterning, conditioned by an awareness of the conventions of the genre and the numerological traditions upon which earlier authors of epithalamia drew so extensively. Another pattern is apparent in the poem's handling of rhyme. The first two stanzas rhyme *abba*. With stanzas three and four this rhyme-scheme is replaced by a pattern of *abab*. The change corresponds to a transition of thought. The first two stanzas (in enclosed rhyme) deal with bride, groom and bridesmaids. As the poem's focus widens to include the wedding guests, alternate rhyme replaces closed rhyme. As the poem begins with bride and groom, so it returns to them at its close—a further symmetry is effected.

For all its structural subtleties the poem is, in many other respects, relatively straightforward. Its central symbols are familiar from other poems of Warner. That love should be identified with light is no surprise; that it should be seen as part of a cycle of natural growth is a familar enough topos. The wedding takes place 'in a ring of green fields'—the wedding ring externalized, as it were, by the fields that encircle the church. Gifts and giving are recurrent motifs in the poem. The poet's bride is a 'dancing gift' from heaven; the sheep, in an apt and resonantly pastoral gesture, 'stray up close leaving wool on the hedges, / Their gifts for her future'. House-martins, those most domestic of birds, bring song as their gift. Stanza IV, ending, as we have seen, the first major structural unit of the poem, affirms that

> The rice will be scattered, her blossom will glow
> As new garland, and sheaf, and the berry-bright trees,
> And the laughter of friends, and the families grow;
> And our spring-wind will dance on the grandparents'
> knees.

The image in this final line links the marriage and its offspring to the creative (using the word with its full range of meanings) concerns of Warner's *Living Creation*, especially to its analysis of Botticelli's 'Primavera', the myth of which is there explained by Poliziano and the painter himself:

POLIZIANO   . . . Ovid tells how Zephyr, the spring wind,
               Breathed, seized on Chloris—nymph all winter-
               bare—
               And turned her into Spring. 'I who was Chloris
               Now am called Flora.'

SANDRO   Yes. The year's new bride.[43]

In the 'Epithalamium' the gifts of nature and of 'town friends' are, as it were, increased and returned—marriage, like a lens focussing sunlight, is a focus intensifying human and natural growth. The second major structural unit of the poem, ending with stanza VII, acknowledges that the particular moment of focus, which is this wedding celebration, is itself necessarily destined to disappear within the larger movements of time—'Later today we'll be scattered away'. Yet what that moment means can endure, the scattering is of seeds that may take root, and the moment itself can find its eternity in the poem, seeking to provide 'for short time an endlesse moniment'.[44] The wish expressed in the Envoy is that the 'posy of song' should

> live on to sweeten years
> To come, when winter's shears
> Harvest the loveliness about us now—
> Take the pink rosebuds from the bridesmaids' cheeks,
> And the white garland from my darling's brow.

The pastoral imagery which earlier spoke of the moment's perfection serves here to register the inescapable awareness of that moment's transience. The poet offers his 'posy' of song—posy bearing the senses both of 'poesy' (the O.E.D.'s first definition of posy is 'a syncopated form of poesy') and of 'a bunch of flowers, a bouquet'. The beautiful flower imagery of stanza VI is here picked up. The flowers themselves will fade, the posy of song may endure. The ancient association of flowers and poems (implicit in the very word anthology) is invoked. The iconographic and symbolic associations need not, perhaps, be explored in any detail. They are, in any case, subordinate to the larger outlines of the poem, which I have endeavoured to clarify above.

The poems considered in this chapter have illustrated some of the ways in which Warner's poetry acquires meaning and form from its classical models. The poems, evidently, are not the work of an author who feels himself confined and limited by these models. In all the instances we have examined, Warner's poems, insofar as they have a literary genesis, might be said to be only the indirect offspring of Latin and

Greek poetry. The interpretation and development of classical models at the hands of the Renaissance intervene in every case. Warner's own time and society have also left their distinctive marks on the poems; they are by no means merely bookish. These are not, then, simply copies of ancient figures, mere neo-classical statuary. We might better think of them as palimpsests, where the layers of classical, Renaissance and modern inscriptions blur into one very individual texture. A similar effect characterizes *Perennia*.

CHAPTER 3
Perennia

Perennia first appeared in an elegant edition published by the Golden Head Press in 1962. Two years later it was published a second time in the author's *Early Poems*. Of Warner's poems based on classical models, this is the longest. The term 'epyllion' is not one that now seems to be in favour with classical scholars.[1] As the designation of a genre it may only have come into use in the nineteenth century, but it seems as good a way as any of referring to a series of classical and post-classical poems, of the kind discussed by Crump in *The Epyllion from Theocritus to Ovid*.[2] Probably of Alexandrian invention, the epyllia were short (around six hundred lines seems to have been the maximum acceptable length) narrative poems, relating mythological episodes, and usually having a substantial erotic or amorous content. Elaborate and colourful description was a common and important feature. The epyllia of Euphorion and Callimachus are lost, though examples survive in the work of Theocritus. Catullus 64, the *Marriage of Peleus and Thetis*, is perhaps the best known Latin example. One might argue that the story of Hercules and Cacus in Book VIII of the *Aeneid* is a kind of inset epyllion, and Ovid's *Metamorphoses* is clearly much indebted to the genre. It is in the Elizabethan poetry of the 1590's, in poems such as Lodge's *Scillaes Metamorphosis*, Heywood's *Oenone and Paris* or Edwards' *Cephalus and Procris* that the epyllion may first be said to find an English equivalent.[3] A good case can be made out for regarding such later poems as Landor's *Dryope*, Tennyson's *Oenone* or the *Marpessa* of Stephen Phillips as a continuation of the genre in English. It is in such a tradition that *Perennia* belongs. Its employment of the Spenserian stanza naturally aligns it particularly (though not exclusively) with the Elizabethan works in the genre.

The poem's narrative of Perennia and Eros is obviously a variation on the tale of Cupid and Psyche. The earliest literary version of this story is found in the *Metamorphoses* or *Golden Ass* of Apuleius (born c.127 A.D.). Apuleius did not invent the story. Its sources in folklore are now well established, and have been extensively studied.[4] Nor is it only a matter of sources. Analogues have been pointed to in (amongst others) Welsh, Indian, African and Red Indian folktales.[5] Long before Apuleius the story was being illustrated by artists in a variety of media. A fascinating study by Carl Schlam[6] examines representations of the story from the fourth and fifth centuries B.C. onwards, on reliefs, wall-paintings, mosaics, sarcophagi, statuettes and a variety of other locations and objects. The most famous example is the marble sculpture of Eros and Psyche in the Capitoline Museum. This appears to be one of several Roman copies of an original of the second century B.C. A tale with such evidently archetypal force and with such an apparent attraction to very diverse audiences was hardly likely to end its career with its first literary telling by Apuleius. Writing in 1812 Robert Southey could observe that 'the beautiful story of Cupid and Psyche has been represented in every possible form by poets, prosers, painters, sculptors, and opera dancers', and proceed to summarize a version by Calderón in an *Auto sacramental*.[7] Cupid and Psyche long continued to be, as Southey implies, a favourite theme in the visual arts. Raphael's work in the loggia of the Villa Farnesina, most notably 'The Wedding of Cupid and Psyche', stands as the major Renaissance treatment of the theme. Simon Vouet's 'Cupid and Psyche' (c.1615), now in the Musée des Beaux Arts in Lyons, is a delightful and atmospheric piece. Van Dyck's 'Cupid and Psyche' of the 1630's (in the Royal Collection) is a strikingly powerful composition. Such neoclassical sculptors as Canova, Pajou, and Thorvaldsen all returned repeatedly to the subject. Earlier, the Château de Chantilly had been adorned by a stained-glass narrative in its Galerie de Psyché. A more famous French version of the story is perhaps Rodin's 'Cupid and Psyche'. As Southey observes, it is not only the painters and sculptors who have been fascinated by the story. Cupid and Psyche have found incarnations so many and various that we can do no more here than glance at a few examples, by way of illustrating the range of material. There are, for example, Marino's characteristically conceited version in the fourth canto of *L'Adone*; Lully's *Psyché* of 1656, with a libretto to which Corneille, Fontenelle, Molière and Quinault all made contributions; La Fontaine's *Les amours de Psyché et de Cupidon* which appeared in 1669; Thomas Heywood's *Love's Mistris* (1636); Pater's *Marius the Epicurean*;[8] the novels of the Dutchman Louis Couperus; [9] the adaptation by C.S. Lewis in his *Till We Have Faces: A Myth Retold* (1956).[10]

Warner, it will readily be seen, was hardly pursuing originality in his choice of story. Of course, the same could be said of the authors of the Elizabethan epyllia. When Shakespeare chose to write a *Venus and Adonis*, or when Drayton and Shirley approached, respectively, their narratives of *Endimion and Phoebe* and *Narcissus*, they did so, like Warner with *Perennia*, in the full knowledge that their story was one which had been handled by a number of masters before them. In English poetry alone, Warner had had a considerable number of predecessors. It is perhaps surprising that there was not an Elizabethan epyllion devoted to this particular story. Spenser does tell the tale briefly in Book III of the *Faerie Queene*: Cupid's

> true love faire *Psyche* with him playes,
> Faire *Psyche* to him lately reconcyld,
> After long troubles and unmeet upbrayes,
> With which his mother *Venus* her revyled,
> And eke himselfe her cruelly exyld:
> But now in stedfast love and happy state
> She with him lives, and hath him borne a chyld,
> *Pleasure*, that doth both gods and men aggrate,
> *Pleasure*, the daughter of *Cupid* and *Psyche* late.[11]

The first extended narrative in English (leaving aside the highly inventive masque, *Loves Mistris*, produced by Heywood in 1636) appears to be that by Shakerley Marmion. Marmion published his *Cupid* and *Psiche, or an epick Poem of*

Cupid, and his Mistress in 1637 (it includes prefatory verses by Heywood).[12] Marmion's is an admirable retelling of the familiar tale. There have been many later English poetic versions, including ones by Glocester Ridley in 1747 and Mrs Tighe in 1805 (both in Spenserian stanza. Mrs Tighe's version was familiar to Keats), by Hudson Gurney (1799), Thomas Ashe (1864), Willam Morris (in *The Earthly Paradise*, 1868), Lewis Morris (in *The Epic of Hades*, 1877), and Robert Bridges (1886).

The story of Cupid and Psyche has been the subject of allegorical interpretation at least since the sixth-century Fulgentius Planciades, who discussed and expounded the story (along with a great many others) in his *Mythologiarum Libri III*.[13] Fulgentius identifies the King and Queen (parents of Psyche) as God and Matter. Her sisters are the Flesh and Free Will. Psyche herself is the Soul. Venus is Lust and Eros Desire. The 'Mythology: or, Explanation of the Argument' which Marmion places before his poem belongs very much in the line of interpretation established by Fulgentius and will serve well to represent it:

By the City is meant the World; by the King and Queen, God and Nature; by the two elder Sisters, the Flesh and the Will; by the last, the Soul, which is the most beautiful, and the youngest, since she is infused after the body is fashioned. Venus, by which is understood Lust, is feigned to envy her, and stir up Cupid, which is Desire, to destroy her; but because Desire has equal relation both to Good and Evil, he is here brought in to love the Soul, and to be joined with her, whom also he persuades not to see his face, that is, not to learn his delights and vanities: for Adam, though he were naked, yet he saw it not, till he had eaten of the Tree of Concupiscence. And whereas she is said to burn him with the despumation of the Lamp; by that is understood, that she vomits out the flames of desire which was hid in her breast; for desire, the more it is kindled the more it burns, and makes, as it were, a blister in the mind. Thus, like Eve, being made naked through desire, She is cast out of all happiness, exiled from her house, and tossed with many dangers . . . In the separation of several grains, is understood the act of the Soul, which is recollection, and the substance of that act, her forepast sins. By her going to hell, and those several occurrences, are meant the many degrees of despair; by the Stygian water, the tears of repentance: and by the Golden Fleece, her forgiveness. All which . . . being by Divine Providence accomplished, she is married to her Spouse in Heaven.[14]

That fascinating and influential figure Thomas Taylor published in 1795 *The Fable of Cupid and Psyche, Translated from the Latin of Apuleius.* He provided an introduction 'in which the Meaning of the Fable is Unfolded'. The general purpose of the tale is, he suggests, 'to represent the lapse of the human soul from the intelligible world to the earth'. Psyche, of course, is the Soul. Her descent into the valley 'signifies the descent of the soul from the intelligible world into a mundane condition of being, but yet without abandoning its establishment in the Heavens'. Psyche's sisters, in Taylor's interpretation, 'signify imagination and nature, just in the same manner as reason is signified by Psyche'. When Psyche heeds the advice of her sisters 'the rational part, through the incentives of phantasy and the vegetable power, becomes united with impure or terrene desire'. The tasks imposed by Venus are 'images of the mighty toils and anxious cares which the soul must necessarily endure after her lapse, in order to atone for her guilt, and recover her residence in the intelligible world'. Taylor's interpretation is undoubtedly familiar to Warner.[15] We shall return to it later.

Warner's immediate, and chief, source in *Perennia* is Apuleius. *The Golden Ass* contains what its Elizabethan translator, William Adlington, describes as 'the most pleasant and delectable tale of the marriage of Cupid and Psyches'.[16] Warner's version of this 'delectable tale' is a variant rather than an imitation. *Perennia* re-narrates only a small section of the larger arc described by Apuleius' narrative. *Perennia* makes no mention of Psyche's parentage, or, therefore, of her father's consultation of the Oracle of Apollo. In Warner's narrative we (and Perennia herself) are told:

> You have been carried by the wind, unseen,
> And set away from cheering crowds apart;
> For Hespera, the jealous Goddess Queen,
> By you has lost her rule over Man's heart.

In Apuleius, the jealousy of Venus is followed by the Oracular pronouncement:

> Let Psyches corps be clad in mourning weed,
> And set on rocke of yonder hill aloft:
> Her husband is no wight of humane seed,
> But Serpent dire and fierce as might be thought.

Apuleius' narrative of Psyche's exposure on the mountain and of her rescue by the wind is therefore rather different in tone from the abbreviated version of events in *Perennia*:

Then they brought her to the appointed rocke of the high hill, and set [her] hereon, and so departed. The Torches and lights were put out with the tears of the people, and every man gone home, the miserable Parents well nigh consumed with sorrow, gave themselves to everlasting darknes.

Thus poor Psyches being left alone, weeping and trembling on the toppe of the rocke, was blowne by the gentle aire and of shrilling Zephyrus, and caried from the hill with a meek winde, which retained her garments up, and by little and little brought her downe into a deepe valley, where she was laid in a bed of most sweet and fragrant flowers.[17]

In *Perennia* the dominant sense is not so much of escape from looming danger as of punishment by a jealous goddess. In her beautiful valley Apuleius' Psyche finds and enters 'a princely Edifice, wrought and builded not by the art or hand of man, but by the mighty power of God'.[18] Warner's Perennia has no palace in which to make her home; rather she is promised, by 'an ivy-covered oak / Older than all the forest' and gifted with speech, that

> Perennia will live amongst us, free
> To make her peace here. Let her never lack
> Shelter or food, clothing or company.
> When she calls music, echoes will blow back
> Your bird-songs from hill-hollows till they pack
> The sunbeams full of sounds. When she needs food
> Fetch her ripe nuts and let small squirrels crack
> Them for her. Mice, bring hedge-wine newly
>   brewed,
> And birds of prey, protect her as your tender brood.

> These hill-slopes, lady, and this cave are yours,
> Where every night Eros, unseen, will come
> To be your close companion.[19]

Delicious as the promised comforts are, they are of a decidedly different order to Psyche's magical palace with its 'storehouses wrought exceedingly fine, and replenished with aboundance of riches' and its staff of invisible servants. Warner's is a pastoral, rather than a regal setting, a setting introduced previously in the first seven stanzas of the poem. These stanzas introduce the narrator of this particular dream-vision. It is not only in the adoption of a pastoral setting that this early stage of *Perennia* differs rather strikingly from its source in Apuleius. In the Latin narrative Psyche has no such helpful informant as Perennia's oak tree. She moves in a more mysterious world where little or nothing is explained, in a palace where 'though there were no maner of person, yet seemed she in the midst of a multitude of people'.[20] She retires, somewhat afraid, to bed. Apuleius continues, rather baldly:

Then came her unknowne husband and lay with her: and after that hee had made a perfect consummation of the marriage, he rose in the morning before day, and departed.[21]

Perennia's first meeting with her lover is an altogether more delicate and innocent affair. Perennia falls asleep. Eros, 'a boyish figure', unsuspecting arrives at where she sleeps:

> Entranced he gazed, his goatskin slung across
> His body while he stood and wondered long
> Whether this creature sleeping on the moss,
> Warmed by the sun and lulled by insects' song,
> Was mortal or a goddess, to belong
> In such tranquil surroundings; if some freak
> Of Nature had united weak with strong
> To make perfection. Aching now to speak,
> Yet fearful to disturb her rest, he kissed her cheek. . .

> She felt the touch upon her cheek and saw
> The boy-god's face a moment over her
> So brilliant that she blinked; but saw no more,
> For he had vanished without sound or stir.

The episode is a kind of inverted anticipation of Eros' later awakening. It has no model in Apuleius, though it is strongly reminiscent of a beautiful moment in a different, more pastoral, romance of the late classical period, the *Daphnis and Chloe* of Longus. In the first book of Longus' romance the innocent Daphnis (a goatherd, as Warner's Eros wears a goatskin) finds the sleeping Chloe. He

laid down his Pipe; and without any shame or fear, was bold to view her all over, and every limb, insatiably, and withall spoke softly thus:
What sweet Eyes are those that sleep? How sweetly breathes that rosie mouth? The Apples smell not like to it, nor the flowery lawnes, and thickets. But I am afraid to kisse her. For her kisse stings to my heart, and makes me mad, like new honey.[22]

Much of the charm of *Daphnis and Chloe* resides in the naivety of the two lovers. Warner's Eros is also

As yet too young to know his archery,
His heart was filled with love of purest fire
And all his soaring spirits, once so free,
Were anchored now in innocent desire.

His affinity is with Daphnis, rather than with Apuleius' Cupid. Cupid, as we have seen, seems to have a complete familiarity with his 'archery'. When Warner's Perennia and Eros lie down side by side to pass the night in the cave it is so that they might 'spend the hours in happiness and play / Of childish innocence'. There is no suggestion that their love is consummated. Far from it, indeed; Eros does not understand the nature of his own feelings. On the ensuing day he is 'deeply stirred / Within his heart' and

wondered the reason why
His pulse beat restlessly and mouth seemed dry,
And all his sports and pleasures seemed to cloy
After his night spent in the cave near by
With pure Perennia.

Their innocence, however, has already found its enemy, its would-be destroyer, in the shape of Perennia's sister. In Apuleius Psyche has two, unnamed, sisters. The two are

scarcely differentiated and though there are good folkloric
reasons for there being two of them, it is hard to see that they
serve distinct artistic purposes. Warner reduces the two
sisters to one, and gives that one a name—'salt Salacia'. The
name may perhaps be an unconscious reminiscence of 'Salita
with her bosome full of fish', one of the daughters of Nereus
in an attractive passage in Apuleius; [23] more significantly it is
derived from the Latin adjective *salax*, meaning 'salacious,
lustful . . . lust-provoking'. In *Perennia* as in *The Golden Ass*
it is the wind which carries the sister(s) to Perennia / Psyche.
Salacia is immediately, but covertly, jealous of her sister's
surroundings of 'plenty and peace'. Like her twin models in
Apuleius, her strategy is to try to rob her sister of her
innocent trustfulness, to cast disturbing doubts in her mind.
In an almost Blakean sense it is the voice of Experience
corrupting the soul of Innocence. [24] Before Salacia speaks we
have been offered some pictures of a natural world gathering,
with a virtually paradisal fecundity, to pay homage to Perennia: [25]

> Then birds of all descriptions gathered round
> At peace with one another—hedge-sparrows
> And bunting, wrens and larks flew to the ground
> Fearlessly mingling with the hawks and crows.
> Ibis and lapwing spread their summer shows
> Of multicoloured feathers, and with these
> Peregrine falcons from far Iceland snows
> And eagles from the golden Pyrenees
> Settled upon a branch or circled round her knees.
>
> And animals of many breeds and kinds,
> Rabbits and does, foxes and water-voles,
> Hedgehogs and donkeys, kingly stags and hinds,
> Earthworms and beetles, blindly burrowing moles,
> Pushed through their tunnels or crept from their
>   holes,
> Or travelled from thick forests and wide parks
> To see her with their young—mares with their foals,
> Goats bringing kids with strange, distinctive marks,
> And sheepdogs guiding lambs and sheep with careful
>   barks.

It is an image of the natural world in a state of perfected peace, of the human soul at home in a world of perfected instinct, and capable, therefore, of communion with the divine. It is reminiscent of Blake's 'Little Girl Lost', with Perennia guarded much as Lyca is in that poem. To Salacia, the mind of worldly Experience, such magical scenes are no more than a trivial sideshow, an entertainment to be condescendingly dismissed from serious consideration:

> 'Sweet sister,' soon she smiled, 'this luxury
> Of animals and birds for retinue
> May fascinate; but can your Eros be
> So radiant that he must hide from you
> In stealthy midnight visitings his true
> Form? Can he be a pure, immortal child
> Such as you say? If he is fine to view,
> Why does he hide a body that is mild
> And harmless? He may be a beast, gross and defiled.

> 'For many a satyr has an easy charm
> And glowing look, insinuating trust
> That merely leads us on to our own harm
> Till we are prostituted to its lust
> And every passionate and goatish gust
> That shudders through its body.

Her own salaciousness is very clear. There seem to be excited 'shudders' in her own contemplation of the lust of which she declares her disapproval. In Apuleius Psyche is persuaded that her husband is no other than that 'great serpent full of deadly poyson, with a ravenous and gaping throat'[26] that was pronounced her doom by the Oracle of Apollo. The images planted in the minds of Psyche and Perennia may be different, but their purposes and effects are well-nigh identical. Each exists to rob the innocent soul of the certainty of faith, and to exchange it for, in Taylor's words, a state in which it is 'fascinated with outward form'.[27] (It is more than simply a coincidence that Salacia should see the world in terms of 'fascination'.) Psyche's sisters urge her, with her husband asleep in the darkness, to behead (with 'a sharpe razor') the supposed serpent. Salacia's prompting is for Perennia to 'destroy' her sleeping companion with a burning branch.

Before any such plan can be put into action, however,
Warner's poem introduces a vivid episode which has no
parallel in Apuleius. Salacia herself overhears Eros, sighing
out his perplexity. Her jealousy spies an obvious and
immediate possibility of expression. She sees in the situation
an opportunity to bring her own salacious experience to bear
upon Eros, just as she has already endeavoured to destroy
Perennia's innocence. She approaches Eros:

> Gently she whispered, 'Young god, in distress
> When all your kingdom loves to wake and sing—
> What is it that disturbs your happiness?
> Have you not, with my sister, everything
> You could desire? Perhaps some hidden spring
> Wells up within to trouble you, although
> You cannot yet describe it. Does this bring
> You sighing to this bank? If that is so
> Come to your loved one's sister: learn what I will show.
>
> 'For you must lie by me and kiss me as
> You did your own Perennia, and I
> Will teach you secrets that the grown man has
> But hides from childhood's uncorrupted eye;
> And all your misery will pass you by
> As golden daybreak floods your youthful heart.'
> In unsuspecting ignorance of why
> Salacia should scheme to make them part
> He lay, though still unseen, to learn this lady's art.

Apuleius' Cupid is, as we have seen, not in need of such
doubtful tuition. Salacia offers the very dubious benefits of
her experience in the initiation, sexually, of Eros. The
attempt upon Eros' 'innocence' is, in fact, the moment of her
own inevitable destruction. It is at a later stage in Apuleius'
narrative that one (and later the other) of Psyche's sisters,
tempted by Psyche's false stories that Cupid has expressed an
interest in her, is 'pierced with the pricke of carnall desire'.[28]
In the grip of this desire she casts herself 'headlong from the
mountaine: but shee fell not into the valley neither alive nor
dead, for all the members of her body were torne amongst the
rockes'.[29] Salacia suffers a different, perhaps even more

dreadful, dismemberment, and suffers it not in jealous anticipation but in the very moment of intercourse:

A mighty vision burst within her head
As mortal with immortal was combined.
She dreamed she saw a flying waggon led
By two great horses and controlled behind
By Eros tugging at the reins, confined
Within his chariot. The right-hand horse
Was white as snow and knew the driver's mind:
The black one plunged and reared up in its course
Dragging its driver down with devastating force.

Then blasted with milk of eternity
Her body scattered in a thunderflash
Over the hill-slopes far out to the sea.

The imagery in which Salacia's experience presents itself to her (and us) is derived, of course, from one of the most famous of all the Platonic myths. It is a myth which continued to exert its fascination upon Warner long after its appearance in this early poem,[30] and which was of central importance in the thought of that philosopher of Renaissance neo-Platonism who has, above all others, fascinated Warner—Marsilio Ficino.[31] The myth, as expounded in the *Phaedrus*, is so central to Warner's work that it merits quotation at some length here. Socrates presents the myth in an attempt to illustrate the nature of the soul:

To explain what the soul is, would be a long and most assuredly a god-like labour; to say what it resembles, is a shorter and a human task. Let us attempt then the latter; let us say that the soul resembles the combined efficacy of a pair of winged steeds and a charioteer. Now the horses and drivers of the gods are all both good themselves and of good extraction, but the character and breed of all others is mixed. In the first place, with us men the supreme ruler has a pair of horses to manage, and then of these horses he finds one generous and of generous breed, the other of opposite descent and opposite character. And thus it necessarily follows that driving in our case is no easy or agreeable work.[32]

Socrates later elaborates upon the significance of his simile:

Now of the horses one, if you remember, we said, was good, and the other bad; but wherein consists the goodness of the one, and the badness of the other, is a point which, not distinguished then, must be stated now. That horse of the two which occupies the nobler rank, is in form erect and firmly knit, high-necked, hooknosed, white-coloured, black-eyed; he loves honour with temperance and modesty, and, a votary of genuine glory, he is driven without stroke of the whip by voice and reason alone. The bad horse, on the other hand, is crooked, bulky, clumsily put together, with thick neck, short throat, flat face, black coat, grey and bloodshot eyes, a friend to all riot and insolence, shaggy about the ears, dull of hearing, scarce yielding to lash and goad united.[33]

This description turns into a narrative of human behaviour as Socrates proceeds, with great vividness, to relate how this ill-matched pair and their driver react when they see 'the sight which inspires love'. Then, when the driver's soul

is surcharged with irritation and the stings of desire, the obedient horse, yielding then as ever to the check of shame, restrains himself from springing on the loved one; but the other pays heed no longer to his driver's goad or lash, but struggles on with unruly bounds, and doing all violence to his yoke-fellow and master, forces them to approach the beautiful youth, and bethink themselves of the joys of dalliance.[34]

Socrates' account of the ensuing struggle, beautiful and powerful as it is, is too long to be quoted in full here.[35] Salacia cannot see the 'beautiful youth' (Eros remains 'unseen') but the 'joys of dalliance' are more than a matter of mere thought in her encounter with Eros. Eros is both startled and frightened by what has happened to Salacia—and frightened of the very power of sexual union.[36]

When Eros returns to Perennia after his initiation by Salacia, it is still to lie by her side 'in unmistrusting love and simple faith'. It is Perennia who has been corrupted by Salacia and who now lacks these qualities of trusting love and simple faith. Like Salacia, and thanks to Salacia, her mind is troubled now by dreams. The curiosity to which she has been prompted is inseparable from an impulse, however unconscious, to destruction. The lighted branch simultaneously reveals and damages the beauty of Eros (in *Perennia* the comparison with the earlier episode of Eros looking at a sleeping Perennia enables us to make some significant distinctions):

> She lifted up the brand in breathless stealth:
> It faded low. She blew, and a bright spark
> Flew like a comet showing all the wealth
> And beauty of his body through the dark,
> Falling to burn his shoulder with a mark
> That seared into the skin.

Eros' disappearance in *Perennia* is more abrupt than the corresponding departure of Cupid in *The Golden Ass*. Perennia is immediately aware of her culpability, struck with sorrow at her 'betrayal of his love'.

In presenting the aftermath of that betrayal Warner departs considerably from his 'source' in Apuleius. There is no equivalent to the very picturesque moment in *The Golden Ass* when a gull reveals to Venus the love between her son and Psyche. Warner's Hespera seems, rather, to deduce how matters stand from the observation of Eros after he has (as in Apuleius) been 'plucked back to heaven'. In Apuleius' narrative Psyche seeks (and is refused) aid from Juno and Ceres, and receives advice from Pan. At Venus' command Psyche is sought and imprisoned. Indeed she is physically assaulted by Venus. Perennia, on the other hand, is allowed to remain in her beautiful pastoral setting. Like Psyche, however, she is set a series of difficult tasks. Here again Warner makes significant changes from Apuleius. Both narratives involve four tasks. Venus demands, as a first task, that Psyche should sort a heap of 'wheat, of barly, poppy seede, peason, lintles, and beanes . . . disposing them orderly in their quantity'. Psyche performs the task with the aid of 'the little pismire the emote . . . [and] . . . all her friends'.[37] Venus, wrongly, suspects that Eros has performed the task for her. Venus instructs her as to the second task she must perform:

Seest thou yonder Forest that extendeth out in length with the river? there be great sheepe shining like gold, and kept by no manner of person. I command thee that thou go thither and bring me home some of their wooll of their fleeces.[38]

Psyche completes the task thanks to the advice of 'a green reed inspired by divine inspiration'.[39] Next Venus demands of her that she climbs a 'great hill' where there run 'waters of blacke and deadly colour, which nourisheth the floods of Stix',[40] and returns with a bottle of the water. The hill is protected by dragons. She is, once again, able to perform the task thanks, this time, to the assistance of 'the royall bird of great Jupiter, the Eagle'.[41] Venus assigns her a fourth and final task:

Take this box and to Hell to Proserpina, and desire her to send me a little of her beauty, as much as will serve me the space of one day.[42]

Advice is offered once more, this time from the very tower ('as inspired') from which she had thought to throw herself in despair. She carries appropriate talismans and obeys the tower's advice in detail.

Perennia is also allotted four trials. The first has obvious parallels with Psyche's first task. Perennia is required to search 'all the river-bed to count / The hairs upon the lily-stalks'. Where the ants had aided Psyche, it is the creatures of the water whose apt assistance comes to the aid of Perennia:

> The falling moonbeams made the pebbles shine
> White in the pools and shallows as she heard
> The bitter task that Hespera in fine
> And flattering phrases sent her by this bird.
> She stared down where a water-spider stirred
> Beneath the surface near his bubble trap,
> Seeing her own reflection miniatured
> Within his airy prison, while the lap
> Of water seemed so pure she felt her mind would snap.

> A newt disturbed a clump of meadow-sweet
> And peered through clusters of marsh-marigold
> To catch a caddis-fly. His weblike feet
> Darted round crowfoot stems to find a hold,
> Or paused among those loosestrife buds which fold
> The purple flowers close within their leaves
> To shield them from night vapours and the cold.
> She watched him jerk and scamper by degrees
> On to a full-lipped lily, where he seemed to freeze.

She started up. Along the water's edge
Thousands of tiny creatures had appeared:
Lizards and newts crawled from the willow-sedge,
And daphnia and water-boatmen steered
Among the traces water-mites had cleared.
Fat bullfrogs made their way, with brook lamprey
And softest moths blown from the old-man's-beard
To settle on this lily carpetry,
While fishes searched the mud and depths they could not see.

By such means Perennia gives Hespera her answer, and is
immediately sent a second task, the messenger being one of
Hespera's own doves:

Hespera heard her answer, but in hate
Ordered a second task—that she should send
An apple plucked from where grey, desolate
Crags on the mountain towered to contend
With piling clouds.

There are evident resemblances here to the third of Psyche's
tasks, and the similarity extends to the way in which each
problem is solved. Here too it is an eagle which releases the
heroine from her difficulties:

from her side a golden eagle soared
Into the sun to find the fruit for her,
And circling where the precipices roared
Severed the apple for Perennia,
Flying in feathered bold regalia
Northwards again to lay it at her feet.

The third of Hespera's impositions upon Perennia has no
model in Apuleius. Hespera subjects Perennia to a trial by
fire; she is to be enclosed inside the cave she has shared with
Eros and, like St.Cecilia, must face 'a bath of flambes rede'.[43]
Once more Perennia finds comfort and assistance in her time
of trial:

A thousand silkworms spun a thick cocoon
Over her body, and the phoenix came
To give her courage from his magic tune,
While ancient salamanders, blind and lame,
Gave her their power to withstand the flame—

> Secret for untold weary centuries.
> She tremblingly endured the pain and shame
> Through crawling hours that stretched eternities,
> Till release came at last with morning's certainties.

Perennia's final task is, in outline at any rate, identical with the last of the tasks which Venus imposes upon Psyche in *The Golden Ass*. Perennia too

> must descend into the grave to find
> And bring back Beauty from the world below,
> Beyond that stream where lethal waters flow,
> Venturing to the kingdom of the shades.

Psyche received advice from the tower from which she had intended to cast herself. Perennia, too, struck with terror at the prospect of such a journey 'turned to die rather than try to cull / Trophies from lands where even gods grew pale and dull':

> Her gentle river, that had washed her heart
> So many times with music of content,
> Would surely understand, and take her part
> While she dissolved her body, and prevent
> The suffering that drowned souls underwent.
> This river knew her thoughts and, with a stir
> That hardly rippled, asked her to relent,
> Taking upon the quest that piece of fur
> That Eros, when he first appeared, had left with her.

Perennia's journey (narrated in much less detail than the corresponding journey of Psyche in *The Golden Ass*) culminates (like Psyche's) in the receipt of the precious casket. Both are enjoined not to open the casket. Both are unable to resist the temptation to do so. If we compare Apuleius' account of the episode with Warner's adaptation of it, it is evident how much detail the poet has added to the relatively perfunctory treatment in the romance. Apuleius has little or no interest in circumstance or description:

When Psyches was returned from hell, to the light of the world, shee was ravished with great desire, saying, Am not I a foole, that knowing that I carrie heere the divine beauty, will not take a little thereof to garnish my face, to please my love withall? And by and by she opened the boxe where she could perceive no beauty nor any thing else, save onely an infernall and deadly sleepe, which immediately invaded all her members as soone as the boxe was uncovered, in such sort that shee fell downe upon the ground, and lay there as a sleeping corps.

But Cupid being now healed of his wound and Maladie, not able to endure the absence of Psyches, got him secretly out at a window of the chamber where hee was enclosed and (receiving his wings,) tooke his flight towards his loving wife, whom when he had found, hee wiped away the sleepe from her face, and put it againe into the boxe, and awaked her with the tip of one of his arrows.[44]

Warner's treatment of these two episodes spans some six stanzas in *Perennia*. Where Apuleius affords Psyche's return to the earth nothing beyond the observation that she was once more in 'the light of the world', Warner lavishes detailed description on the moment, and on the effects of Perennia's apparent death upon the natural world of which she has now become 'mistress':

> when she
> Returned, as she had come, to where sleek herds
> Of cattle grazed beneath the wych-elm tree,
> And saw again all nature's artistry,
> She longed to take some beauty from the case
> To win her Eros back again, that he
> Loving her would forgive all her disgrace.
> She opened it; and fell like death upon her face.
>
> The little mist of beauty had enclosed
> Her vital spirits till she lay so cold
> That all her living kingdom round supposed
> Their mistress dead. Ravens and night-owls tolled
> Their evensong, and sad marsh-marigold
> Lowered their petalled heads to touch the brook,
> While clouds across the sun seemed to enfold
> The world in mourning till it made it look
> As though the tears of life were in each leaf that shook.

But Eros, now recovered from his burn,
Yearning to see Perennia once more
Watched for a moment when he might return
Unnoticed by his mother, to restore
The laughter that her eyes had held before
When both together they had mocked the rain,
Slept in the sun and run along the shore
Like young gazelles, untouched by hate or pain,
Resting only to wake to happiness again.

He came back to the stream—but all was changed.
No birds, no animals bathed in the sun.
Where herds of sheep and goats before had ranged
Browsing within the meadows, now not one
Appeared. The very fishes seemed to shun
The surface where the lily-leaves were spread
In rich profusion. Silence seemed to stun
His senses. Then, by where the elm-tree shed
Its leaves he saw his love lying as one struck dead.

And yet no agony was in her face:
Beauty had calmed her brow in perfect peace.
The harshest sufferings had left no trace
Upon her cheeks, for sleep had brought release
From all her miseries, and made them cease.
Unutterable love surged in his heart
As, bending down, and taking off his fleece
To cover her, he saw her earthly part
Outshone the brightest miracle of heaven's art.

He brushed away the mist with gentle breath;
Then, trembling in her eyes, she saw him stand
In all his radiance.

This is an awakening (the recurrent motif of *Perennia*) for
both of them. Eros, an immortal, sees something of that
natural beauty which the poet has so vividly evoked and
celebrated. The emphasis is important in relation to the very
distinctive climax towards which Warner leads his version of
the story.

When Adlington translated *The Golden Ass*, that part of it
which dealt with Cupid and Psyche was headed 'The Marriage of Cupid and Psyches'. In Apuleius the narrative ends
with Jupiter's intervention on behalf of the lovers. Psyche is

brought up to Heaven and granted immortality. There are splendid marriage celebrations. Apuleius informs us, finally, that 'she was delivered of a child whom we call Pleasure'.[45] Most later versions of the story similarly treat this marriage, and the resulting offspring, as the natural climax of the narrative. So Shakerley Marmion's *Legend of Cupid and Psyche* concludes as follows:

> Thus Cupid had his Love, and not long after
> Her womb, by Juno's help, brought forth a daughter,
> A child by nature different from all,
> That laugh'd when she was born, and men did call
> Her Pleasure, one that does exhilarate
> Both gods and men, and doth herself dilate
> Through all societies, chiefly the best,
> Where there is any triumph, or a feast.
> She was the author that did first invent
> All kind of sport, conceits and merriment:
> And since to all men's humours does incline,
> Whether that they be sensual or divine.
> Is of a modest and a loose behaviour,
> And of a settled and a wanton favour;
> Most dangerous when she appears most kind,
> For then she'll part and leave a sting behind:
> But happy they that can her still detain,
> For where she is most fix'd she is least vain.[46]

Milton's beautiful introduction of the story at the close of *Comus* (a work of densely allusive mythological texture) also places its emphasis upon the marriage and the children produced by it:

> on the ground
> Sadly sits th'*Assyrian* Queen;
> But farr above in spangled sheen
> Celestial *Cupid* her fam'd Son advanc't,
> Holds his dear *Psyche* sweet intranc't
> After her wandring labours long,
> Till free consent the gods among
> Make her his eternal Bride,
> And from her fair unspotted side
> Two blissful twins are to be born,
> Youth and Joy; so *Jove* hath sworn.[47]

For Marmion and Milton, and for many others, one of the most important features of the story is its aetiology of Pleasure and its narrative prelude, the marriage. Both are absent from *Perennia*. Warner's poem stops short of any possible marriage, and certainly of any possible conception of Pleasure. *Perennia's* emphasis and climax are rather different and have been prepared for by the changes made in the tasks assigned to Perennia.

Perennia's four tasks are each characterized by their involvement of one of the four elements; the lily-stalks of the river-bed (water); the apple to be reached only by an eagle's flight (air); the burning cave (fire); the descent into the grave (earth). Surviving—and completing—all four tasks, now re-awakened by Eros, Perennia sings an ecstatic lyric, at a moment when 'the whole of nature burst to life with cries / Of rapture'. Something of the language and imagery of this song is anticipated in the second and third stanzas of the poem (as are its dactylic rhythms). The echoes set up a formal parallelism between beginning and end of the poem. Perennia's lyric is that of a soul that has journeyed 'to the very extremity of things'.[48] It is the song of a soul that has has lived the life of the elements themselves, explored the motions of the natural world to the full. Transcendence is discovered in the absolute fulfilment of the material. The lyric becomes one more, and perhaps the most enraptured, of Warner's poems of pastoral invitation. It has links with 'The Passionate Goatherd to His Love' and 'Jet Pastoral', though its idioms are more obviously individual:

> I have danced, with eternity dawning,
>   lain between delicate petals of night,
> Stroked the blue butterfly-wings of the morning,
>   tiptoed the moon on a cobweb of light,
> Washed in the waterfall, made my limbs moister,
>   tickled a slippery trout by the gills,
> Plunged with the otter and yawned with the oyster,
>   ridden a stallion over the hills.
>
> Ride on with me to the lands of tomorrow,
>   sail where our souls will be sundered no more,
> Far from where breakers of parting and sorrow
>   pound on the heart like the waves on the shore.

The poet-dreamer awakens (last in the poem's series of awakenings). *Perennia* has, thus, a lyrical rather than a strictly narrative climax. It had begun with a poet who, like so many mediaeval predecessors, presents himself in a sunlit setting by a river. Later poetry provides its models too. The stanzas in which the poet of *Perennia* plays his flute, hears 'gentle flute music . . . / From all the hill around in soft reply' and sees

> a woman by a small flood-lake
> Weeping into the stream as if her heart would break

perhaps remember a passage in *Il Penseroso*:

> There in close covert by som Brook,
> Where no profaner eye may look,
> Hide me from Day's garish eie,
> While the Bee with Honied thie,
> That at her flowry work doth sing,
> And the Waters murmuring
> With such consort as they keep,
> Entice the dewy-feather'd Sleep;
> And let some strange mysterous dream,
> Wave at his Wings in Airy stream,
> Of lively portrature display'd,
> Softly on my eye-lids laid.
> And as I wake, sweet musick breath
> Above, about, or underneath,
> Sent by som spirit to mortals good,
> Or th'unseen Genius of the Wood.[49]

The landscape here in *Perennia* is described in loving and sensuous detail and in verse which delightfully exploits the varied music of the Spenserian stanza:

> The river idled in among the weeds,
> Eddying round each obstacle that came,
> And lulled the sycamore's slow-falling seeds
> That fluttered down to make a teasing game
> For hungry minnows, searching for a grain
> Or water-fly. The clouds borne in the stream
> Drank in the sunlight and threw back again
> Flashes of warmth from where cool trout and bream
> Slept while the liquid music murmured through their dream.

The device of placing a poet-figure in such a riparian landscape as a means of introducing one's main narrative had
already been used in the English epyllion. One might parallel
Warner's device from at least two English Renaissance
epyllia—Thomas Lodge's *Scillaes Metamorphosis* and Phin-
eas Fletcher's *Venus and Anchises*. The latter presents its poet
as Thirsil by the banks of the Cam (like the poet of
Perennia—though the dreamer himself is by the banks of the
Mole); Lodge's poet-narrator begins his poem by the banks
of the Isis. *Perennia* opens thus:

> I stretched and lay beside the stepping-stones
> Down on the grass beneath a rowan tree.

The poem's final lines return us to the rowan tree:

> I knew that I had seen reality
> Lying upon that bank beneath the rowan tree.

In Celtic lore the rowan tree is a sacred tree with magical
properties. It is in the light of such traditions that we should
view the tree's prominence in *Perennia*. An immediate
source is perhaps to be found in Kathleen Raine's 'Northum-
brian Sequence':

> The sleeper at the rowan's foot
> Dreams the darkness at the root,
> Dreams the flow that ascends the vein
> And fills with world the dreamer's brain.[50]

Perennia carries as epigraph a quotation from Edgar
Wind's *Pagan Mysteries in the Renaissance*:

Only by looking towards the Beyond as the true goal of ecstasy can
man become balanced in the present. Balance depends on ecstasy.

The quotation is taken from Chapter III of Wind's volume,
'The medal of Pico della Mirandola', a study of the neo-
Platonic understanding of the three Graces. Wind examines
the triad Pulchritudo-Amor-Voluptas, which is inscribed on
Pico's medal and much discussed in the work of Ficino.[51]
Amor is understood as the mediator between Pulchritudo

and Voluptas. In Ficino's thought, as Wind explains, 'only by the vivifying rapture of Amor do the contraries of Pulchritudo and Voluptas become united'.[52] Amor's importance leads to an emphasis upon the middle term of the triad, and on the virtue of balance. It is against such a background that Wind comes to employ the words which Warner has appropriated as an epigraph:

In the *Shepheardes Calender*, Spenser expressed the union of balance and transcendence, which he knew from his study of Italian Neoplatonists, by juxtaposing two seemingly incompatible mottoes: *in medio virtus—in summo felicitas*. For an explanation the Gloss referred to 'the saying of olde Philosophers, that vertue dwelleth in the middest . . . with continuance of the same Philosophers opinion, that albeit all bountye dwelleth in mediocritie, yet perfect felicitye dwelleth in supremacie'. Pico explained the connexion of 'mediocrity' with 'supremacy' by man's affinity and distance to God: 'There is this diversity between God and man, that God contains in himself all things because he is their source, whereas man contains all things because he is their centre.' *Est autem haec diversitas inter Deum et hominem, quod Deus in se omnia continet uti omnium principium, homo autem in se omnia continet uti omnium medium*. The aim of Ficino's doctrine of divine love was to teach man to feel his affinity with God, and thereby become aware of his own centre. With the shrewdness of an experienced physician, he conceived of transcendence as an integrating force, and a source of temporal well-being. Only by looking towards the Beyond as the true goal of ecstasy can man become balanced in the present. Balance depends upon ecstasy.[53]

Perennia has discovered both her distance from, and her affinity with, the divine. She has realized, as her final ecstatic lyric makes clear, the sense in which she 'contains all things'. In her discovery is wisdom for the poet of this dream-vision. He can awake, must awake, to the details of the river-bank on which he fell asleep. His vision, though, has allowed him to pierce the accidents of the world around him, to make contact, however briefly, with that which is perennial, beyond the mutable surface of things and yet only to be apprehended through them:

And with her song still ringing in my ears,
I woke beside the Box Hill stepping-stones.
My flute had slipped among some travellers'-tears,
Where in the evening wind brown autumn cones
Dropped through the weeds and made wide, rippling
    zones.
A bonfire flamed and crackled cheerfully
Scenting the air with smoke, till in my bones
I knew that I had seen reality
Lying upon that bank beneath the rowan tree.

CHAPTER 4
Beyond the Classical

The two preceding chapters have discussed some of the ways in which Francis Warner's poetry has made use of models and genres which are ultimately classical in origin. This chapter will deal, in the main, with poems which are indebted to non-classical traditions, either native or, in one or two cases, exotic.

Three of Warner's poems unmistakably derive from the traditions of the ballad: 'The Escape of Princess Mary Tudor', 'The Ballad of Brendan Behan' and 'Ballad from "Riot", an abandoned play'. English ballads can, for the sake of convenience, be divided into three crude categories, though one must realize that the boundaries between such categories can only be approximate and fluid: traditional ballads, street ballads, and literary ballads. The characteristic forms of the traditional ballads—the typical ballad stanzas of couplet or quatrain, for example—were perhaps Norman in origin. The ballads were produced in environments where the written or printed word was not dominant. The identities of their original authors are long lost, and the texts, being transmitted orally, have usually undergone a constant process of change. Most traditional ballads were probably composed in the period 1450-1600. 'Street' ballads, or broadsheet ballads, were probably more often the work of professional journalists or writers. In tone they are generally less romantic than the traditional ballad. The broadsheet ballad, unlike the traditional ballad, was produced in a literate (or at any rate semi-literate) environment, and in predominantly urban communities. Its popularity depended on the availability of relatively cheap printing. Its heyday was perhaps the seventeenth century, though it continued to thrive at least until the end of the nineteenth century. The literary ballad, as its name implies, is a ballad written by an educated, self-conscious poet, taking up and employing the manners and forms of the earlier 'popular' ballad poets. The literary ballad can perhaps be dated from the first half of the eighteenth century and its development can be traced from Addison's famous essays on ballads in *The Spectator* (1711), through the publication of ballad collections, most famously Bishop Percy's *Reliques of Ancient English Poetry* (1765), and through its increasing use by poets of the pre-Romantic and Romantic generations—poets such as Tickell, Goldsmith, Lewis, Campbell and, of course, Wordsworth, Coleridge and Keats. The ballad has, ever since, remained an attractive form for many English poets. Swinburne and Morris were but two of the distinguished Victorian authors of ballads; Auden and Yeats provide modern instances. In contemporary American poetry, Helen Adam has made brilliant and freshly creative use of the possibilities of the form. One attraction for the early writers of the literary ballad was the sense that the form led them beyond and away from the inherited classical models. It offered an alternative tradition. So William Cowper could counterpoise the classical ode and the native ballad:

The ballad is a species of poetry I believe peculiar to this country, equally adapted to the drollest and most tragical subjects. Simplicity and ease are its proper characteristics. Our forefathers excelled in it; but we moderns have lost the art. It is observed that we have few good English odes. But to make amends we have many excellent ballads, not inferior perhaps in true poetical merit to some of the very best odes that the Greek or Latin languages have to boast of. It is a sort of composition I was ever fond of, and if grave matters had not called me another way, should have addicted myself to it more than to any other.[1]

In exploring the non-classical possibilities of the form, Warner's literary ballads reflect each of the earlier ballad traditions. Though it perhaps involves a degree of simplification, we may perhaps say that 'The Escape of Mary Tudor' owes most to the traditional ballad—as does 'The lonely fens are dark tonight', the ballad inset into 'Plainsong' (lines 196-219)—while its companions are more heavily indebted to the broadside ballad.

'The Escape of Princess Mary Tudor' employs the quatrain made up of first and third lines of iambic tetrameter and
second and fourth lines of iambic trimeter, which is the most
frequently used of traditional ballad forms. Warner rhymes
his quatrains *abab*, where most traditional ballads employ a
rhyme scheme of *abcb*. (The *abab* pattern occurs more
frequently in the poems of the ballad revival). 'The Escape of
Princess Mary Tudor' narrates an episode with some historical basis, however legend may later have embellished it. The
poem's relation to historical fact might be compared to that
of such traditional ballads as 'Earl Bothwell', 'Sir Andrew
Barton', or 'The Bonny Earl of Murray', or that of such
literary ballads as Mickle's 'Cumnor Hall' (about Amy
Robsart) or Aytoun's 'The Execution of Montrose'. When
the young Edward VI was on his deathbed, Northumberland
manoeuvred to disinherit both Mary and Elizabeth, so as to
put his own daughter-in-law, Lady Jane Grey, on the throne.
Concealing immediate news of Edward's death he sent a
message to Mary, telling her to visit her brother in his
sickness. On her way to London she was met by a messenger,
possibly sent by Sir Nicholas Throckmorton. The messenger, meeting Mary at Hoddesdon, advised her of the true
situation. She took shelter at Sawston Hall, the home of John
Huddleston. Legend has it that after spending one night
there, the citizens of Cambridge, or at any rate the puritans
amongst them, moved to attack the house, and Mary left the
house in the early morning, disguised. The mob fired the
house behind her. Thomas Fuller narrates part of the episode in his brief biography of Huddleston:

He was highly honored . . . by Queen Mary, and deservedly. Such
the trust she reposed in him, that (when Jane Grey was proclaimed
Queen) she came privately to him to Salston, and rid thence behind
his servant (the better to disguise herself from discovery) to
Framlingham Castle. She afterwards made him (as I have heard)
her Privy-Councellor, and (besides other *great boones*) bestowed
the *bigger part* of Cambridge castle (then much ruined) upon him,
with the stones whereof he built his fair house in this County.[2]

One modern account of the episode, by F.M.Prestcott,[3]
makes it clear that the burning of the house was probably not

the work of the people of Cambridge, but of Northumberland himself. The Victoria County History takes the same view:

> The most likely culprit was the duke of Northumberland . . . who left London for Cambridge on 14 July and began pillaging and burning the houses of Mary's supporters; a mass-book and grail used by her were taken from Sawston, and by 18 July one of Huddleston's tenants was spreading news that 'the tyrant hath burned good Master Huddleston's house and spoiled his goods'.[4]

The recent brief biography of Huddleston in S.T.Bindoff's *History of Parliament* confirms this as the likeliest sequence of events.[5] Edward died on the 6th July. It was clearly some weeks later that Sawston Hall was burned. The legendary version, however, has all the advantages of dramatic compression so far as the poet is concerned. Oddly enough, the events with which Warner's poem begins had once previously received poetic treatment, albeit in very feeble fashion. In the British Library is the manuscript of an anonymous poem, 'The Legend of Sir Nicholas Throckmorton'. Some 1400 lines long, it is a monologue spoken by the ghost of Throckmorton, in the manner of the *Mirror for Magistrates*. A few of its clumsy stanzas deal with Throckmorton's sending of a warning to Princess Mary. Throckmorton's ghost relates that at Edward's death:

> Mourning from Greenwich I didd strayt departe
> To London, to an house which bore our name.
> My brethren guessed by my heavie hearte
> The King was dead, and I confess'd the same:
> The hushing of his death I didd unfolde,
> Their meaninge to proclaime queen Jane I tolde.

> And, though I lik'd not the religion
> Which all her life queene Marye had profest,
> Yett in my mind that wicked motion
> Right heires for to displace I did detest.
> Causeless to proffer any injurie,
> I meant it not, but sought for remedie.

> Wherefore from four of us the newes was sent,
>   How that her brother hee was dead and gone;
> In post her goldsmith then from London went,
>   By whome the message was dispatcht anon.
>   Shee asked, 'If wee knew it certainlie?'
>   Whoe said, 'Sir Nicholas knew it verilie.'[6]

It is not to pay 'The Escape of Princess Mary Tudor' much of a compliment to say that it relates events in rather better fashion than is managed by the alleged ghostly reminiscences of Sir Nicholas Throckmorton. In fact, Warner's poem has a number of the virtues of traditional ballad narrative. The impersonal narrative voice of its opening and its characteristically ballad-like employment of dialogue wherever possible give it the sharp outlines and much of the dramatic immediacy of its models:

> King Edward on his death-bed lay,
>   His young eyes dim and chill:
> 'Lord, save my Sister. This I pray,
>   Preserve us all from ill.'
>
> The boy king died; but word was sent
>   By false Northumberland:
> 'Come, Mary, ere his life be spent
>   And kiss his dying hand.
>
> Speed, Mary! Turn your horse again,
>   By all must you be seen.'
> Meanwhile in London, Lady Jane
>   Is nominated Queen.
>
> At Hunsdon town, not far from Ware,
>   The Princess heard his tale,
> And taking five brave men with her
>   Rode through the wind and hail.
>
> But good Throckmorton sends a man;
>   At Hoddesdon bridge they meet:
> 'Your Brother's dead! 'Tis the Duke's plan
>   To weave your winding-sheet.'

The doubling of adjectives in 'dim and chill' in the first stanza, and of nouns, 'wind and hail' in the fourth stanza, are characteristic features of ballad style. The pathetic repetitions of the ninth stanza are also familiar from the authentic ballads:

> Weary, weary was the Queen,
> And weary were they all.
> The hearths were warm, the stables clean,
> Tapestries hung the wall.

Like many a balladeer before him, Warner gives weight to telling symbolic detail, while not wholly neglecting historical fidelity. The final stanza illustrates both impulses:

> John Huddleston was knighted;
> His stone hall stands there still:
> And where the Queen alighted
> Gorse grows on Pampisford Hill.

Huddleston was, indeed, knighted—on the second of October, 1553; the grant of stones from Cambridge castle is also documented; perhaps it would be rather more difficult to find documentary evidence of Mary's responsibility for the presence of gorse on Pampisford Hill. The 'romantic' and the 'real' are neighbours in most successful ballads.

In 'The Ballad of Brendan Behan' it is of the street-ballad that we are more often reminded. Its opening summons to attention adapts a common formula—'Come all ye . . . '—in the broadside ballads. It shares with many street ballads a less dramatic style of narrative than that which characterizes the traditional ballads. Its sensibility is essentially urban and the 'virtues' it celebrates are in no simple sense 'heroic' or 'romantic'. The street ballad is more prone than the traditional ballad to celebrate the un-heroic joys of laughter and alcohol. The poem was written on the day of Behan's death—Friday, March 20th 1964—and was broadcast, on Anglia T.V., early on the same evening. It records and re-creates Behan's career and personality as

> The boy with laughter in his eyes,
> And liquor in his veins.

Behan was, of course, one of those artists whose very character was perhaps a richer and greater creation than any of their individual works. Behan's writings are registered here. His 'laughing prison book' (*Borstal Boy*), and 'hanging play' (*The Quare Fellow*) as well as his 'singing play / About a cockney soldier / Shot by the I.R.A.' (*The Hostage*) are alluded to in the eight-stanza summary of the man. So are his political attitudes and his spells of imprisonment. Yet it is as public 'roaring boy' that he emerges most forcefully, the laughing and singing rebel:

> From morn again to twilight
> He'd laugh and sing and say
> 'Mock all the world, my darlin's,
> But back the I.R.A.'

The ballad has Behan's vigour and conjures up his mixture of seriousness and irresponsibility. The Irish ballad tradition is, of course, one of the richest in European literature, and it might be said to inform Behan's own dramatic work—especially *The Hostage*. The broadside ballads have always been inseparable from Irish political struggles,[7] and the 'literary' poets have often been much influenced by the broadside ballads. Yeats is an obvious case in point. Such poems as 'The Rose Tree' and 'Sixteen Dead Men' would have been impossible without the traditions of popular political ballad. There is a three-fold aptness—theatrical, political and personal—in the choice of the ballad form as that in which to pay tribute to Behan. It is hard, certainly, to imagine Behan well served by the formalities of a more classical elegy. The looser confines of the ballad allow for a greater variety of tone, a more fitting mixture of jest and earnest. There is room here for the 'neon lights', for 'The Shaky Man' and Mooney's bar, as well as for the moral injunction and brute ballad force of the closing lines:

> And love like him, forgive like him,
> Till Death knocks out your brains.

The 'Ballad' from Warner's abandoned play *Riot* also has affinities with the broadside ballads. Warner's poem belongs with the early nineteenth-century street ballads of social criticism, represented by such poems as 'Come all you swaggering farmers, whoever you may be' or the 'Song of the

Lower Classes' by the Chartist poet, Ernest Jones.[8] Jones' poem dates from the 1840s, but speaks of a situation closely akin to that within which Warner's poem, set in 1816, is located:

> We plough and sow—we're so very, very low,
> That we delve in the dirty clay,
> Till we bless the plain—with the golden grain,
> And the vale with the fragrant hay,
> Our place we know, —we're so very low,
> 'Tis down at the landlord's feet:
> We're not too low—the bread to grow,
> But too low the bread to eat.[9]

Warner's 'Ballad' bears the date of 1816. In that year there were extensive riots by agricultural labourers in Littleport, Ely, and Downham Market. The mention of the 'fen' in stanza two suggests that it is these riots that Warner had in mind. The riots have been the subject of a fascinating modern study by A.J. Peacock.[10] In the years after the Napoleonic Wars the conditions of the agricultural labourer became increasingly difficult. Farming was rapidly becoming more and more capitalistic; labourers became landless employees. Prices increased rapidly. The demobilization of something approaching a quarter of a million soldiers could simply not be accomodated in the rural labour market. Enclosure's effects were thus compounded. It was against such a background that the riots took place. Driven by hunger and by a sense that they had been robbed of their traditional rights, the agricultural labourers resorted to direct action against the wealth and commercial activity they could see around them:

The crowd at Brandon, for instance, said 'they wanted their rights . . . Cheap Bread, a Cheap Loaf and Provisions Cheaper', and a Mr. Norman, a miller, was accused of forcing up the price of flour. At Ely, Norwich and Downham Market mills were broken into, millers and butchers attacked and food distributed among the crowd.'[11]

Poaching gangs became an important phenomenon,[12] and the battle between gamekeeper and poacher developed to a

pitch of intensity not previously known. Warner's 'Ballad'
reflects these historical circumstances in language that is
entirely true (given the inevitable 'distortions' of the literary
ballad) to the idioms of the nineteenth-century broadside
ballad:

> When Jack was a youngster he had a fine house,
> And linen and carpets and beds;
> He fished and he hunted and shot his own grouse,
> Drank vintage and baked his own breads.
> But Johnny-boy-soldier went off to the wars
> All dressed in his tunic and boots;
> And when he came back they had ransacked his stores
> And pulled up his trees by the roots.

> Lie down, my small darling, I'll sing you a tune,
> > for shadows move dark in the wood;
> Your daddy is out by the light of the moon,
> > and he walks where the gamekeeper stood.

> Now Johnny-boy-soldier, he rides all alone
> And knows every track of the fen;
> He's a bright baby daughter and lady called Joan,
> And a coat cut in velvet again.
> Oh, the inn-keepers welcome his tap at the door,
> And the millers mount guard on their mill:
> But they'll never catch Johnny in ten years or more
> Though the gibbet stands high on the hill.

> Lie down, my small darling, no candle must flame,
> > lie close as you hear what I'll sing;
> For Johnny your daddy has got a new name
> > which the wayfarers call Captain Swing.

By the end of the poem 'Johnny' has, as it were, undergone a
metamorphosis; now he is 'Captain Swing'. He has become
the very spirit and symbol of the agrarian movement in
ensuing years, for 'Captain Swing' was the name which
appeared on the threatening letters which were dispatched
during the rural uprisings of late 1830.[13] The most characteristic 'voice' of Warner's poetry is lyrical and private; only
a relatively small number of poems—such as *'Pax Britan-
nica'* or the sonnet for 'Remembrance Day'—are truly
'public' poems. His ballads, perhaps especially the one from

Riot, foreshadow his later union of lyrical and 'public' in his verse dramas.

In an essay published in 1965 Warner presented the ballad and the carol as contrasting but complementary forms;

. . . in the medieval world it was the carol that sang of summer, of dancing and the open air; and in direct contrast to it was the ballad. Whereas the form of the carol depended on a *burden* which was external to the narrative stanzas (and its definition depended on this *burden*), the ballad either had no chorus at all, or, if it had one, it was a part of the stanzas themselves . . . The atmosphere conjured up by the ballad was one of darkness and unease, of a single singer on a winter night, standing by the fire after a communal feast, relating tales of sudden violence and unquiet graves to a silent company . . . But in place of one man singing to the listening darkness, the carol presupposed open-air and gaiety, young folk holding hands and singing their own music for the dance . . . Where the ballad is impartial and doom-laden, the carols sing of more intimate and lyrical subjects—of lovers, of mothers suckling children, and hence, on occasion, of the Virgin Mary and her Child.[14]

Warner's *Collected Poems* contains three carols. The early poem 'The Love of God' (not itself a carol) gives lyrical expression to what Suheil Bushrui describes as a faith 'deliberately unsophisticated and inspired by what is most natural and immediate to the senses':[15]

> No priest, with sanctuary bell,
> No rhetoric of demagogue,
> No missionary infidel
> Brings me to the love of God.
>
> But a simpler state of mind,
> Seeing less, perceives the truth:
> A milkboy, whistling down the wind,
> Theologically uncouth,
>
> Knowing nothing of the strange
> Orthodox uncertainties
> That perplex the subtle brains
> Of divine nonentities,

> Innocent of party ties,
> Weather-worried at the most,
> Lives and loves and laughs, and dies
> Welcomed by the Holy Ghost.

None of Warner's three carols falls within the terms of the strictest definition of the genre. In his magisterial study of the pre-Reformation English carol, R.L.Greene defines a carol as 'a song on any subject, composed of uniform stanzas and provided with a burden'.[16] Greene sees the burden as the very essence of the carol:

The burden makes and marks the carol. The presence of an invariable line or group of lines which is to be sung before the first stanza and after all stanzas is the feature which distinguishes the carol from all other forms of Middle English lyric.[17]

None of Warner's carols makes use of such a burden. His are carols in the looser, more popular, use of the term—'a song or hymn of joy sung at Christmas in celebration of the nativity' in the words of the Oxford English Dictionary. Of Warner's three carols it is the 'Carol for Two Boys' Voices' which owes most to medieval models:

> The wet nose of the donkey
>   The wet warmth of your breast—
> But what strange shadow leans over
>   My strawy nest?
>
> Young farmhands come to bless my sweet
>   With freshness from the field.
> Like butterflies that wake too soon
>   Your eyelids yield.
>
> The roofbeams bear the winter
>   Of all the wilding world;
> I see them, and the shepherds—
>   But what strange scurry swirled?
>
> Your father scrapes snow from the door
>   As politicians shed
> Wonders I do not understand
>   About our bed.

Mother, the lamb is crying
We both of us need milk—
Who is that last that brushes us
With midnight silk?

We cannot understand, my babe,
These strange foreshadowings.
Now all have left, come take my milk;
Sleep, while your mother sings:

Lullaby, lily-lullay,
Hold my finger in your palm
Tight now all the world is still.
Stay you safe from cold and harm
As within your father's arm
Sleeps the lamb brought from the hill.

The dialogue structure here—alternating stanzas spoken (sung?) by the Infant Christ and the Virgin Mary—is one for which there are many precedents amongst the mediaeval carols; the dialogue carol is most frequently found, significantly, in mediaeval carols of the nativity. Greene's collection includes several examples of lullaby carols in dialogue form.[18] Warner has also adopted one of the most common features of the burdens in such mediaeval lullaby carols[19]— the onomatopoeic 'lullay' from which the modern term 'lullaby' itself derives. Greene observes that the carol writer's use of 'lullay'

is, of course, in imitation of real folk-lullabies; a similar sound was used by those first-century nurses whom Persius reports as singing to their charges:

Lálla lálla lálla, aút dormí aut lacté,

and doubtless by many generations before them.[20]

Though the printed form of the poem does not offer any guidance on the matter, the final six lines of Warner's poem could very well serve as a burden. It would, of course, be unusual for a burden to be longer than the stanza form of the main body of the carol, but it would not be without precedent.[21] If Warner's carol were to be performed, as its title suggests, by two boys' voices, then one imagines that the burden could be sung by both together, each otherwise singing the words of either the Infant Christ or the Virgin

Mary. 'Carol for Two Boys' Voices' has not, so far as I know, received a musical setting as yet. The earlier poem, 'A Legend's Carol', was set to music by Leon Coates.[22]

'A Legend's Carol' has affinities with sixteenth- and seventeenth-century English poems on the Nativity—such as Southwell's 'Behold a silly tender babe' or Herrick's 'In numbers, and but these few'—rather than with the pre-Reformation carol. Though very different in mode and manner its concerns are not without their relation to those of Milton's 'On the Morning of Christ's Nativity'. 'A Legend's Carol' combines lyrical and narrative. Its stanza has been described as original,[23] but is in fact that of Alexander Montgomerie's 'The Cherrie and the Slae', a stanza later employed by both Allan Ramsay and Robert Burns.[24] C.S. Lewis described it as 'a delightful stanza in itself' but with Montgomerie's poem in mind observed that 'this tumble-home is unendurable in a prolonged narrative, and still more in a prolonged debate'.[25] There can surely be little doubt of its suitability for Warner's purposes. Basically iambic, the stanza might be represented, where letters indicate the rhyme-scheme and figures the number of syllables, as follows: a^8 a^8 b^4 c^8 c^8 b^4 d^8 e^6 d^8 e^6 f^6 g^6 h^6 g^6. The two unrhymed lines, here marked as f and h, contain internal feminine rhymes. The pattern invites a number of different relationships between syntax and stanza. The final four lines are, most clearly, a self-contained unit, and in every one of the eleven stanzas of 'A Legend's Carol' the last four lines constitute a separate sentence. The opening six lines of the stanza invite either division into three plus three (where the two rhyming couplets are each seen as establishing a separate structural unit) or treatment as one unit of six lines (where the rhyme link of third and sixth lines is seen as overriding the potential division). In 'A Legend's Carol' six stanzas (2, 3, 4, 5, 7, 11) make a syntactical break after three lines; the remainder do not, giving an attractive variety to the movement of the poem. In all but three (5, 8, 9) of the poem's eleven stanzas, the quatrain made up by lines 7 to 10 is a discrete unit of syntax.

The first five stanzas of the poem are concerned with events before the birth of Christ; stanzas seven to eleven deal with the consequences of that birth. The birth itself is, therefore, quite literally central to the poem, its occurrence being obliquely narrated in the poem's sixth and middle stanza. Such central placement has a clear and important significance. The central place, traditionally, was the place of sovereignty. It is a motif especially associated with what H.P. L'Orange calls 'the iconography of Cosmic Kingship'.[26] Biblical exegesis in the Middle Ages and the Renaissance frequently stressed the sovereign importance of the central position. It was important that the tree of knowledge was 'in the midst of the garden'.[27] A much quoted text was taken from God's address to Moses—'thou mayest know that I am the Lord in the midst of the earth'.[28] When Christ is, as he so often is in the art and literature of the period, expressed by the symbol of the sun, the motif of centrality derives added force from another tradition. The Ptolemaic order of planets—Saturn, Jupiter, Mars, Sun, Venus, Mercury, Moon—after all made the sun the central planet in the line of planets. In 'A Legend's Carol' Christ's birth is given the sovereign central position for obvious theological reasons. The poem's pattern of temporal imagery and, especially, of light and dark, reinforces the pattern. 'A Legend's Carol' begins in darkness, albeit starlit:

> The air was purified with frost,
> And many a lonely mariner lost
>   Upon the sea
> Raised a numb hand to shield his sight,
> And stared up at the starry night
>   In reverie.

The opening five stanzas narrate the events of the night, and such natural darkness is deepened by the Holy Family's entry into a cave. It is, once more, in the central stanza of the poem, the stanza of Christ's birth, that light suddenly floods the poem:

> But when they came back to the hill
> A blinding cloud came down to fill
>   The cave with light
> And dazzled them, until at last
> The flame, its blaze of fury passed,
>   Shone clear and bright.

The ensuing stanzas chart a movement from dawn to night.
Stanza seven opens with a delightful dawn picture, with all the
clarity and innocence of a mediaeval Italian Nativity scene:

> Some streaks of day spread through the sky
> As Mary sang a lullaby
>   To her new-born.
> Linnets and starlings perched around
> Waking all nature with their sound
>   And din of dawn:
> The orchards and the olive-groves
>   Filled with fresh-waking noise,
> And early cattle passed in droves
>   Driven by sleepy boys.
>   Then tramping and stamping
>   Some shepherds asked if they
>   Might enter; they sent her
>   A lamb this holy-day.

The emphatic importance which the poem gives to its central
stanza carries with it implications of a larger kind of symmetry. We should expect, for example, to find connections
between first and last stanzas. One connection, obviously
enough, is that each is a stanza of night; the symmetry
registers the poem's movement from night to night. Still
more important is that the opening lines of the poem, quoted
earlier, should begin with 'a lonely mariner' at sea, and thus
prepare us for the symmetrically necessary completion of
this motif in the final stanza:

> And late that night, when all had left,
> A helmsman nodding on his chest
>   Woke with alarm:
> A sudden wind from off the shore
> Beat on his sails a bitter roar
>   That broke the calm.
> He saw his rigging torn away
>   And left without a shred,
> And heard a loud lamenting say,
>   'Tell out great Pan is dead!'
>   Then swirling and hurling
>   Its thunder of that name,
>   With calling and falling
>   The wind sank as it came.

If confirmation be needed of Warner's interest in the structuring of literary works by such devices of emphatic centrality, we need look no further than his essay on 'The Poetry of James Joyce'. In it, discussing *Chamber Music*, he quotes one of Joyce's letters to G.Molyneux Palmer;

The central song is XIV after which the movement is all downwards until XXXIV which is vitally the end of the book. XXXV and XXXVI are tailpieces just as I and II are preludes.

Warner elaborates upon Joyce's hint:

We are now in a position to see the work whole. The central climax of the suite is the *Song of Songs*, greatest of all love-poems and neatly versified by Joyce. At the centre of this (thirty-five words before it in a poem of seventy words) is the upstanding and timeless cedar of Lebanon.[29]

It need hardly surprise us that Warner's own poetry should be marked by the same kind of attention to such patterns of centrality and symmetry. Both *Experimental Sonnets* and *Morning Vespers* are marked by similar patterns.[30] Here in 'A Legend's Carol' the central placement of the birth of Christ serves, not only to give the birth its due emphasis, but to link it to that 'legend' which gives the poem its title. The legend is that which is narrated in the poem's final stanza and which seems to derive, ultimately, from Plutarch. Most English readers will perhaps be familiar with the legend as it is narrated by E.K. in a well-known gloss to the *Shepherd's Calendar*.[31] Plutarch's own account is worthy of quotation. He reports the story of Epitherses:

This *Epitherses* was my Fellow-citizen, and had been my Schoolmaster in Grammar, and this narration he related: That minding upon a time to make a voyage by sea into *Italy*, he was imbarqued in a Ship fraught with much merchandize, and having many passengers beside aboord. Now when it drew toward the Evening, they hapned (as they said) to be calmed about the isles *Echinades*; by occasion whereof their Ship lulled with the tides, untill at length it was brought near unto the Islands *Paxae*, whiles most of [the] Passengers were awake, and many of them still drinking after supper: but then, all on a sudden there was heard a voice from one of the Islands of *Paxae*, calling aloud unto one

Thamus; insomuch as there was not one of all our company but he wondred thereat. Now this *Thamus* was a Pilot, and an Egyptian born: but known he was not to many of them in the Ship by that name. At the two first calls, he made no answer; but at the third time he obeyed the voice, and answered: Here I am. Then he who spake, strained his voyce and said unto him: When thou art come to *Palodes*, publish thou and make it known: *That the Great* Pan *is dead*. And as *Epitherses* made report unto us, as many as heard this voyce were wonderfully amazed thereat, and entred into a discourse and disputation about the poynt, whether it were best to do according to this commandement, or rather to let it passe, and not curiously to meddle withall; but neglect it. As for *Thamus*, of this mind he was, and resolved: If the wind served, to sail by the place quietly and say nothing; but if the winds were laid, and that there ensued a calm, to crie and pronounce with a loud voyce that which he heard. Well, when they were come to *Palode*s aforesaid, the winde was down, and they were becalmed, so that the Sea was very still without Waves. Whereupon *Thamus* looking from the poop of the Ship towards the Land, pronounced with a loud voice that which he had heard, and said: *The Great* Pan *is dead*. He had no sooner spoken the word, but there was heard a mighty noyse, not of one but of many together, who seemed to groan and lament, and withall to make a great wonder.[32]

Epitherses' story was, not surprisingly, subject to many and contradictory interpretations in ensuing centuries. The details need not concern us here.[33] It will suffice to know that one school of thought interpreted that 'mighty noise', which closes the passage just quoted, as the lament of the devils upon the overthrow of Satan (Pan) by Christ. On the death of Pan the oracles ceased, their power overthrown. The motif is a common one in seventeenth-century poetry. So Giles Fletcher writes of the new-born Christ:

> The Angell's caroll'd lowd their song of peace,
> The cursed Oracles wear strucken dumb,
> To see their Sheapheard, the poor Sheapheards press,
> To see their King, the Kingly Sophies come,
> And them to guide unto his Masters home,
>   A starre comes dauncing up the orient,
>   That springs for joye over the strawy tent,
> Whear gold, to make their Prince a crowne, they all present.[34]

The movement of Warner's poem is towards an affirmation of the defeat of paganism in the birth of Christ. It moves, that is, to the declaration, less explicitly, of what is celebrated at greater length in the final movement of Milton's 'On the Morning of Christ's Nativity'—stanzas XIX and XX of that poem having an especial relevance to 'A Legend's Carol'. Where Milton aspires to, and achieves, an almost Pindaric high style, Warner's poem works in the humbler idiom of the carol. Homely and human detail has more place here and it has been said, with good reason, that the poem 'celebrates the nativity in realistic terms appropriate to the twentieth century',[35] We should not, though, neglect the larger mythical resonances which the poem also sets up.

All of Warner's three carols are lyrical—they would scarcely merit the name were they not. Within their lyricism, however, there are differences of emphasis. The 'Carol for Two Boys' Voices', with its dialogue of question and answer, has something of the dramatic about it, in however subdued a fashion. 'A Legend's Carol' is essentially narrative. The 'Carol for Two Boys' Voices' is essentially intimate; 'A Legend's Carol' has its scenes of human and domestic detail, but seeks also to explore significances of a more obviously historical nature. The third of Warner's carols, 'Christmas Day Carol for a Child', is different again. Here we have a poem more reflective than dramatic or narrative. This change goes with a change of technique. The 'Carol for Two Boys' Voices' has no narrator, no poet's voice as such. 'A Legend's Carol' has a third person narrative voice, though it is not one which is in any way individualized. 'Christmas Day Carol for a Child' uses the first person plural voice. 'Carol for Two Boys' Voices' made us overhearers, as it were, of an exchange between mother and child. 'A Legend's Carol' asked us to listen to a story, a legend. The 'Christmas Day Carol for a Child' asks us to share in the poet's reflections on Christmas Day—the poem is dated 25th December, 1977. This kind of poem, like 'A Legend's Carol', has its seventeenth-century precedents—such as George Herbert's 'All after pleasures as I rid one day'. The finest English poems on Christmas subjects are chiefly to be found either

amongst the pre-Reformation carols or in the work of
seventeenth-century poets. Warner has availed himself of
the models provided by both. The first stanza of 'Christmas
Day Carol for a Child' ends with a striking picture of the
simultaneous weakness and power of the Infant Christ:

> a baby boy
> Shivering and shut-eyed in rough straw
> Helpless and pink and weak
> Whose playthings are the stars, his door
> Lit by a comet's streak.

The second and third stanzas of the carol imagine a whole
series of 'nativities', an Infant Christ born on each of the
many planets:

> Today perhaps another world,
>   Planet light-years away,
> Welcomes the same Creator, curled
>   In bed more strange than hay,
> Born afresh a tiny thing
>   Suited to that far star
> Where they now sing their new-come king
>   Transformed as we too are.

> And one day every furthest speck
>   Unseen in outer space,
> Every space-mariner on deck,
>   Lonely and out of place,
> Will hear a gong ring through the dark
>   To say that all is done—
> Jesus has planted all his park,
>   The universe is one.

'Jet Pastoral', it was suggested in an earlier chapter, is a poem
which discovers a thoroughly contemporary experience to be
invested with the weight and significance of a classical poetic
genre—finds in the one an apt artistic idiom for the expression of the other. Here in 'Christmas Day Carol for a Child'
the Nativity is taken into the space age. Perhaps it is the way
in which a post-technological age can best express such sense
as it has of the cosmic significance of this 'baby boy /
Shivering and shut-eyed in rough straw'; not for us, alas, that

music of angels and spheres which served the same purpose for an earlier age. The final stanza of Warner's carol returns us to earth, both to celebrate and to find in the 'fantasy' of the previous two stanzas a moral judgement on human behaviour.

All the poems we have so far considered in this chapter have been examples of forms—the ballad and the carol—which in their origins were sung, and which in their later forms still bear unmistakable signs of their musical origins. Of Warner's three ventures into the use of poetical forms drawn from outside the European tradition (a description in need of major qualification in one case), two involve poetic forms inseparable from music. The collection *Madrigals* (1967) contains a pair of related poems—'West Coast Blues' and 'East Coast Calypso'. Both are pleasant, if rather slight, pieces and neither employs with any great fidelity the verse forms alluded to in their title. The Blues—the solo song form of the American Negro—is based on a three-line stanza, in which the second line is a repeat of the first, as in this example from the work of Big Bill Broonzy (1893-1958):

> Look like everybody, mama got a friend but
>   me
> Look like everybody, mama got a friend but
>   me
> I'm a poor boy, baby, mama good as I can be.
> Baby when I'm happy, my friends are happy
>   too
> Baby when I'm happy, my friends are happy
>   too
> Now I've fell in bad luck, mama what am I
>   going to do?
> Babe I'm motherless and I'm fatherless, I'm
>   sisterless and brotherless too
> Babe I'm motherless and I'm fatherless, I'm
>   sisterless and brotherless too
> Baby today I'm so blue baby, I don't know
>   what to do.[36]

As Suheil Bushrui suggests, 'West Coast Blues' is most interesting for the interplay it sets up between elements from the true blues idiom and elements which are clearly the work of a man educated in the European poetic tradition:

The first verse is admirably within the blues idiom, with its colloquialisms ('ease my mind'), while in the second Warner blends in the poetic image ('Dead conversations stifle out the day').[37]

For the most part the poem takes only a slight flavour from the blues, a flavour of idiom and mood. It is not a wholly serious attempt to turn the blues idiom to 'literary' use, of the kind one finds, for example, in the work of Langston Hughes. 'East Coast Calypso' is perhaps a closer approximation to the form and idiom of its originals. The rhyming couplets and the structure of verse and chorus, or call and response, are common features of calypso. Paula Burnett's remarks on the calypso are very helpful as regards the characteristic attitudes and purposes of such calypsonians as 'Mighty Sparrow' or 'Lord Kitchener':

Calypso . . . is in direct descent from the African tradition of satiric song . . . The singer-songwriters are the court-jesters of modern society; they must first entertain, but of equal importance is the serious meaning of what they have to say, so that wit goes hand in hand with perceptive comment, whether on politics, society or the human condition.[38]

Warner's verses fit the bill quite well:

> Kennedy Airport's bright and gay
> Pink floodlight fountains make it look like day
> Everybody's rich and kissing and plush
> But down on the waterfront—hush! hush! hush!
>   New York, New York, slice of life,
>   When you taste it take a fork and knife.
>   Central Park's a peculiar place
>   And violence smiles with a virgin's face . . .
>
> Busy Manhattan's very neat,
> Gardens and ice-rink along the street;
> Down in the subway out of sight
> No spitting's allowed while the dagos fight.
>   New York, New York . . .

With the poem which Warner calls 'Rubaiyat' we leave behind, for the first time in this Chapter, song forms. A *rubai* is a standard form in Persian poetry. It is a quatrain rhyming *aaba* (infrequently *aaaa*). It is important to realize that in Persian poetry the *rubai* is not a stanza form; it is the form in which the poet composes an entire and discrete poem. It is analogous to a fixed form such as, say, the triolet, rather than a stanza form like the Spenserian stanza. One does not compose a poem in a series of triolets. In Persian poetry the term *rubaiat* describes a collection, not a sequence, of *rubai*. The term was made familiar to English readers, of course, by Edward Fitzgerald's *Rubaiyat of Omar Khayyam*. Fitzgerald there produced a more or less continuous poem made up of stanzas rhyming *aaba*. He thus established a new, and distinctively English, form. We might draw an analogy with Cowley's Pindaric Odes. By a misunderstanding (deliberate or otherwise) of his original, Cowley produced a new English form, the irregular Ode. Fitzgerald's new form found a number of Victorian imitators—the best such poem perhaps being Swinburne's 'Laus Veneris'. It remains a lively form in the hands of the right poet—as is witnessed, for example, by John Heath-Stubbs' 'Quatrains' ('The Dog Star now, negating all desires') and Dick Davis' delightful 'Letter to Omar'.[39] The two *rubai* which make up Warner's 'Rubaiyat' form a continuous composition. We are dealing, that is, with a poem that comes from Fitzgerald rather than from Persian poetry itself. Both parts of Warner's 'Rubaiyat' follow a pattern characteristic of many of the best stanzas of Fitzgerald's *Rubaiyat*: a first couplet enjambed, pauses marked by punctuation at the end of lines 2, 3 and 4. Some of Warner's phrasing also echoes Fitzgerald. 'Master of our Fates', for example, seems to conflate phrases from stanzas XXXI, L and LXVIII of Fitzgerald's *Rubaiyat*.[40] In content the poem belongs with the series of poems upon the poet's children, and his relationship with them. The series is discussed in Chapter Nine. The 'Rubaiyat', like others in the series, is concerned with the travels shared by father and daughter. Here, fittingly, these are travels in the Middle East—in

Egypt and in Israel and the Lebanon. The second stanza's vision of a Heaven eventually to be shared by the two fuses neo-Platonism and a conception of the after-life that is influenced by the traditions of Islam:

> Ah, Georgie; you and I have travelled far
> To where the crescent meets the morning star;
> From citadel of David to the Sphinx,
> From Baalbek's sands to Karnak's Amon-Ra;
>
> And when the Master of our Fates decides
> To show the glory that our frail flesh hides,
> One grove, one river in that Paradise,
> Will be our mirage where the Bedouin rides.

Amongst non-classical forms it is evidently the sonnet that has held most appeal for Warner. One other Italianate form requires at least brief discussion. 'American Hotel, Amsterdam' makes assured use of *terza rima*, five triplets rounded off by a couplet. The Dantean associations of the form are counterpointed wittily by the thoroughly modern and ironic content:

> Two girls with legs, one dark, one blonde, outside
> Compel our eyes across the Leidseplein
> Past the Schouwburg until they sit beside
>
> Fern-plants that come between us. We are vain:
> Call 'Ober!' Ask him to convey a pun
> In verse and wait till they respond again.
>
> Their answer is in prose, though they are none.
> We watched them rise with the approaching sun.

Though he shows in the poem a well-developed sense of *terza rima's* very individual capacity to lead the reader on from stanza to stanza (so as to complete the 'leap-frogging' patterns of rhyme) and simultaneously to present each triplet as a self-contained unit (the two outer rhymes asserting this sense), Warner has not chosen to investigate more extensively the potential of this particular form. It is the sonnet which has attracted his continuing interest. Warner's *Collected Poems* contains 59 sonnets; the verse play *Living Creation* includes another 5. Warner's one volume devoted exclusively to sonnets was his *Experimental Sonnets* of 1965. The title suggests something of his attitude to the form. Warner has sought constantly to explore the sonnet's possibilities. He stands at precisely the opposite pole to a dogmatist such as T.W.H. Crosland who could call a chapter of his *English Sonnet* 'Sonnet Legislation' and begin it:

It has been commonly held that poetry is a law unto itself, and that there are no standards whereby it can be judged. Of the sonnet, however, this is certainly not true. The law has written itself explicitly and finally, and the standards have been set up and are irremovable. Of the law we may dispose very briefly. A sonnet consists of fourteen decasyllabic lines, rhymed according to prescription . . . Any poem in any other measure than the decasyllabic is not a sonnet. For this reason, the poem which figures as Sonnet 145 in the Shakespeare series is not a sonnet . . . The prescription for the rhymes of the English sonnet pure and simple may be formulated thus: -

$$a\text{-}b\text{-}a\text{-}b \ c\text{-}d\text{-}c\text{-}d \ e\text{-}f\text{-}e\text{-}f \ g\text{-}g^{41}$$

Warner's flexibility is closer than Crosland's dogmatism to what has actually happened in the writing of the English sonnet. The history of the English sonnet (which has yet to be adequately written) is a history of constant experiment. Most of Wyatt's sonnets conform to already existing Italian models as regards rhyme-schemes. Surrey's work, on the other hand, exhibits a considerable range of sonnet schemes. Some poems, such as 'Love that doth raine and live within my thought', employ, perhaps for the first time, what was later to be known as the pattern of the Shakespearian sonnet; 'Alas, so all thinges nowe doe holde their peace' utilizes a very individual scheme of *abababababababcc*; 'The fansy which that I have served long' makes use of a variant of this—*abababacaccc*; 'The soote season, that bud and blome furth bringes' uses no more than two rhymes disposed in the pattern of *abababababababaa*. Sidney is sufficiently scornful of sonnet 'legislation' to begin *Astrophel and Stella* with a sonnet in alexandrines, an experiment he repeats in numbers 6, 76 and 77 of the sequence. The variety of rhyme

schemes he employs is too great to be examined here, though
mention must be made of the audacious and brilliant 'Now
that of absence the most irksome night' which uses only two
rhyme words—'day' and 'night'. Spenser's invention of a
new rhyme scheme for the sonnets of the *Amoretti* is too
well-known to need illustration here. Later centuries have
seen a whole series of experiments within the framework of
this most remarkable of poetic forms. A few examples may
suffice to show that Warner's innovations do no more than
continue the spirit of experimentation which has long
marked the English sonnet. Wordsworth's 'From low to
high doth dissolution climb' employs a rhyme scheme of
abbaaccadacdca; Coleridge's 'Dear native Brook! wild
Streamlet of the West' offers the innovatory *abbaacdcdcece*;
Keats' 'If by dull rhymes our English must be chained' is
both a meditation upon the possibilities of sonnet rhyme and
the creation of a new sonnet pattern. Some Victorian
sonneteers were distinctly adventurous, either in metre
(Hopkins is the obvious example; others, like John Payne
and Wilfred Scawen Blunt, wrote sonnets in iambic
tetrameters) or rhyme scheme. Hanmer's 'To the short days,
and the great vault of shade' is an interesting variant on the
two-rhymed sonnet: *abbaabbaabbaba*; J.A.Symonds produced at least one interesting experiment in 'One, who
through waiting years of patient pain', with a rhyme scheme
of *aaabaaabcddcdc*. Twentieth-century sonnet experiments
abound. Dylan Thomas' sequence 'Altarwise by Owl-Light'
is rich in innovations; Auden's handling of the form has an
accomplished flexibility. Amongst contemporary poets,
John Fuller has pointed to an interesting example in James
Fenton's sequence *Our Western Furniture* (1968):

This ironic examination of the confrontation of East and West at
the time of Perry's opening of Japan uses its ingenious symmetrical
arrangement of three groups of seven sonnets as a conscious means
of historical and dramatic organization. In part 1 the Japanese
anticipate, and in part 3 the Americans reminisce. In part 2 they
meet, and in the central sonnet of the sequence display their skills
(abcdefggfedcba).[42]

It is in this tradition of diversity and experimentation that we should locate Warner's sonnets. In fact, of the 64 sonnets mentioned above, some 26 are orthodox Shakespearian sonnets. In many of these Warner's organization of idea and image falls very neatly into the typically Shakespearian pattern of three quatrains plus a couplet. One example must suffice—the 'Sonnet inscribed in a Copy of Andrew Young's *The Poet and the Landscape*':

> Come, take this book with me when winter winds
> Blow boisterous through the crucifixion trees
> And tread again those pathways in our minds,
> Our summer's foliage of memories.
> Why, we have set the sun on Helpston church,
> Sought out the resting-place of weary Crabbe,
> Searched in the roof of Diss, where hawks would perch,
> Seen where King Charles and Rochester would drab.
> Ah, many ways we've wandered, you and I,
> Treading the varied haunts of poetry—
> From where Ben Bulben merges mist with sky
> To Blunden's Suffolk, mill-board reverie.
>   Each place we visit's ours, because your mind
>   Makes the past live till life itself seems kind.

Here the units of sense, the sentences, are precisely coincidental with the units of structure. The structure of the rhyme scheme, that is, serves as a clear articulation of the poet's material; syntax and rhyme scheme are indivisible. Where Warner, in those of his sonnets which employ the Shakespearian rhyme scheme, chooses to override the divisions most naturally suggested by that rhyme scheme, it is usually clear why he has done so. So in 'The Imperious Ones' the absence of any pause at the end of the first quatrain is, in effect, a prosodic enactment of that very freedom from constraint which is seen as characteristic of the great artists discussed. Just as, for them, 'objects bend to personality', so the sonnet-form is subordinated to the recording of those personalities. The more regular form of the third quatrain and final couplet register the poet's own 'humbled' choice of a more modest mode:

The imperious ones—Picasso, Bacon, Moore,
Lifted above themselves by certainty,
Exhilarating self-belief so sure
That objects bend to personality,
Proud God-usurpers, dam the darting stream,
Moulding out strength from leaves of daily life,
With X-ray vision of a killer-beam
Burning fresh outlines with a surgeon's knife.
What self-renewing confidence you have!
Renaissance emperors from a broken past.
What arrow of daring there in all you gave
For us who stumble now the gate is fast!
   Humbled, I praise; yet turn, I must confess,
   To Beckett's truth and Blunden's gentleness.

Of Warner's more obviously 'experimental' sonnets, many
of the most striking and successful are discussed elsewhere in
this study, in connection with the sequences or works in
which they appear. Here I shall do no more than point to
some of the kinds of innovation which have been most typical
of Warner's experiments with the form. Most noticeable,
and without parallel in the earlier sonnet writers noted
above, is his frequent use of alternatives to traditional end
rhyme. He has made extensive use both of medial rhyme and
initial rhyme. The rhyme schemes of *Experimental Sonnets*
have been discussed by Ingrid Melander, and her analysis
need not be repeated here.[43] Sometimes Warner dispenses
entirely with end rhyme. So Poem VIII in *Morning Vespers*
makes exclusive use of initial rhymes, the rhyme sounds
located in the first syllable of each line. Poem XI of the same
sequence, on the other hand, makes use both of end rhyme
and initial rhyme. Where Warner does employ end rhyme at
any point in a sonnet he always does so in lines 13 and 14, also
indenting those lines. The 'Shakespearian' final couplet thus
functions as a clear resolution of the poem and also as a visual
and aural signal to the reader that a poem, the rhyme scheme
of which may not be immediately apparent, is a sonnet. It is
not only in his placement of rhymes within and at the
beginning of lines, rather than just at their end, that Warner's innovations are to be found. The *Experimental Sonnets*

contain such rhyme schemes as (where upper case letters
represent end rhymes and lower case letters rhymes placed
elsewhere in the line) *abcabcdefdefGG* (eg.IV) and *ababcdc-
deffeGG* (eg.XIII). The sonnets of *Morning Vespers* and of
Living Creation employ particularly complex rhyme
schemes, and are discussed in the chapters devoted to those
works. Warner is also very fond of combining the traditional
Shakespearian sonnet scheme (using end rhymes) with an
acrostic message. The *Collected Poems* contains at least nine
such instances.[44] Two sonnets ('Elysium' and 'In Hungary')
add to the initial acrostic a further pattern of letters to form a
double acrostic. The second pattern of letters is, for the
necessary convenience of the reader, italicized in each case.
Warner, it is clear, is not a poet afraid of the 'artificial', or
needlessly suspicious of the virtuoso. One imagines him to be
an admirer of the twenty-two identically acrostic *Hymns to
Astraea* which Sir John Davies published in 1599! Yet
Warner is also a poet capable of a kind of simplicity which
most contemporary poets would view with suspicion. In the
tension between these two impulses lies the key to his
individuality as a poet. It also goes some way towards
explaining the diversity of poetic forms on which he has
drawn, both classical and non-classical.

CHAPTER 5
Experimental Sonnets

The Elizabethan poet Samuel Daniel found in the sonnet both an emblem of creative wholeness and a necessary and effective discipline upon extremes of feeling:

for the body of our imagination being as an unformed *Chaos* without fashion, without day, if by the divine power of the spirit it be wrought into an Orbe of order and forme, is it not more pleasing to Nature, that desires a certaintie and comports not with that which is infinite, to have these clozes, rather than not to know where to end, or how farre to goe, especially seeing our passions are often without measure?[1]

For other writers too the sonnet has seemed, not only the natural vehicle for love poetry, but an emblem of that 'wholeness' to which love aspires. It functions so, for example, in the first meeting of Romeo and Juliet who, as is well known, share a sonnet shaped and rewarded by the exchange of kisses. Indeed, there is powerful tragic resonance in the way in which this initial sonnet is immediately succeeded by the first quatrain of another—only to be interrupted and destroyed by the Nurse's 'Madam, your mother craves a word with you'.[2] We need not be so fanciful as to imagine that, uninterrupted, Romeo and Juliet would have communicated in sonnets for ever after, but the episode does clearly set up the antithesis between, on the one hand, the creative impulse to wholeness, articulated as much by the sonnet form as by what is said, and, on the other hand, the destructive pressures of the circumstances which surround it. The sonnet form in these *Experimental Sonnets* is made to function in a related fashion, its 'orbe of order and forme' subjected to distortion and inversion by the pressures of the events of the sequence's own implied narrative. That the form does not, finally, crack, and that it eventually re-asserts

97

itself is an affirmation of the human capacity to endure, and of its power to resist the encroachments of 'unformed chaos'. All that the words of the poems say is tempered by the truths of the form in which they say it.

Daniel's characteristically sensible observation that the form provides a means of organizing and controlling such 'passions' as 'are often without measure' has an aptness here too. It was precisely such a lesson that Wyatt and Surrey learned when, in the words of George Puttenham, 'they greatly pollished our rude & homely maner of vulgar Poesie from that it had bene before'.[3] For a later 'experimental' poet, Hopkins, the sonnet form—in however individual a transformation—can be seen to have offered a necessary means of disciplining innate linguistic extravagance and of providing a sense of 'order and forme' for a poetic mind which, in some other poems, seems 'not to know where to end, or how farre to go'. Here in Francis Warner's *Experimental Sonnets* 'passions . . . without measure' are both the material of, and the pressure exerted upon, an inherited form which offers both a means for their comprehension (in more senses than one) and a constant reminder of a world of order and measure which exists outside their reach.[4]

The first sonnet immediately juxtaposes the fragmentation of parting and the 'wholeness' of love and poetry. Yet the irony is that the wholeness of art can only be created, can only satisfactorily re-create the wholeness of love, by re-enacting the pain of separation as well as its joyous opposite:

> In order that some splinter may remain
> Of all that glory, here, in my poor verse,
> Let me evoke the strained, satanic pain
> Of vivisecting parting, and rehearse
> Those moments of brief immortality
> Lying oblivious and locked in one.

The poet's purpose is declared with clarity. Separation has already happened, separation expressed in the language of physical pain—'vivisecting parting'.[5] The poems can only offer a 'splinter . . . of all that glory'. Glory here carries the sense of 'a great circle of light' (OED), an image of wholeness and also of that identification of love and light which is so repeated a feature of Warner's work. Its appearance here is one of a series of symmetries set up between the opening and closing poems of the sequence. 'All that glory' in the first sonnet is echoed by 'all that splendour' in sonnet 25; 'brief immortality' in line 5 of this opening poem stands in antithesis to the 'weak mortality' of the final poem's second line; the first poem celebrates

> Dark candle-light and soaring solo boy;
> The soft perfection of your dancing eyes.

The last poem of the sequence concedes that

> Darkness must touch these eyes now.

The sense of design, of the poet's control of his material, is never far to seek in these poems, and is a necessary counterweight to the intensity of their emotional life.

The sequence can offer only a 'splinter' of the lost glory. No more than a fragment is promised—and the poet's talk of 'my poor verse' repeats the promise. Though the chronological perspective—looking back on a union achieved and then destroyed—is unusual, the phrasing here is but one of the sequence's many echoes of the Petrarchan tradition. What has been called the topos of affected modesty[6] has antecedents in Classical and Mediaeval writers, but is a characteristic note struck at the opening of many a Renaissance sonnet sequence. To take but a few English examples, the dedicatory sonnet of Daniel's *Delia* offers 'these my humble rhymes'; Robert Tofte's *Laura* opens with talk of 'these verses rudely penned' and the anonymous author of *Zepheria* promises his reader only 'the humble accent of [his] Muse'.[7] That the poet of these *Experimental Sonnets* should hope to create 'some splinter' of lost glory is in keeping with this topos. A splinter is a fragment remaining after a whole has been shattered; it is also, to quote the OED, 'a comparatively thin piece or slender strip of wood . . . used as a torch, or dipped in tallow and used as a candle'. Throughout Warner's plays the candle frequently functions as an emblem of love's survival in surrounding darkness. In an earlier study of those plays I suggested an affinity with the vision of such authors as Francis Quarles:

Self-consuming, and easily snuffed, readily extinguished by the gusts of sorrow, Quarles finds in the candle a fit emblem of mortality:

> No sooner is this lighted Tapour set
> Upon the transitory Stage
> Of eye-bedarkening night,
> But it is straight subjected to the threat
> Of envious winds, whose wastfull rage
> Disturbs her peacefull light,
> And makes her substance wast, and makes her flame
> less bright.[8]

In these lines from Quarles, as in Warner's plays, the candle is ultimately associated with the larger metaphor of human life as a play, of this world as a 'wide and universal theatre'.[9] Here in the first of the *Experimental Sonnets* the poet's promise is to 'rehearse / Those moments of brief immortality'. The verb, in part, anticipates the theatrical imagery of some of the later poems in the sequence, and in part offers another Petrarchan echo. It is a common pattern of poetry in that tradition that the poet-lover should announce that he intends to 'rehearse his woes' to his lady. Words such as 'splinter', 'rehearse' and the later 'candle-light' offer a context in which we might more fully understand the richly oxymoronic 'brief immortality' of line 5. The whole complex of thought surely owes much to Macbeth's

> Out, out brief candle!
> Life's but a walking shadow; a poor player,
> That struts and frets his hour upon the stage,
> And then is heard no more.[10]

As such we have the first of a series of Shakespearian echoes prominent in the *Experimental Sonnets*.

In the poems, then, the poet seeks to keep alight at least a 'splinter' of former love. In this first sonnet the 'dark candle-light' of line 11 encapsulates both the amatory and the Christian significances of the candle. The candle-light's darkness serves both for 'the tiptoed nights of joy' and as a setting for the 'soaring solo boy' of the Cathedral choir. Both are part of the list 'rehearsed' by the poet, the list of moments which, while ephemeral, are yet experienced as apprehensions of the eternal, moments of 'brief immortality'. Now, though, the poet must come to terms with something rather different—'a country new'. The final couplet's declaration of intent is not without its ambiguities. Is the 're-creation' to be entirely a matter of poetic mimesis? Is his concern with the imitation, in art, of what had previously been experienced? Or is there, perhaps, a hope that the evocation in verse might stir in the 'sweet lady' an eagerness to re-create the experience itself? In either case, that which is to be re-created is 'a world' and the word will stand adequately as an image of either kind of re-creation. We talk, after all, of a poet's 'world'—the imaginative landscape he creates and peoples. The love poetry of the Renaissance also employs the same term as a symbol of the wholeness achieved in the unity of love. The lover in Donne's 'The Good-morrow' can declare to his lady:

> Let us possesse one world, each hath one, and is one.

The promise of that world's re-creation, in whatever sense, is made here, in this first poem, in a perfectly regular Shakespearian sonnet. The poem thus states both the principal themes of the sequence and the formal reference by which we need to read and understand all that follows. Sonnet III is also in regular Shakespearian form—though with the distinguishing addition of an acrostic—and after these two early instances the form does not re-emerge until the very last poem of the sequence, sonnet XXV. In between, the poems explore a range of variations on the form, seeking means to reduce 'passions [that] are without measure' to an 'orbe of order and forme', responding to the pressures of experience and memory, to the exigencies of expression and emotion, not simply by abandoning the form, but by allowing that form to live, refusing to accept 'form' as the mere ossification of that which has been done before. In the interplay of tradition and originality is to be found the source alike of the attitudes and forms of these *Experimental Sonnets*.

The second sonnet opens on a note—of sleeplessness—that many a love poet has struck before. Indeed, Andreas

Capellanus in his *Tractatus De Amore* makes it one of the
'rules' of love that 'minus dormit et edit, quem amoris
cogitatio vexat'.[11] Amongst sonneteers there are well-known
poems on the theme by, among others, della Casa, Chariteo,
Desportes, Daniel and Sidney. We are returned, with this
poem of the lover's sleeplessness, to the first stages of the
poet's relationship with his lady. The sequence's sense of
design, which we noted in the parallelisms between the first
and last poems, is further sustained here. This second poem
is a poem of dawn; the penultimate poem, no. XXIV, begins
with 'the breaking dawn'. In the imagery of no. II the motif
of the arts continues. The passing of sleepless nights has,
says the lover, 'etched' his 'brow with music of contempt'.
The poet's imagination is ceaselessly stimulated, but provides him only with teasing fictions:

> Ten thousand times that starlight's pushed my lids
> To demonstrate a breeze is not your hair
> Trailing in lines across my cheek to tease
> And half-create your darkling mockery.

The internal rhyme of 'demonstrate' and 'create' (reinforced
by the reiteration of create's first vowel in 'breeze' and
'tease') throws emphasis on the poet's ability only to 'half-
create' (this is not the re-creation of the first sonnet). 'Half-
create' takes its place with those figures of incompleteness
and fragmentation we have already noted in the first poem,
figures which stand in antithesis to the wholeness of the
worlds of love and art. Here there is no more than a 'semi-
globe'; the poet is but 'one little fragment of the night'. He
can only 'whittle down the ember hours'—whittling being
the activity of cutting shavings from a piece of wood; a
means of passing the time; a means of shaping that 'splinter'
(from the opening of the sequence) which is the poetry
itself. In their incompleteness and imperfection the
sleepless poet's imaginings are no more than fantasy
('moonshine of a lover's fantasy') and must inevitably drift
towards bitterness:

> Imaginings grow worse,
> While God plays snooker with the universe.

This last is one of those abrupt modernizations of an older topos which give the *Experimental Sonnets* their particular character. It is a vision and a metaphor which relates to judgements such as Bosola's that

> We are merely the stars' tennis-balls, struck and banded
> Which way please them[12]

or Sidney's observation that 'mankind . . . are but like tennis balls, tossed by the racket of the higher powers'.[13] The wittiness of Warner's conceit balances an awareness of the statement's final excessiveness with a painful feeling of its present appositeness. Ingrid Melander has noted how this final sentence of the poem serves to widen the sequence's themes:

> Throughout this poem there is an undercurrent of hidden anxiety, which is . . . [here] . . . given a wider perspective by reference to God's indifference towards his creation. The woes of a lover's sleeplessness have been fused here with man's more universal fear of loneliness and separation from God.[14]

The way thus being prepared, Sonnet III considers the motives for life itself, from the febrile perspective of the lover lamenting separation from his lady. In the best Petrarchan tradition the poet 'burns' with love (line 13). That 'burning' may be a restless discomfort, but it is also a motive for life itself, a source, indeed, of the poet's continuing desire to live:

> Living on memory that seems a dream.

The dismissal, as irrelevant, of other possible motives for life is the poem's chief concern. The attractions of finance or capitalism, or of the 'social' virtues of justice and honour are alike dismissed:

> I draw what sustenance still gives me life
> Not from the worldly dust for which men sweat,
> Grinding in busy streets—the smiling strife
> And vampire business-deals that breed on debt;
> . . . Nor from high hopes of honourable age,
> Justice, or social platitude—that cloak
> Invoked by petty minds to ape the sage.

Similarly rejected is 'the eunuch-mystic's incense smoke'. What is rejected here is the apparatus of a false mysticism— its falsity apparent in its sexlessness, its sterility. Warner's verse always places a great positive value on sexuality— prime image of human creativity—while never being without a pained and painful sense of its dangers. The harsh satirical note of rejection in these central lines of the sonnet is significantly tempered in the polite formality of the poem's final couplet:

> Lacking such spurs, another makes me burn;
> Look in the left-hand column, dear, and learn.

Until we reach the twenty-fifth and final poem of the sequence, this is the last regular Shakespearian sonnet that we shall encounter. The poem is invested with an additional formality, a further sense of a poet entirely in control of the disposition of his material, by the presence of that acrostic to which the final line of the poem directs us. That the poem should fulfil two pre-ordained formal patterns serves to suggest that for all his intensity of feeling the poet is still very clearly in control of his emotions, and of the direction and shape of his 'imaginings'. The 'passions' have been brought within the bounds of a traditional form.

All the more startling, in consequence, is the formal and emotional distortion which characterizes the fourth poem in the sequence. What was incipiently febrile in III now 'becomes fever-bout' (line 7) in IV. Poems I and III were regular Shakespearian sonnets, as we have seen. Poem II did, in the words of the sequence's prefatory note 'change the traditional form by bringing many of the rhyme-words in from the end of lines, usually to the centre'. The rhyme-pattern thus produced was, however, still that of the Shakespearian sonnet, the 'norm' which poem I had established. This is clear from examination, by way of example, of the first four lines:

> No, I've not *slept* or rested, though it must   *a*
> Be dawn by *now*, for daylight hints the room;   *b*
> The clocks have *kept* each patient quarter-hour   *a*
> And etched my *brow* with music of contempt.   *b*

In Poem IV, however, this Shakespearian norm is much less fully in evidence—the 'form' comes close to fragmentation under the pressure of extreme emotion. The basic structure of three quatrains plus a couplet has now vanished, as the following analysis will show:

Sick with this *black* despair of loving you,	*a*
Absent, desper*ate* for your company,	*b*
Your voice, your *eyes*; knowing you with another,	*c*
Snared by a mocking *pack* that's hunting still,	*a*
Your undefended *bait* their leering sport,	*b*
Their grinned and greasy *sty* new-fanged your trap,	*c*
Time becomes fever-*bout*, fleshed broken glass,	*d*
A purgatory *pace* around the skull,	*e*
A plain with *walls* and ceiling closing in	*f*
As hope ebbs *out* and candles gutter down	*d*
And such dis*grace* scars incapacity	*e*
It *scalds* raw, dislocated, ransacked mind	*f*
Until I know there is no deeper *hell*	*g*
Than this, sweet Christ! of loving you too *well.*	*g*

Only the closing couplet, in its neatness and certainty, remains to insist upon the Shakespearian sonnet, to assert its continued presence as a formal point of reference, even if these fourteen lines have not fallen into its pattern. The first twelve lines here, as far as rhyme-scheme is concerned, are organised as four triplets rather than three quatrains. Even so, we should note that the rhyme-fellows in each case are four lines apart—*a*bc*a*, *b*ca*b*, etc. The shadow of organisation by quatrains remains, but not the substance. The poem's opening seems little more than the stock Petrarchan lament for an absent lady. From the middle of the third line, however, the tone changes disturbingly and menacingly. Just as behind the poem's formal organisation there lingers the shadow of a traditional form, so behind the imagery of lines 3-6 (a kind of quatrain hinted at by the rhyme *eyes-sty*) lies the shadow of a traditional motif—but a shadow become grotesque. The 'hunt of love' is a common subject in the love poetry of the Middle Ages and the Renaissance. It will be familiar to most readers from Wyatt's 'Whoso list to hunt I know where is an hind' or Petrarch's 'Una candida cerva

sopra l'erba'. In various transmutations it appears quite
frequently in the work of the Elizabethan sonneteers, or in a
popular song like the anonymous 'Blow thy horn, hunter'.
The notion that involvement in that hunt may lead to
suffering is never very far away. Samuel Daniel, in the
sonnets to *Delia*, presents a hunter-lover who has become the
victim of his own capacity for thought:

> Whilst youth and error led my wandring minde,
> And set my thoughts in heedeles waies to range:
> All unawares a Goddesse chaste I finde,
> Diana-like, to worke my suddaine change.
> For her no sooner had my view bewrayd,
> But with disdaine to see me in that place:
> With fairest hand, the most unkindest maide,
> Castes water-cold disdaine upon my face.
> Which turn'd my sport into a Harts dispaire,
> Which still is chac'd, whilst I have any breath,
> By mine owne thoughts: set on me by my faire,
> My thoughts like houndes, pursue me to my death.
> > Those that I fostred of mine owne accord,
> > Are made by her to murther thus their Lord.[15]

Tormented by his 'thoughts like houndes', sunk in 'a Harts
despair' in the fourth of these *Experimental Sonnets*, the poet
imagines his lady as the object—but the seemingly willing
object—of a 'pack that's hunting still'. She is herself the 'bait'
that encourages 'their leering sport'. The word 'bait' effectively transports us to another very *un*Petrarchan sonnet, no.
129 of Shakespeare's *Sonnets*, that dreadful meditation upon
lust, before and after 'action':

> Past reason hunted, and no sooner had,
> Past reason hated as a swallowed bait.

The 'hunting' here is close in tone and purpose to that
imagined in Warner's poem. It is worth noting that this
fourth sonnet employs in its final couplet precisely the
rhyme-words (albeit in reverse order) of Shakespeare's
closing couplet:

> All this the world well knows, yet none knows well
> To shun the heav'n that leads men to this hell.[16]

The 'hunt' in this fourth sonnet of Warner's begins in line 3; 'knowing' in that line introduces a description which is to be read, surely, not as knowledge of something which is objectively true, but as the fruits of an obsessed and jealous mind. Here, indeed, is evidence of the second sonnet's warning that 'imaginings grow worse'. These are thoroughly unpleasant 'imaginings'—the 'mocking pack', 'leering', the 'grinned and greasy sty'—all are vivid evidence of that 'fever-bout' which is named in line 7. The poem's final couplet, with its talk of 'loving you too well', is very relevant here. The final phrase sets up distinct literary echoes. It alludes, unmistakably, to Othello's final speech, to his injunction that he should be remembered as 'one that lov'd not wisely, but too well'.[17] Othello's 'unwisdom' was primarily that of jealousy, and in the dramatic expression of jealousy the 'imaginings' of Shakespeare's characters frequently find articulation in just the kind of animal imagery which we have encountered here in the fourth of these *Experimental Sonnets*. Desdemona was, as we know, innocent of all that that imagery implied about her. Its 'truth' related more to the mental state of those who employed it than to the behaviour or character of Desdemona. It seems reasonable to assume that here, too, in this fourth sonnet, the truth of such images resides in their fidelity to the state of the poet's mind, in the 'fever-bout' of his jealousy and frustration, rather than in any 'objective' truth that they might express about the behaviour of the woman he loves. As the sonnet continues its concern is more and more with the state of the poet's soul. The second half of the poem is governed by a series of terms which carry what one might, loosely, call 'theological' overtones—purgatory, hope, candles, (dis) grace, hell, Christ. A key link between the amatory and the religious dimensions of the poem is provided by the word 'disgrace'. Its significance is complex. The poet feels himself 'disgraced'—humiliated by his apparent rejection; insofar as that rejection 'scars' (line 11) him, it mars the 'grace' of his own human dignity. In Petrarchan poetry, the lover woos his lady in the hope of winning her 'grace', her favour. So Sidney, in the opening lines of *Astrophil and Stella* provides

Astrophil with the motive for the composition of the ensuing poems:

> Loving in truth, and fain in verse my love to show,
> That she (dear she) might take some pleasure of my pain;
> Pleasure might cause her read, reading might make
>   her know;
> Knowledge might pity win, and pity grace obtain.[18]

The poet-lover excluded from his lady's favour is, it follows, in a state of dis-grace. Naturally the spiritual overtones of such diction are not to be overlooked. 'Grace' became a key word in the vocabulary of Renaissance love poetry, as it was in the courtly-love poetry of the Middle Ages. To be deprived of the lady's 'grace' is to be in the darkness beyond the light of love, that darkness where 'candles gutter down' (line 10). In the first of the *Experimental Sonnets* the light of the candle had both erotic and spiritual significance. Here too its extinguishing locates the poet in a position of deprivation which has spiritual as well as amorous dimensions. The fever and physical pain of line 7 ('fleshed broken glass') is followed by the sense of mental confinement—'a purgatory pace around the skull'. The sense of imprisonment and restriction increases in the following lines, and the 'purgatory' of line 8 becomes the 'hell' of line 13. That fragmentation which, throughout the sequence, stands in antithesis to the wholeness of love is forcefully present in the 'dislocated' and 'ransacked' of line 12, while the same line's 'scalds' both anticipates sonnet VI and makes almost grotesquely literal the familiar Petrarchan conceit of the unhappy lover who 'burns'. This fourth sonnet is one of the finest in the sequence, rich both in the personally immediate and in the texture of allusion. In its final couplet, indeed, we are offered a reminder not only of Othello (apt in the context of jealousy), but also of another tragic hero, Marlowe's Doctor Faustus (apt in the context of damnation). The final line's 'sweet Christ!' echoes Faustus' favourite adjective and his final cry to Christ.[19] The theatrical resonances which we have noted in earlier sonnets are here developed in ways that broaden the sequence's concerns. Increasingly the poems seek to examine, not merely the position of the lover, but what that position suggests about the nature of human experience understood more broadly. The next sonnet, no.V, ends with a ringing phrase which might serve as a formulation of one of the central insights of the tragic tradition—the 'splendour of man's insignificance'.

Sonnet V takes, once more, the poet's sense of his inability to exist, independent of the woman, as its starting point. Like the Donne of 'A Nocturnall upon St. Lucies Day' the poet-lover seeks to define his condition in terms of 'things which are not':

> What can I do, what can I think or say
> Without you? What tight wrench of mind can twist
> Even one simple operation plain
> Undedicated to your distant thought,
> Unshadowed by your lightning; unrehearsed . . .

'Undedicated . . . unshadowed . . . unrehearsed'; the accumulating negative prefixes invert some of the sequence's positive values. It is impossible for the poet to conceive of the present absence being readily overcome—'we shall meet, only to part'. That meeting, and parting, may be understood as a specifically sexual encounter or merely as a brief re-affirmation of the happiness of love. Poetically the force is carried by the contrasts of imagery. The 'anvil' tortures are coupled with the 'blackness' of the pit—taking us back to the 'hell' of the previous sonnet. The pit also shares a verb—'to leer'—with the 'mocking pack' of no. IV. The heavy and bestial imagery of that poem—reinforced by a different kind of weight in the 'anvil' of the present sonnet—stands in stark contrast to the light and lightness (of movement) in the eleventh and twelfth lines of sonnet V:

> Till the next kingfisher moment cut the dark
> In meteor career down to the sea.

The presence of simultaneous polarities (albeit only for a 'moment') is here evoked with considerable power. The image evokes a painting like, say, Barnett Newman's *Onement V*, with its single central line of light, a metaphorical expression of traditional creation myths, the separation of light from darkness. In such a context the final couplet's approach to metaphysical generalization, striking after the concreteness of the preceding lines, seems entirely natural. In terms of the sequence's larger design, it should be noted that this couplet, closing the fifth sonnet from the beginning, is directly reflected by that of no. XXI, the fifth sonnet from the end of the sequence. The two couplets read thus:

> Strange comment by that phantom circumstance
> On splendour of man's insignificance (V)

and

> Ah, comedy divine, man's tragedy—
> Why make us gambol in our agony? (XXI)

The two might very reasonably be seen as symmetrical wings of a triptych, whose central panel is provided by the final couplet of the medial poem of the sequence, no. XIII:

> Is there a reason behind human care?
> What is the acreage of its despair.

Sonnets VI and VII of the sequence hold in precarious balance despair and, in its antithesis, faith. The presence of that balance, however ephemeral its achievement, is echoed in the re-adoption of the Shakespearian sonnet form— though in each case the quatrains involve medial rhyme rather than end rhyme. In VI the couplet, which thus stands out as the most traditionally regular formal unit in the poem, is also distinguished by its fitting use of more traditionally 'poetic' diction:

> If this prime, envied bud of life is ours,
> Why do we catalogue our thorns and briars?

The rose, though not actually named, is the governing image in these lines, and its employment evokes a whole tradition of love poetry—in the *Roman de la Rose*, in Waller, in Shakespeare's *Sonnets*, in Yeats. Yet the rose of perfected love in these lines (no more than a bud as yet) is seemingly inaccessible behind its barrier of thorns and briars. The opening lines of the sonnet register, with an image of disturbing physical force, that devastation of innocence which is the experience of love defeated or betrayed:

> There are some moments when the mind is scorched
> More than a kettle down a baby's face,
> Or spark in eye.

In despite of such experiences, the lover, unless hopelessly 'cynicized' (VII), attempts once more the act of trust that is love, encouraged by 'that transcendental meeting'— referring back to the meeting of sonnet V, and to the 'transcendent flame' of sonnet VIII. To make such an attempt is, of course, to expose oneself to danger, to uncover one's most essential being:

> Undefended, unrestrained, in love
> And vulnerable, keeping nothing hid.

With those lines the second quatrain comes to a close, on a note of 'hesitating trust'. The violence of line 9 thus effects a *volta*-like change of direction:

> A whip-crack at that delicately balanced
> Perfected instant cataracts the nerve
> And snaps the backbone like a cygnet's wing
> In tortured wince and catastrophic end.

As a statement this third quatrain is open to interpretation both as the presentation of a generalized truth—at any such moment of extreme vulnerability rejection or betrayal are likely to be beyond bearing—or as a narrative of events in the particular relationship which is the immediate subject of these poems. The lines repeat the sequence's earlier juxtaposition of wholeness and fragmentation; the 'perfected instant' is snapped 'like a cygnet's wing'—this last a powerful echo of the poem's opening image of innocence and aspiration violently marred. The final couplet's question is not merely rhetorical. One answer to it lies in the inescapability of the briars:

Roses have thorns, and silver fountains mud.

Innocence, in a fallen world, must discover that

Rough winds do shake the darling buds of May.

It is naivety rather than innocence that anticipates 'roses, roses all the way'.[20] The thorns and briars that surround love's rose in this sonnet sequence are experienced and articulated in imagery of considerable violence, as we have seen. In the significance of that violence resides another answer to the poet's own question as to 'why . . . we catalogue our thorns and briars?'. In an essay published in 1965—the very same year as *Experimental Sonnets*—Francis Warner addressed himself to the topic of 'Violence and Contemporary Poetry'.[21] One concern of that essay is to wonder whether poetry has not, too often, ignored an important area of human experience that may, perhaps, conceal some insight of value:

Violence is an undeniable fact of human existence, and in the psychology of every individual, however peace-loving. It is usually latent, controlled towards some civilised end. But is the humanist missing something of value when he sees it only in an evil light? Yeats's most famous statement on the change he believed had to come in English poetry . . . is in his last great poem, *Under Ben Bulben*:

> You that Mitchel's prayer have heard,
> 'Send war in our time, O Lord!'
> Know that when all words are said
> And a man is fighting mad,
> Something drops from eyes long blind,
> He completes his partial mind,
> For an instant stands at ease,
> Laughs aloud, his heart at peace.
> Even the wisest man grows tense
> With some sort of violence
> Before he can accomplish fate,
> Know his work or choose his mate.

To grant this argument is to understand why the poet must 'catalogue' the thorns and briars. In sonnet VII the violence resides in the similes offered for its own condition by a mind

given over to 'irrational fright'. The irrationality of that fear
is acknowledged in its designation as 'a restless fear beneath
my brain'. In the fear is the loss of that trust and confidence
towards which the previous sonnet had shown the poet
taking 'hesitating' steps. Separation from the loved one
becomes a kind of imprisonment—a variation on that sense
of 'walls and ceiling closing in' that we met in no. IV. The
'confidence' the poet sought in sonnet VI is now subjected to
the cynical jeers his own 'panicking thoughts' provoke. Gone
is any trust, any confidence that love can endure absence:

> Love like a natural scene evaporates
> When the horizon's clanged its gates.

Though the diction and imagery may be peculiarly modern
('the blackboard chalk' and the 'sparrow stamped upon / By
hob-nailed schoolboy') the theme is a recurrent one in
Renaissance sonnet sequences. Once again the poems provoke a particular kind of doubleness of focus, a constant
sense of their being simultaneously traditional and innovatory.

Much the same might be said of the next sonnet in the
sequence. Poem VIII leaves behind the doubts which characterize its predecessor. The final couplet of VII leaves us
reflecting on a disturbing gap between the rhetoric and
reality of love, between what is said and what is felt. The gap
is due, not to dishonesty, but to the difficulty of absolute
faith:

> I say our faith is mutual, and sure;
> And yet I fear, lest yours may not endure.

Very different is the ringing confidence and declamatory
manner of Sonnet VIII:

> From the creation of that evening, when
> Shipwrecked by chaosed winds, our new-touched lives
> Flashed and leaped high in one transcendent flame,
> Not isolation, distance, weakness, fear,
> Restless, cycloning minds, physically
> Separated by irony of past
> Yet anchored each within the other's brain—

Mockery, silence, disease, temptation; nothing
Has sullied absolute relationship.
Yet this leech world conspires against such light,
Seeks to snuff down and squeeze under its slime
Those who are not brutalized to despair.
Will may corrode and pain can split the bone;
Nothing eradicates what we have known.

Many of the sequence's themes, treated separately in other
sonnets, come together here. The catalogue of love's
enemies, the 'thorns and briars', takes the form of an uncom-
fortably insistent list of nouns. The poem's point of departure, however, is the 'creation of that evening'—presumably
the 'transcendental meeting' of Sonnet VI. The word 'creation' brings with it some of those ambiguities which were
earlier raised by the final couplet of Sonnet I. The lovers'
meeting was creative—it created 'all that glory' (I); the noun
used here envisages that creative moment as analogous to
cosmic creation itself, and to the creative activity of the
artist. Prior to their meeting the lovers had been 'shipwrecked by chaosed winds'. The imagery takes a good deal of
its force from its re-employment of the stock materials of
Petrarchan love poetry. The metaphor involved is common
in Petrarch's own work. It is familiar from, say, no. 80 of the
Canzoniere ('Chi è fermato di menar sua vita') or from the
opening of no. 317:

> Tranquillo porto avea mostrato Amore
> a la mia lunga et torbida tempesta.

No. 189 of the *Canzoniere* is well known to English readers
from its imitation by Wyatt in 'My galy charged with for-
getfulness'. Spenser's use of the motif in the *Amoretti* is less
closely tied to Petrarch:

> Lyke as a ship that through the Ocean wyde,
>   by conduct of some star doth make her way,
>   whenas a storme hath dimd her trusty guyde,
>   out of her course doth wander far astray.
> So I whose star, that wont with her bright ray,
>   me to direct, with cloudes is overcast,
>   doe wander now in darkness and dismay,
>   through hidden perils round about me plast.

Yet hope I well, that when this storme is past
    my *Helice* the lodestar of my lyfe
    will shine again, and looke on me at last,
    with lovely light to cleare my cloudy grief.
Till then I wander carefull comfortlesse,
    in secret sorrow and sad pensiveness.[22]

It is in this tradition that much in sonnet VIII belongs, not
only the shipwreck and winds of line 2, but also line 7 with its
assertion that the two lovers are 'anchored each within the
other's brain'. Oddly enough, in a poem published only one
year later, Seamus Heaney was to produce a related updating
of this same Petrarchan motif:

Lady with the frilled blouse
And simple tartan skirt,
Since you have left the house
Its emptiness has hurt
All thought. In your presence
Time rode easy, anchored
On a smile; but absence
Rocked love's balance, unmoored
The days. They buck and bound
Across the calendar
Pitched from the quiet sound
Of your flower-tender
Voice. Need breaks on my strand;
You've gone, I am at sea.
Until you resume command
Self is in mutiny.[23]

In the eighth of Warner's *Experimental Sonnets* the adjective
applied to the winds which make their contribution to the
'torbida tempesta' serves to widen the significance of the
image. 'Chaosed' relates to 'creation' in line 1 to suggest that
what is here created is a 'world' ('each hath one and is one')
which can offer a positive value to stand against the 'leech
world' of the third quatrain of the poem. In the moment of
'creation' the lovers' 'new-touched lives / Flashed and leaped
high in one transcendent flame'. The 'flame' of love is a
common motif in Renaissance love poetry. In Donne's

'Love's Deitie', for example, reciprocal love is that moment 'when an even flame two hearts did touch'. Donne's verb is also here in Warner's sonnet. It involves many of the same ambiguities of meaning which Sidney exploits in his use of the word in the ninth sonnet of *Astrophil and Stella*. The lovers' lives take on a new emotional intensity, and they have been 'fired' (as with a touch-paper) into this new and 'transcendent' flame. The image takes us back to the splinter and candles of the first sonnet, as well as anticipating the unnamed candle of the final quatrain here. The verbs 'flashed and leaped', though, have an energy and intensity which serve rather to associate the image, in its sudden blaze of light against surrounding darkness, with, say, the separation of light and dark in sonnet V—that 'kingfisher moment' which can 'cut the dark'. Volpone travesties the positive values of light and creation in the opening speech of Jonson's play, but the language he there uses has considerable power. The object of his praises:

> Shew'st like a flame by night, or like the day
> Struck out of chaos, when all darkness fled
> Unto the centre.[24]

In Warner's poem 'the creation of that evening' is also like 'the day / Struck out of chaos'. We are necessarily reminded of Daniel's words on the achievements of art, with which this chapter began, with its image of 'the body of our imagination . . . as an unformed *Chaos*'. The poet's experience of life without the woman he loves is that it is lived amongst 'chaosed winds'.[25] The 'orbe of order and forme' is absent and can be found only in the experience of fulfilled love, that created 'whole' which is analogous to the created whole of the finished poem. Each, in its wholeness, has the capacity to stand up against its enemies and to endure. Love faces the dangers of 'isolation, distance, weakness, fear', of 'mockery, silence, disease, temptation'. For the moment, at any rate, the poet is confident of their love's power to remain above the threats of either time or space. It is its own world of light. Yet that 'world' must exist within the context of another world, and that other world 'conspires against such light'. Once more the light of love is symbolized by a candle, a candle which the darkness-loving world seeks to 'snuff down'. The writer's sense is of a world where all is 'bleared, smeared'.[26] 'Slime' stands in sharp opposition to 'absolute relationship'. The world's desire to put out the light, to cover it with slime, produces a 'despair' which is 'brutalized' because it is less than fully and properly human. The poem's couplet, though, while recognizing the world's power ('Will may corrode and pain can split the bone') also recognizes the limitations of that power, since 'nothing eradicates what we have known'. In art and in memory, at least, love has no dealings with the 'rags of time'.[27]

It is natural that such an affirmation should be followed by an attempt to understand what it is in the beloved that enables such faith (just as natural as that other sonnets should seek to locate the sources of love's betrayal). Given the governing images of sonnet VIII, it is hardly surprising that its successor should identify the lady as a custodian of the 'flame' of love:

> Is it a certain gentleness, a touch
> Of unmistakable nobility
> Under your curtain and façade of life
> That breaks discourtesy, complete respect?
> Or exercise of unobtrusive taste;
> A tact, finding beneath this hell of strain,
> Instinctively, one small, elusive joy
> Guttering in the heath-storm of the mind;
> And cherishes, until the rain-blown spark
> Curls to new radiance, throws back the night,
> Beacons from hill to hill, transcends the sun,
> Hurls suffering to insignificance?
>   Is it a certain quality of soul?
>   Yes, all of these; for you have made me whole.

The woman's quality resides in her capacity to recognize the light beneath the slime, beneath the 'hell of strain', to see the candle 'guttering in the heath-storm of the mind'. A candle melts away rapidly when it gutters; its light is frighteningly fragile against the Lear-like heath storm, but in the woman's tact there exists a power to renew and

strengthen it, so that it might take on a greatly increased
power, as it

> Curls to new radiance, throws back the night.

Here is the 'creation' of the previous sonnet echoed afresh;
indeed, as the light's power increases and spreads, as it
'beacons from hill to hill' (Warner's use of this verb perhaps
owes something to Shelley's *Adonais*)[28] it may act as a guide
to those presently in danger of being 'shipwrecked by
chaosed winds'. The creative power of love is restorative and
redemptive. In these poems of fulfilled love it is the force
which 'hurls suffering to insignificance' and makes the poet
'whole'.

Sonnet X takes as its subject a rather different encounter
with darkness. The poet (and presumably the woman) are in
a car travelling through the countryside at night. The poem
does not deal exclusively, or necessarily, with the lovers'
relationship. It is not a love poem in the direct sense that its
predecessors are. The poem has been well discussed by both
Suheil Bushrui and Ingrid Melander.[29] Bushrui finds in the
owl which looms from the darkness 'the visitation of a nature
spirit'.[30] Certainly the sonnet evokes with considerable
vividness—though with a slightly blurred quality, befitting a
dark and misty night—the life of owl and rabbit in a time and
place where there is 'no prate of peopled England'. Inside the
metal and glass of their car, however, the human visitors are
alienated from their surroundings. That alienation is recorded in words such as 'widow' and 'shroud'. Bushrui points,
tellingly, to lines in Coleridge's 'Dejection':

> And in our life alone does Nature live:
> Ours is her wedding garment, ours her shroud[31]

In this tenth sonnet the relationship of man and nature is
symbolized more aptly by the shroud than by the wedding-
garment. Yet the poem does raise the possibility that men
(and women) might 'unkiss the shroud and lift the latch of
dark'. In the relationship with nature, as in the relationship
of human love, there lies the 'promise' of renewal, of a

redemption from alienation. In sonnet VIII the lovers' lives were 'new-touched'. Now

> New senses register. Re-live all these
> As moving emblems of our sympathies.

Nature's activity becomes a kind of moving picture-book of emblems (precisely what it was, for example, for the writers of the Bestiaries). Its emblems are also emotionally 'moving'; they speak of 'sympathies' which have their significance in other realms too.

Fittingly, sonnet XI is another night-piece. This, though, is very much an interior, and very explicitly a love-poem:

> When day's ranked, echoing pageantry is furled,
> Yielding me benediction of your breast,
> A prisoner flanked in nipple sentinels,
> Full dereliction by the universe
> Cannot disturb this bedside candle's flame,
> Or break the quiet of your mystery:
> No war perturb, no butcher-doubts usurp
> The spirit's diet of love's harvestry.
> Your pillowed calm breeds life, and can renew
> Oceans and continents in a caress
> Where all the motions of eternity
> Touch the still trembling pity of your peace.
>> Beside such miracle, why, earth's crammed store
>> To rim of outer space is beggared poor.

The activities of the social day are the lesser reality. The pageantry involves much waving of flags, but it is an 'insubstantial pageant', perhaps even a 'crumbling pageant'.[32] 'Ranked' introduces a chain of military images—'yielding . . . a prisoner . . . sentinels'. Such imagery has, of course, been common in love poetry since, at least, Ovid. Here it also stands in antithesis to the non-figurative use of 'war' in line 7. In its presentation of the lovers in bed, the poem mixes tonal effects very attractively. That he should be 'a prisoner flanked in nipple sentinels' is a conceit in the tradition of Baroque anatomical wit. Its playfulness is somewhat moderated by the 'benediction' of line 2. In that benediction—anticipating 'mystery' in line 6 and 'miracle' in line 13—is a strength and richness that cannot be disturbed by 'war' or 'butcher-doubts'. The physical activities of others ('war') or the 'cycloning minds' (VIII) of the lovers themselves are alike unable to 'disturb this bedside candle's flame'. The candle, which is so effectively reiterated an image in these poems, is here at its most stable—neither 'guttering in the heath-storm of the mind' nor bursting into new radiance. Sonnet XI is perhaps the calmest and most emotionally assured in the sequence. It seems to speak from a full experience of 'the spirit's diet of love's harvestry'. The capacity of love and beauty to renew and restore is beautifully celebrated in the poem's third quatrain. No merely natural riches can compete with this 'harvestry' of love:

> Beside such miracle, why, earth's crammed store
> To rim of outer space is beggared poor.

As so often in the sequence love is seen in terms of a cosmic analogy. The woman's 'pillowed calm' renews 'oceans and continents'. In the presence of her beauty the poet experiences the very 'motions of eternity'. Here the dominant note is of a freshly achieved and experienced serenity. Sonnet XII is very different in tone and purpose.

The lucid calm of its predecessor is replaced in sonnet XII by a tense complexity perhaps greater than at any other point in this sequence of poems. Syntactically the poem is complex. Ingrid Melander writes of the first quatrain:

These four lines, which introduce the central theme, contain a series of major anticipatory constituents: two -ing participle clauses (line 1), three verbless adjective clauses (lines 2 and 3), and a verbless adverbial clause (line 4). Not until line 5 does the main clause begin by the introduction of the addressee.[33]

That addressee is the 'lonely impulse' of line 5. The verb of this main clause—'illumine'—does not appear until line 7. This 'lonely impulse' is, we are told, 'warm without form' and 'outside the cradle and bier of mammocked creation'. This last phrase is striking for its use of the word 'mammocked'. The reader is likely to be familiar with the word— the verb to 'mammock' means to tear to pieces—only from

Shakespeare's use of it in *Coriolanus*, in Valeria's description of the young Marcius:

I saw him run after a gilded butterfly; and when he caught it, he let it go again; and after it again; and over and over he comes, and up again; catched it again; or whether his fall enraged him, or how 'twas, he did so set his teeth, and tear it. O, I warrant, how he mammocked it.[34]

A 'creation' for which 'mammocked' is the appropriate adjective is one which one might, indeed, prefer to stay out of. 'Doubtful of wintry world', why leave one's formless warmth? The 'lonely impulse', it appears, is a possible human existence, a new human life 'hesitant whether to exist'. The poem is addressed to the unborn, potential, child which may be brought into being by the two lovers. They are 'anchored in tangible substance', very much inside 'the cradle and bier of mammocked creation'. Their lives are a 'fardel of drives and inherited flesh'. The word fardel activates another Shakesperean allusion. Hamlet's soliloquy in Act III Scene i finds him wondering

> Who would fardels bear,
> To grunt and sweat under a weary life,
> But that the dread of something after death,
> The undiscover'd country, from whose bourn
> No traveller returns, puzzles the will,
> And makes us rather bear those ills we have
> Than fly to others that we know not of?

Hamlet must decide 'to be or not to be' in the face of fears as to what may be beyond death. The addressee of this sonnet—'grappling with fear, riding the razor-edge / Of being, hesitant whether to exist'—must make its choice in the face of fears as to what lies beyond birth. It must decide whether to 'receive the catastrophe of human day'. 'Catastrophe' here has both its popular sense, and its technical sense of the denouement of a drama. The metaphor which will later govern sonnet XXIV is here anticipated. There is, even so, the sense that if this 'impulse' accepts the poet's plea, it will be a 'warrant' of their existence; it will be that which gives authority to their lives, by which they might imagine them-

selves 'reaching beyond the cloyed and derangeable cosmos'.
For all its complexity it is clear that the sonnet continues that
same interplay between different senses of the concept of
'creation' which we have traced in earlier poems. This is the
point at which their human experience can be at its most
profound, their point of closest contact with the 'nexus of
void and becoming'. Not for the first time the sequence
proceeds by offering an abrupt contrast in the next poem.[35]

Sonnet XIII is a bleak statement of human isolation and
alienation. It sets the poet in a hotel room—modern urban
symbol of transience and rootlessness. The contrast is stark
both with the natural and 'moving emblems of our sympathies' explored in sonnet X, and with the mutuality affirmed
in sonnet XI (and even, allowing for a considerable difference in tone, in sonnet XII). Alone, in a world of discrete
and unconnected objects, the poet's is a death-like experience, a kind of 'nightmare life-in-death', to borrow a Coler-
idgean phrase once more: [36]

> A towel; suitcase; this a hotel room.
> Each object, élite, curiously numb:
> Clean, empty place of unreality,
> All singly neat. Mad traffic hurtling on,
> Metal, below, The bed's bare winding-sheets.

The bed is now a death-bed, emblem not of 'sympathies' but
of sterility. No longer a bed of love, it stands also as an
emblem, as we might by now expect, of another kind of loss
of creativity. Such an environment—and what it says of the
human condition—makes the writer abandon his own creative activity:

> Why sit down
> To throw an understatement on a page?

Sanity seems hard to maintain, numbness the best defence.
In numbness of feeling and articulation—'force the hand
still'—lies a possible defence, but the inevitable price of such
a defence against immediate suffering is despair. There may
indeed be a 'reason' behind human care and despair. Despair

may be a defence against even greater pain. The sonnet's final couplet poses the question in terms that demand both theological and psychological answers. If this sonnet's 'solution' is forced upon us, then there is, indeed, no 'reason behind human care', our condition becomes a wholly and frighteningly irrational one. But this is not the conclusion of the sequence, only the question posed by its numerically central poem. We need not be surprised that its successor should be a poem in which positive values and 'reasons' are discovered.

The natural world is again important in sonnet XIV. It is the background against which the poet's beloved is seen; more precisely she is seen against the background of a mountain waterfall, emblem of the endlessly changing but never-changed. The poet is analytical observer, she is innocent participant, the antithesis articulated in the 'aware' of line 1 and the 'unaware' of line 8:

> Aware, across this mountain baritoned
> Moss-bearded waterfall, that as you bend
> Carefree beside the green-eyed, weeping race,
> Even the elusive moments comprehend
> Only in retrospect; becoming, change:
> That thought destroys, though desperately preserves;
> And each flecked leaf's baptized in a free grace
> Caught in your unaware, cascading joy.

She is 'unaware', her joy 'cascading'. She is as much a natural phenomenon as the cascading waters of the waterfall itself. The poet, in his awareness, can experience the 'elusive moments' only in the analytical activity of thought. His very activity as a poet involves an attempt to preserve and celebrate the elusive moment. Yet that attempt, being necessarily an intellectual activity, actually serves to destroy the moment *as experience*: 'thought destroys, though desperately preserves'. He, and his works of art, can never have that 'free grace' which 'each flecked leaf' possesses. It is they that are 'baptized', sharing in the woman's instinctive joy. It is in her activity that there is an apprehension of something 'beyond the cloyed and derangeable cosmos' (XII), but it is an apprehension which she makes no attempt to comprehend. In doing so she is 'holy and unique'. Unconsciously she affirms 'value' and 'truth'. The poet remains bound in a 'profane' intellectual self-awareness. The antithesis of sacred and profane survives no further than the final line of the poem. Sonnet XV abruptly changes direction, most notably in its assessment of the woman:

> Yes, you are flesh and blood all right. My God!
> And do I know it. Scorn convention's track
> Yet follow it, inclining to conform
> When cautious pressure from a hackneyed world
> Threats in my absence. So, proud stamina
> Steps into line and licks the boots of law;
> Simpers authority and worships straw;
> Ventures, in prudence; pioneers, in bed—
> Jesus! What zombie's this? What carcass-thief
> Postures this attitude? Nods, mutters back
> Exactitude of platitude, and fears
> A pontiff's ransom of unborn regret?
>   Is the high lark, dawn's song-drenched accolade,
>   Only a small grey hopper round a spade?

Central to sonnet XIV was a sense of the woman's simplicity—the absence in her nature of any doubleness. Now, though, it is her all too human doubleness that is at the heart of the poet's response to her. What he now 'knows' and the mode of knowledge involved are both very different. She is now seen, very definitely, as 'profane', very much of the world. What disturbs the lover most is the gap between the protestations she makes in his presence and her behaviour in his absence. Her seeming 'scorn' for convention is replaced by a conformity to the ways of the 'hackneyed world'. The 'unaware, cascading joy', the sense of 'each moment stilled new in [her] arm or eye', are replaced by his perception of her as another incarnation of death-in-life, a 'zombie', a 'carcass-thief'. Disillusionment is well-nigh absolute. The final couplet employs another Shakespearian allusion as an ironic means of registering that disillusionment. Warner's couplet clearly echoes Shakespeare's 29th sonnet:

> When in disgrace with fortune and men's eyes,
> I all alone beweep my outcast state,
> And trouble deaf heav'n with my bootless cries,
> And look upon myself and curse my fate,
> Wishing me like to one more rich in hope,
> Featured like him, like him with friends possessed,
> Desiring this man's art, and that man's scope,
> With what I most enjoy contented least;
> Yet in these thoughts myself almost despising,
> Haply I think on thee, and then my state,
> Like to the lark at break of day arising
> From sullen earth, sings hymns at heaven's gate;
>> For thy sweet love rememb'red such wealth brings,
>> That then I scorn to change my state with kings.

In Shakespeare's sonnet the lark 'at break of day arising' is a symbol of the way the mere thought of the beloved is enough to raise the spirits of the poet, to raise him to the highest pitch of contentment. In Warner's *Experimental Sonnets* we have seen the lady capable of exercising a similar power. But no more. What had seemed a 'lark' now appears no more than 'a small grey hopper round a spade'. No dizzying ascent, merely an earth-bound hopping and the spade of the earth-bound human, perhaps even of the grave-digger. Certainly the grave and its contents loom large in the succeeding sonnet, no. XVI.

Separation from the woman he loves has already been presented as a kind of death-in-life earlier in the sequence. Here in the opening lines of sonnet XVI the metaphor takes on a gothic gruesomeness:

> With you I can do anything. Without
> The sodden shroud, the rough planks, hard beneath,
> Over stared eyes, binding the elbows in;
> Fouled, waterlogging dew; the white, gorged worm;
> Inevitable dark; rank, crumpled flesh;
> Grit, blinding dust and everlasting cold
> Feel.

There seems to be no possibility that one might 'unkiss the shroud' (X); the 'bed's bare winding-sheets' (XIII) now enfold the corpse; the 'worldly dust for which men sweat'

(III) is now the 'blinding dust' of the grave. 'Day's ranked, echoing pageantry' (XI) has been reduced to 'rank, crumpled flesh'. The analogy between death and night is a frequent one in Renaissance poetry. In Shakespeare's *Sonnets* night is 'death's second self'.[37] Here in the sixteenth of the *Experimental Sonnets* the analogy serves as the hinge upon which the poem turns. The lines quoted above have taken us to the half-way point of the poem. (The ambiguity of 'feel', both sensory and emotional, marks the turn). The charnel language of the first half of the poem is succeeded by the phrase 'death's mockery hours'. We move from death to its 'image'—night. More specifically we move to the nights of love which the lovers have shared. These have been 'death's mockery hours' in the further sense that they have involved a conviction that death could be overcome, that he posed no threat to them. They felt with Donne that

> All other things, to their destruction draw,
> Only our love hath no decay.[38]

It was then that their 'shared warmth' put them at the greatest distance from the 'everlasting cold / feel' of the grave. Their 'breathing calm' (phrasing reminiscent of sonnet XI) was such that the 'world's oppressions' could 'disturb no dockleaf' (the verb another echo of sonnet XI). In their mutuality 'courtesy and constancy' were matched and 'love of beauty' made the lady beautiful. That mutuality has gone, faith in its possibility has disappeared, as sonnet XV has melodramatically demonstrated. Yet the poet's mood here is different. The poem's final couplet ends, though not without a sense of a straining for conviction, on a note of defiance:

> Then mailed fist of fate can smash our skulls,
> For we can ridicule all death annuls.

It is ironic that this couplet should be followed, in the opening lines of sonnet XVII, by the quieter assertion that:

> Our passion is no bold extravagance
> Or cultivation of hyperbole.

The assertion prompts, in turn, the observation that

> There is no poetry save what we live.

Indeed the frequently heightened and expressionist language of earlier poems is here notable by its absence. The tone is quieter, less anguished, almost resigned. What has happened, and continues to happen to the poet and the woman is, it seems, beyond the control of their own wills. Rather it is

> Bred of no choice, but brought out like the grain
> Elicited with seasoned polishing
> Of teak.

The poet becomes, like his fellow men and women, an 'object' made by the events, emotional and otherwise, of his life. He becomes something created, rather than being himself a creator. Love itself is similarly 'polished' (which need not necessarily be a very comfortable or enjoyable process) until it too can be seen and thought of in terms of art:

> And let our love, like deepest art, be seen
> To be inevitable, strong, and clean.

This final couplet seems not to be a wish for the future condition of their love. Indeed that love, after the savageries of sonnet XV, seems to have no future. It is rather a wish as to how their love might be perceived, presumably by themselves in retrospect, and by readers of the poems. Its course acknowledged as 'inevitable', ordained by forces beyond their control, the burden of individual guilt may be eluded, as, indeed, may the horribly tempting desire to find ways of throwing that burden upon one's former partner. The implicit suggestion—backed up by so much of the sequence's imagery, before and after this point—is that the two of them have been like actors in a play, their roles determined by the author and director, only their own responsibility in a lesser or secondary sense. It is a strategy which enables the writer, temporarily at least, to achieve an aesthetic distance from his pain, to see himself and his erstwhile lover not so much as suffering human individuals as the materials of a work of art, part of some pattern larger than their own individual joy or misery. It is in such terms that sonnet XVIII presents their changing relationship, as the musical imagery of the first quatrain is succeeded by the painterly language of the second:

> As our fates navigate their destined route
> In modulations of intensity,
> And times necessitate a change of time
> Not in relationship but counterpoint;
> As each new stroke is added by the brush
> Of that practitioner of artistry,
> And though we wear the cloak, yet do not know
> The composition, or the epigraph;
> As each new moment beats upon the pulse,
> Let us resolve to try whatever comes,
> Not in heat's self-paralysis of hate,
> But with compassion's quiet certainty;
> > And neither flinch, nor find across our course
> > Memories of unmitigated remorse.

The poem seeks to achieve a calmness of mind, escaping from 'heat's self-paralysis of hate', by means of the perspective of art in which it places the relationship so heatedly discussed in the previous seventeen sonnets. It is fitting and effective, then, that the poem should be the most 'regular' in form since the Shakespearian sonnet of no. III and before that form's final re-emergence in the last poem of the sequence. No. XVIII is built upon centre-rhymes, arranged in three quatrains and with a final couplet employing the customary end-rhymes. The reader is unlikely to overlook this pattern, since its presence is reinforced by the poem's syntactical organisation. Each of the three quatrains is terminated by a semi-colon; these are the heaviest punctuation marks prior to the full-stop which closes the poem. The structural pattern is emphasized by the poem's pattern of verbal parallelism. The first quatrain opens 'as our fates . . .'; the second 'as each new stroke . . .'; the third 'as each new moment . . .'. This clarity of structure offers visible enactment of the poet's claim to have discerned a pattern of order and form in the seeming contradictions of his experience. The first line's verb—'navigate'—echoes the earlier use (especially in sonnet VIII) of the Petrarchan conceit of the storm-tossed ship. 'Navigate', though, suggests an altogether greater degree of control—albeit the control of 'fate' pursuing a 'destined route'. The lovers 'wear the cloak', they are central participants in the unfolding design, but they 'do not know / The composition, or the epigraph', they are not themselves responsible for the principles on which that design is built or for the significance it can finally be seen to possess. In an earlier 'modulation' of happiness, their lives were described as 'new-touched' (VIII). Retrospectively one can see in that phrase another image of a controlling 'artistic' activity—'touch' is, after all, 'the act or manner of touching a musical instrument, so as to bring out its tones' and to touch is 'in drawing, painting, etc: to mark, draw, delineate (a detail of the work) by touching the surface with the pencil, brush etc; also to modify or alter by such touches' (both definitions from the OED). Here in sonnet XVIII the changes in their lives are registered in the metaphor of 'each new stroke . . . added by the brush'. That such parallels of imagery (shipwrecked / navigate / new-touched / new stroke) should exist between sonnets VIII and XVIII is another instance of that larger symmetry in the sequence which was considered earlier, since no. XVIII is, of course, the eighth sonnet from the end. Such symmetries serve to reinforce the poet's insistence that he and the woman he loves are themselves part of a larger 'counterpoint'. From such an approach the poet draws a resolution to deal compassionately with 'whatever comes', to avoid 'memories of unmitigated remorse'. The resolution is, perhaps inevitably, a precarious one. Given the kind of near-manic changes of mood which characterize this sequence of poems, it is not at all surprising that the next sonnet should present us with a poet-lover struggling with agonies of guilt.

No. XIX moves away from the kind of composure (self-composition?) sought by its immediate predecessor. Aptly enough the metrical smoothness and regularity of no. XVIII is also fragmented and distorted, by emotional and moral pressures, in its successor. Perhaps more than any other poem in the series, no. XIX establishes a tension, a rhythmical dialogue, between a metrical ideal and the specific patterns of the poem's words. The reader's endeavours to reconcile, or any rate to hear at one and the same time, the metrical idea and the rhythmic practice, mimic the poet's attempts to reconcile two conflicting impulses in his own nature. Neither, it must be said, bears much resemblance to that 'quiet certainty' of compassion to which the close of sonnet XVIII had found him aspiring. Sonnet XIX is constructed as a dialogue between two inner voices. It will perhaps be easier to see this if the arrangement of the poem's first two quatrains is modified so as to separate these two voices:

> Night wins. The realizing dark
> Granites that knife along eternity.
> Who sins? What is this idle guilt?
>
> Father forgive by Thy Gethsemane.
>
> Eat, drink, riot today and forget!
>
> By Thine agony and bloody sweat—
>
> Come, try at the wheel; spin, wager a bet!
>
> Ransom my core from catastrophic debt.

The final six lines of the sonnet are perhaps best regarded as 'spoken', not by either of these disputing 'voices', but by, as it were, the 'full' voice of the poet, recording in prayer his resolution of the conflict which the octave has dramatically presented:

> If I must live with this full-earned abyss,
> If I must face my moral holocaust,
> Father, forgive, though I know what I do,
> Forgive my sin against the Holy Ghost.
> The worst is done; the last brutality:
> And mine the sole responsibility.

Out of context we should not be inclined to imagine that this was a poem that dealt with human love—or at any rate not specifically or exclusively so. The focus of the sequence is, indeed, widening. Not until the final poem of the sequence will the poet return explicitly to the subject matter of the first eighteen sonnets. Sonnet XIX, perhaps on the model (though there is no direct imitation) of Shakespeare's sonnet 146, centres upon the moral and spiritual significance of the kind of amatory experiences which (in both cases) the earlier poems of the respective sequences have been concerned to outline. Warner's nineteenth sonnet is a kind of twentieth-century version of mediaeval verse dialogues between Body and Soul. As such it serves as transition to a series of poems that have no direct bearing on the poet's experience as a lover, save insofar as that experience has brought him to a point where he recognizes in it an emblem of wider truths about the human condition.

Sonnet XX explores the poet-lover's own sense of loss in terms of the universal human experience of bereavement. This sixth sonnet from the end of the sequence is linked, both in terms of form and content, to the sixth sonnet from the beginning. Both are constructed in quatrains employing centre-rhyme. No. VI began by comparing the lover's pain to the burning of a baby's face by the boiling water of a kettle. This later sonnet deals with parental reaction to the death of a child. For all the episode's horror it has about it a kind of domesticity never approached by the sequence's central relationship. Its details are gentle and poignant, not violent and fierce as so often in the poems of this sequence. A mother refusing to clean away the fingermarks her dead child has left upon a window; the small child's chatter and eagerness; his shoes 'tugged off . . . still knotted' and left by the fire. The octave of the sonnet (again we have a poem structured in a series of statements introduced by 'as' in lines 1, 9 and 12) deals chiefly with the mother's reaction. The final quatrain turns to the father, similarly unable to express his grief, reduced to pointless or consciously futile activity. We are left to relate this to what we have seen of the poet's own state of mind; he himself makes no explicit connections. The final couplet comes closest to doing so in its generalization upon the preceding 'narrative':

> As such emotion dreads to be betrayed,
> So, in the silent grief, one part's afraid.

In so predominantly simple a sonnet it is perhaps wrong to complicate matters, but it is hard to resist the belief that in the final line we have another of Warner's many allusions to the English dramatic tradition. The phrase 'silent grief' picks up a famous line from John Ford's *The Broken Heart*. Confronted during a feast with news 'of death, and death, and death' the heroine Calantha seems, at first, to be unaffected by the news. When the feast is done, however, she takes the necessary action and then disposes herself for death, saying that

> They are the silent griefs which cut the heartstrings.[39]

Sonnet XX makes a more oblique statement than most of its fellows if one reads it as a comment by the poet upon how circumstances have cut his own 'heartstrings'. Its concern though, as has been suggested, is not exclusively with the poet's own condition; it and its four successors are notable for the relative absence from them of the personal pronoun 'I'.

In sonnet XXI the participant is not identified by the personal pronoun. The kind of diction and imagery employed enable us to recognize in him many affinities with the poetic persona we have met earlier. The absence of the first person pronoun liberates us from any compulsion to make such an identification. Rather, the poem offers us metaphors for an alienated humanity:

> Outside, stuttering hate snarls down the blade
> As a pneumatic drill rapes the dead quay:
> Inside, recreated, as a shaft
> Of black light penetrates the opened soul.
> Somewhere a plumber saws his piece of lead;
> A ribbed and creaking boat heels on the sand;
> Nearer, a drawing-pin studs in the eye
> Of mind, as vessel, float, all disappear.
> Down, down as they go, the bubbles rise,
> The drowned's report upon experience.
> Up, up expanding hope replies
> Until exploded by the drill's retort.
>   Ah comedy divine, man's tragedy—
>   Why make us gambol in our agony?

Like the poet inside his hotel room in sonnet XIII, the participant here is indoors. Unlike sonnet X, what is outside is not a series of 'moving emblems' which might revitalize human sympathies. Instead

> Outside, stuttering hate snarls down the blade
> As a pneumatic drill rapes the dead quay.

The earth is dead, concrete. Man and his machinery 'rapes' it in a paroxysm of seeming hatred. This disturbing outer landscape, a perversion, with its images of hatred, rape and necrophilia, of the human desire for love, is 'recreated' in the mind of the man indoors, hearing the drill's noise. The sense of a perversion of love is re-inforced by the way in which lines 3 and 4 invert one of Warner's most frequently used symbols for the creative power of love. The 'shaft / Of black light' is a grim inversion of the affirmation made by Quark in *Killing Time*:

> The universe spins on a shaft of light
> Whose name is love.[40]

This is unmistakably an echo of the Platonic myth of Er in Book Ten of the *Republic*. There, after seven days in the meadow, the company of souls moved on:

And on the fourth day afterwards they came to a place whence they could see a straight shaft of light, like a pillar, stretching from above throughout heaven and earth, more like the rainbow than anything else, but brighter and purer.[41]

Elsewhere in Warner's plays this same 'shaft of light' becomes, by inversion, a symbol of human lovelessness, 'the shafting darkness'.[42] Here in the twenty-first sonnet the 'shaft / Of black light' penetrates the 'opened soul'. We are reminded (especially in the context of line five's image of the plumber 'who saws his piece of lead') of the sequence's earlier image of 'vivisecting parting' (I), of how, in sonnet VI, the whip-crack 'snaps the backbone', or mention in sonnet VIII of how 'will may corrode and pain can split the bone'. Now it is the soul itself which bears an open wound. The physical and the mental are alike assaulted by savage pain—'a drawing-pin studs in the eye / Of mind'. The world outside the mind seems to disappear from cognitive range; yet, as it vanishes, as its occupants and objects sink from awareness, 'the bubbles rise'. However ephemeral they may be, the bubbles register the vanished presences; the 'rise' of the bubbles, counterbalancing the 'down, down' which begins line 9, offers a brief emblem of aspiration and hope. Its brevity is guaranteed by 'the drill's retort'. The recognition is of human life as inseparably and simultaneously a matter both of the 'gambol' and the 'agony'. It is a 'comedy divine' and it is 'man's tragedy'. The antithetical phrases take us back, of course, to theatricality; neither phrase, though, is exclusively theatrical in its significance. The phrase 'comedy divine' invites interpretation as a judgement of human life as an absurdity, providing laughter for divine spectators, of the human individual as no more than a 'sport' for the 'President of the Immortals'.[43] However, Warner's phrase might equally be thought to offer itself as a reminder of Dante. The *Divina Commedia* affirms the 'comedy' of providence; Dante's dedicatory letter to Can Grande della Scala explains the appropriateness of the word 'commedia':

Nam si ad materiam respiciamus, a principio horribilis et foetida est, quia *Infernus*; in fine prospera, desiderabilis et grata, quia *Paradisus*.[44]

In that perspective, 'man's tragedy' merely awaits its 'comic' denouement. Warner's phrasing by no means authorizes us to make such an assumption, though it raises the possibility. If it did more than that it would rob the sequence of the very tension which fuels it.

Of the final four poems of the sequence, only the very last makes any specific mention of the relationship of love which was the starting-point. The opening lines of sonnet XXV will, though, serve to show that sonnets XXII-XXIV are intimately connected to the experience of that relationship. Sonnet XXV begins with a series of questions:

> And can it be? Has all that splendour passed—
> Was it too pure for weak mortality?
> Was I demanding, hoping it might last;
> Now disillusioned with humanity?

It is with the poet's disillusioned encounter with humanity, product of the failure of love, that sonnets XXII-XXIV are concerned. All three focus on human limitations and weaknesses. In the first of them the subject might be defined as the limited range of traditional aesthetic aspirations and a suspicion that such aspirations have involved a neglect of important areas of human experience; that they have, perhaps, promoted a false and dangerously illusory ideology. The poet's present emotional condition prompts him to re-assess the nature and purposes of artistic activity, examining the question in terms both of music and painting:

> Should we preserve intensity alone?
> The string vibrating at the 'cello's bridge?
> Or stretch to nerve the fingerboard's full range
> In orchestrating waste's cacophonics?
> Is poignancy of beauty's transience
> As time runs over an apple in the stream—
> The hesitancy of a summer's dusk
> When night-stock stuns with scent—ours to forgo?
> Must we desert court-ladies on the grass,
> Their sunlit-dappled breasts and lovers' lutes?
> The skill of craftsman-wrought, firm, rounded themes;
> The guests of Mozart, Purcell, and Watteau?
>   Bear with me if I leave such scenes behind:
>   The dark offstage preoccupies my mind.

The first quatrain offers the alternatives the poet now finds before him. Is the artist to 'preserve' only those moments of greatest and most perfect intensity in images of beauty and grace? Or has he to find ways of 'orchestrating waste's cacophonics' rather than simply producing artefacts of euphony to stand in opposition to the surrounding cacophony? Can he, indeed, 'forgo' the art which produces images of transient beauty—is such an abandonment not perhaps an abandonment of art itself? The poet—like any good rhetorician—plays less than wholly fair with the available evidence. In the third quatrain he represents the achievements of art by 'craftsman-wrought, firm, rounded themes', by the work of 'Mozart, Purcell, and Watteau', and, even more tellingly, by the social world of which their

art speaks, a world of 'court-ladies on the grass' with 'their
sunlit-dappled breasts and lovers' lutes'. He does not, in
short, offer us (or himself) symbols of the whole range of art's
capacity. There is no Michelangelo here, no Beethoven's
Ninth, no *King Lear*. It is not art that the poet rejects in the
sonnet's final couplet, but a particular and partial conception
of it. This is, after all, implied in the very use of the
sequence's recurrent theatrical metaphor:

> Bear with me if I leave such scenes behind:
> The dark offstage preoccupies my mind.

The artistic world of Watteau does, indeed, leave unexplored
much that is dark in human affairs. The same might be said
of the average Renaissance sonnet sequence. It is at those
limitations that the poet seems now to be chafing. That sense
of confinement, that need to extend the boundaries of his art
may, as I have suggested elsewhere, contain the seed of the
Requiem plays.[45] In those plays 'waste's cacophonics' are
fully examined and the 'fingerboard's full range' is employed
in their extravagant eclecticism of form and technique.
Where sonnet XXII considers the limitations of art and
beauty, its successor turns to the limitations of man himself,
whether he is artist or not.

Sonnet XXIII takes as its theme the physical fragility of
man. The mind, his 'diviner part', with its 'restless empiry',
is finally at the mercy of that bodily mechanism which
confines it. The body, inevitably, 'betrays the mind'; the
'throb' of its mechanism falters; the brain becomes a 'grey
waste of intricacy's heritage'. When it does, then

> The vermin rob immortal artistry
> And wisdom, fleshless, reels into the dust.

Ingrid Melander points to parallels in the tragedies of
Chapman[46] and certainly the recognition is one that is central
to Renaissance Stoicism. The 'empiry' of the mind is a notion
strongly reminiscent of Seneca's affirmation that 'mens bona
regnum possidet'.[47] We need not, of course, look so far for
parallels. The same recognition finds particularly vivid
expression in some sentences of Hardy:

Hurt my tooth at breakfast-time. I look in the glass. Am conscious of the humiliating sorriness of my earthly tabernacle, and of the sad fact that the best of parents could do no better for me . . . Why should a man's mind have been thrown into such close, sad, sensational, inexplicable relations with such a precarious object as his own body![48]

The mind may be 'loath to depart' but is entirely 'powerless to stay'; the 'melody' (the word picks up the images of the previous sonnet, and seems here to symbolize poetry itself) is 'disbursed' 'like pollen blown'. The mental faculties, we are obliged to acknowledge, are simultaneously 'endowed to growth and destined to decay'. The recognition is that in everything human 'time that gave doth now his gift confound'.[49] The recognition may be humiliating; or it may, just as readily, stir us to futile anger:

> Abrasive anger at such impotence
> To help the frailer by diviner part
> Engineers atrophy of maimed desire
> And nails inevitable reconciled.
> So dialectics isolate the flaw.
> So small a key unlocks so great a door.

The anger is not only futile; it plays its part in the inevitable death, as it 'engineers' (the image of the mechanism, replaced in the second quatrain by the natural imagery associated with the healthier activities of the mind, here returns) the 'atrophy of maimed desire'.

The processes of 'time's injurious hand'[50] are again to the forefront in sonnet XXIV. It begins by tracing the stages of human life, from birth to the very edge of death:

> The breaking dawn, the cry upon the bed;
> Tottering infancy and gangling youth;
> Mandarin manhood. Anarchy of age
> At last, raving, forlorn and groping back,
> Fearing the icy wind's strangling grip,
> To corridors of constant journeying.

There is no talk now of any capacity to 'ridicule all death annuls' (XVI). As man approaches 'the dark offstage'(XXII) he clutches at earthly illusions, at possessions and pleasures

(such as the 'laconic labials' which are, presumably, kisses),
investing them with spurious dignity and importance. All
this 'ranked, echoing pageantry' (XI) is, in truth, no more
than the 'panoply of rust':

> The secret prides and flattering self-denials;
> Laconic labials, fantasy's deceit;
> Books, Bibles, bidets; halls, hills, cottages;
> Flow and ebb of bodily seasons' tides;
> Those motley macaronics day and night;
> Companions—all the panoply of rust.

The mind's attempted self-deceptions bear no fruit. The
objects with which we surround ourselves become 'élite' and
'curiously numb' (XIII). The 'books, Bibles, bidets' of line 9
are as randomly accumulated and as emptied of all distinctions of value as the contents of Belinda's dressing-table, the
'puffs, powders, patches, bibles, billet-doux'. Time's passing itself becomes a confusing babble. Day and night are
mere 'motley macaronics'—a discourse combining elements
from two distinct languages. Since Teofilo Folengo's *Macar-
roneae* early in the sixteenth century, macaronic verse has
traditionally been the idiom of mock-heroic. Certainly there
seem to be no heroic values to be affirmed at this point in
Warner's sequence. We have entered the world of
'motley'—of costumed folly. In the sonnet's final couplet the
theatrical imagery which has made repeated contributions to
the sequence receives its fullest and fiercest expression:

> No intermission from this pantomime
> Till termination bring an end to time.

Neither 'comedy' nor 'tragedy'—each, after all, a genre of
some dignity—human life now seems better designated a
'pantomime'. The judgement is a traditional one, here
expressed with particular force as the couplet's detached
neatness follows the complexities of the first twelve lines.
Though Warner's terms of reference are not identical, the
position here reached is one that takes us back to the moral
imagery of an earlier age. Just as the form of these poems
enacts a constant interplay between traditional and modern,

so their governing sentiments fuse modern disillusionment and the *contemptus mundi* of earlier times. So, in these two sonnets, we are close, for example, to the judgements and language of Bishop Henry King:

> What is th' Existence of Man's Life?
> But open Warr, or Slumber'd Strife.
> Where Sicknes to his Sense presents
> The Combat of the Elements:
> And never feeles a perfect Peace
> Till Death's cold hand signes his release.
>
> It is a Storme, where the hott Bloud
> Out-vyes in Rage the boyling Floud:
> And each loud Passion of the Mind
> Is like a furious gust of Wind,
> Which beates his Bark with many a Wave
> Till he casts Anchor in the Grave . . .
>
> It is a weary Enterlude,
> Which doth short Joyes, long Woes include.
> The World the Stage, the Prologue Teares,
> The Actes vaine Hope and vary'd Feares:
> The Scaene shutts up with Losse of breath,
> And leaves no Epilogue but Death.[51]

The epilogue of these *Experimental Sonnets*—no. XXV—is not death, but valediction. We return to the elegiac impulse which began the sequence. In the first sonnet the poet sought to memorialize 'all that glory'. Now he must face the truth:

> And can it be? Has all that splendour passed?

The truth is not an easy or a comfortable one. The full acknowledgement of its significance is difficult to make:

> It seems impossible so firm a joy,
> A love so rooted in a summer's day,
> Shared tasks, shared wanderings, should like a toy
> A child has wearied of be tossed away.

The aspiration to permanence has inevitably been defeated. Here the poet's individual experience has been an enactment of Donne's generalization:

> So, lovers dreame a rich and long delight,
> But get a winter-seeming summers night.[52]

The seasonal imagery in Warner's sonnet is double-edged in its significance. It leaves open the possibility of renewal. For the moment, though, a 'delight' which promised to be so rich and long now seems merely to have been a 'toy'. If the love itself is evanescent, so too, in a different way, is the artistic activity which has been inseparable from it in these poems:

> And can this paper be the last that you
> Will hold of mine, these words end passion's qualms?

If the 'splinter' of poetry expires, then the darkness takes over—'darkness must touch these eyes'. Where the first poem of the sequence had celebrated

> Those moments of brief immortality
> Lying oblivious and locked in one

this final poem can now only anticipate 'lonely nights' and 'empty arms'. The closing note is not of 'immortality' (however 'brief') but of 'mutability'. The poet has taken a close look at his experience and reached the conclusion that many have reached before him:

> What man that sees the ever-whirling wheele
> Of *Change*, the which all mortall things doth sway,
> But that thereby doth find, and plainely feele,
> How MUTABILITY in them doth play
> Her cruell sports, to many mens decay?[53]

All that man can be and do is in the 'sway' of mutability. All that he can imagine, too; whether those imaginings be anticipations of a future and enduring happiness, or whether they be the images he produces as an artist:

> Strange how the mutability of things
> Evaporates all man's imaginings.

The paradox of the human condition is that man chooses, even so, not to be confined by that recognition. Its truth will be continually denied and defied, however well it may be known. The sequence as a whole constitutes such a defiance. It is in the tension between the defiance and the knowledge that the poetry exists.

CHAPTER 6

Lucca Quartet

The *Lucca Quartet* is unique amongst Warner's works in existing in three different published forms with substantive differences. It first appeared in a limited edition in 1975, published by Omphalos Press. It then consisted of four poems: 'Camaiore', 'Choriambics', 'Canzone' and 'Madrigal'. Two years later, in 1977, Tim Prentki's collection of essays under the title *Francis Warner. Poet and Dramatist* contained an essay on the *Lucca Quartet* by Warner's good friend, the late Edward Malins. This essay was prefaced by a reprinting of the 1975 text of the *Lucca Quartet* and was followed by a sonnet beginning 'Was it mere chance that brought the mating hare' which Malins introduced thus:

I am pleased to have permission to print here for the first time a sonnet which is not part of the *Lucca Quartet* but which was written between 'Canzone' and 'Madrigal' and is related to the same theme.[1]

By the time of the *Collected Poems* (1985) the *Lucca Quartet* had taken yet another form. It now consisted of six poems. The first four are those which were included in the 1975 publication, in the same order as they then appeared. They are now followed by two sonnets, simply headed 'Sonnet I' and 'Sonnet II'. 'Sonnet I' is new, but 'Sonnet II' is the one which Malins had published in 1977. It will be seen that the poem which Malins then described as 'not part of the *Lucca Quartet*' has now become its conclusion. If Malins was correct in saying that this sonnet was 'written between "Canzone" and "Madrigal"' it is clear that the final order of the poems in the *Collected Poems* version of the *Lucca Quartet* is dictated by reasons other than those merely of the chronology of composition. In the following discussion I shall treat the 1985 text as the definitive version and shall not address

141

myself to the question of how far the difference between the 1975 and 1985 versions represents a significant change of authorial intention.

Edward Malins' essay on the the *Lucca Quartet* is a characteristically sensitive piece, and is particularly valuable for the way in which it provides the reader of the sequence with the kind of narrative background which he might not readily discern from the poems themselves. His account begins as follows:

In April 1975 Francis had not started on the last play of his double trilogy, which was to be performed at the Edinburgh Festival that autumn. So he decided he would try to take his two daughters abroad to some quiet place to get the job done during the Easter holiday. After mentioning his predicament to his friend Henry Moore, he was immediately offered Mary Moore's *casa colonica* at Camaiore in northern Tuscany for two weeks. It was an ideal season in which to go there. Browning, who knew the district well, described how

> You've summer all at once;
> In a day he leaps complete with a few strong April
> suns.

An ideal setting too: an old stone house, roughly plastered over, with shaded terrace, backed by extensive woodland, and overlooking the steep wooded hills, vineyards, and valleys of the Lucchese plain.[2]

Malins observes that the *Lucca Quartet* 'is so called because there are four poems and four characters in them'.[3] The sequence's later history, as outlined above, has obviously rendered the first of these reasons invalid, but the second retains its significance. The poet and his two daughters provide three of the *dramatis personae*; Malins explains that the fourth character is the poet's 'lover Lorraine, who had asked whether she might go with them'.[4]

Lucca and the surrounding districts have long associations with the English and with English literature in particular. Milton spent some time there, Lucca being the original home of Charles Diodati's paternal family.[5] Lucca, the spa of Bagni di Lucca, and the countryside around, were favourite

haunts of several of the English Romantics. Shelley and
Mary spent time in the area, and Shelley's poem 'The Boat
on the Serchio' records his impressions of the area. Readers
of Byron's letters will be familiar with the episode of the man
who, it was rumoured, was 'to be burnt at Lucca for sacri-
lege'.[6] Browning spent several summers in the vicinity.
Jakob Korg, in his study of Browning's relations with Italy,
provides an amusing account of Bagni di Lucca in the
mid-nineteenth century:

High in the Tuscan hills . . . the popular summering place for the
English from Florence, [it] was overrun with an English population bent on gambling, dancing, bathing, gossiping, and flirting
. . . It was intersected by many small paths that led over the hills to
little villages and good sites for picnics. A stout old lady named Mrs
Clotilda Elizabeth Stisted presided over public entertainments as
Queen of the Baths. She played the harp—without, however,
making any sound—and sent her crimson chair ahead when she
visited . . . The Brownings took a secluded house, high on the hill
over the town, and deep in the woods. It was in this house that
Elizabeth first showed Browning *Sonnets from the Portuguese*.[7]

Browning frequently composed here. 'In a Balcony' was
written here in 1853.[8] In 'By the Fireside' from *Men and
Women* of 1855 the landscape of the area around Lucca
becomes, in Korg's words, 'involved in the psychological
processes of lovers'.[9] It is a retrospective piece in which a
married man recalls a visit to the area made in the company of
the woman he loves. To quote Korg once more:

The setting plays its part by preparing the lovers for their moment
of spiritual recognition, and then, by withdrawing its influence,
committing them to each other.[10]

Whether or not it was consciously designed as such, the
Lucca Quartet effectively constitutes the other panel of a
diptych with 'By the Fireside'. In Browning's poem the hills
of Tuscany enable two lovers to come to full understanding
of and with one another. Even when the location is left
behind, there abides that which it has achieved. In the *Lucca
Quartet* the same hills are witness to a pair of lovers who
declare

> We've discovered the best. Here let us rest,
>   living complete content.

In their case, however, that 'best' does not endure the departure from Tuscany.

Browning was not, of course, the only Victorian to value Lucca and its environs. For Ruskin, Lucca was the scene of a turning-point in his life. In an epilogue to *Modern Painters*, written in 1883, Ruskin recounts a visit made to Lucca in 1845. He describes himself as full of 'new knowledge and freshness of acceptancy', and explains that it was in visiting the churches of Lucca that

> then and there on the instant, I began . . . the course of architectural study which reduced under accurate law the vague enthusiasm of my childish taste, and has been ever since a method with me, guardian of all my other work in natural and moral philosophy.[11]

Lucca remained a place of special importance to Ruskin. In his Diaries he consistently writes with particular warmth of this part of Tuscany:

> 1874 July 28th Tuesday LUCCA. The happiest walk in moonlight I have had, this twenty years, in this blessed place, still preserved to me, last night.[12]

His descriptions of autumn in the area form an attractive partner to the spring scenes in the first two poems of the *Lucca Quartet*:

> . . . climbed to the ridge of the marble mountains in afternoon—past the convent with its great ilex, and the perfect cottage with its well under the chestnuts, and so up to the terraced fields . . . sat long watching the soft, sun-lighted terraces of grass, and tenderly classic hills, plumed and downy with wood, and the burning russet of fallen chestnuts for foreground—thinking how lovely the world was in its light, when given . . . drove to foot of hills across Serchio, where we rested among olive-woods with low cypress avenues mingled—green terraces under the olive trees quite rich in grass, and the cyclamen in masses on the shady pink banks with full bright crimson pink everywhere, and peppermint in vivid blue, I looking for forget-me-nots. View of Lucca, of course, too lovely to draw . . . had lovely afternoon walk on hills beyond

Serchio, with skies bright and sublime, changing continually, and warm sun and sweet air, and vignettes of new and perfect composition in Italian villa and mountain, every moment.[13]

The poems of the *Lucca Quartet* do not, on the whole, offer any great difficulties of interpretation. The first two celebrate a scene of happiness and contentment shared by the four figures of this quartet. The third poem returns us to the poet's 'room in Oxford'.[14] The idyll of Camaiore is threatened and doubtful; the poet can only wish anxiously that the 'best' should be re-achieved. The fourth poem presents the children's unease and uncertainty, and the poet's attempt to offer them some degree of comfort and explanation. The final two sonnets are addressed directly to the lady (after the interlude of 'Madrigal'—a dialogue between poet and children conducted in the lady's absence) and concern the choice facing her, between the possibilities aroused by their 'fresh meeting' and 'guilt, subterfuge, despair'. Such, in outline, is the narrative and 'dramatic' thrust of this short sequence.

In some ways more striking than its narrative content is the *Lucca Quartet's* pattern of formal development. Its six poems incorporate five different verse forms and patterns of versification. 'Camaiore' is written in anapaestic and dactylic dimeters (though the rhyme scheme invites the possibility of reading it in terms of tetrameter lines made up from the combination of these). The second poem makes use of another classical metre, choriambics. The third turns, rather, to the mediaeval form of the canzone. The fourth is in another Italianate form, the madrigal, and the sequence ends with two sonnets. The six poems, looked at thus, are discernibly arranged in a kind of historical sequence, beginning with exercises in classical metres, proceeding through a Dantean canzone, and finishing with three poems belonging at least as much to the Renaissance as to the late Middle Ages. It is worth noting that the two poems set in Italy are the ones which employ classical metres, metres which have never been fully assimilated into the mainstream of English poetry. The poem, 'Canzone', which most explicitly looks back at an Italian experience from an English location, employs an Italian verse form which has had its influence on English poetry (*e.g.* Spenser's *Epithalamion*, Milton's 'Upon the Circumcision') but cannot be said to have become established as an *English* verse form. The final three poems, most thoroughly 'English' in their subject matter, are in verse forms which, while Italian in origin, have also distinct traditions in English poetic history. Looked at in this light, the sequence provides both a narrative of this individual poet's coming to terms with an Italian experience and a kind of model of English poetry's relations with the traditions of Italian poetry.

Of the five stanzas of 'Camaiore', the first three are largely concerned to describe and locate the setting in which the poet and his lover find themselves. The interaction of outer landscape and inner happiness is well evoked. In the opening lines the absence of punctuation allows a syntactical ambiguity very relevant to this interdependence:

> Peace in the afternoon
> Sparkling eyes;

Is sparkling an adjective, giving us thus two statements separated by the line-ending? Or is it a verb, with 'peace' as its subject and 'eyes' as its object? The dominant notes in these opening stanzas are of contentment and light. Nature is essentially protective of human concerns:

> Pinetree and olive
> Watch the hearth.
> Farmyards of Tuscany
> Cupped in hills . . .
> Dark wine for cover
> And lover's screen.

In the valley below the church, bells extend a benediction to human activities, both everyday and festal—a distinction which seems almost without significance:

> A baby is sleeping
> Through distant bells,
> A bride in the valley sings.
> Smoke curls
> From a weather-worn building
> Tiled in sun.

It is by a comparison with this distantly observed building that the poet effects a transition to his personal concerns and to the interior of *this* building:

> Smoke curls
> From a weather-worn building
> Tiled in sun
> Like your cheeks when happiness
> Is done.
>
> Calm and elation
> Create this room.

The 'calm' and 'elation' are the qualities of the contented lovers. They may also be understood as relating to the activities of the two children, the one calmly at her paint-box, the other excitedly clamouring for activity:

> One child paints flowers
> The other soon
> Will call from the dusty track
> 'Wake up! Let's start!'

The poet's lover evidently has behind her some years of unhappiness. Present contentment is mingled with remembered sadness and the resultant bitter-sweet quality might be said to be the characteristic tone of the sequence as a whole. The innocence of the children constitutes a reminder of the state the poet wishes this lover to rediscover:

> May wings stretch over you,
> Spring touch your vein,
> Loveliness lighten
> To childhood again.

The external light of the first three stanzas has here taken on a metaphorical import. In related fashion, the Italian spring (the sequence bears the date 11-14 April 1975) outside is invoked as an agent of spiritual and emotional regeneration. The first line of this last stanza adopts an image particularly common in the *Psalms*, the protective wings of God. The two passages of most obvious relevance occur in Psalms Seventeen and Thirty-Six:

Shew thy marvellous loving-kindness, O thou that savest by thy
right hand them which put their trust in thee from those that rise
up against them.
    Keep me as the apple of the eye, hide me under the shadow of thy
wings,
    From the wicked that oppress me, from my deadly enemies, who
compass me about.

(17.7-9)

How excellent is thy loving kindness, O God! therefore the
children of men put their trust under the shadow of thy wings.
    They shall be abundantly satisfied with the fatness of thy house;
and thou shalt make them drink of the river of thy pleasures.
    For with thee is the fountain of life; in thy light shall we see light.

(36.7-9)

'Camaiore' has already offered us its images of a house of
abundant satisfaction and of a light which makes love visible.
Both passages from the *Psalms* are part of petitions in which
the innocent seek Divine help against their more worldly
neighbours. 'Camaiore's' allusion to these verses thus
anticipates the moment in 'Canzone'

> When envy creeps up through our doors and shutters
> Damning our sins, preaching anathemata
> In hate of spring's cantata

(There is perhaps an echo here of *Jeremiah* 9.21: 'For death is
come up into our windows, and is entered into our palaces').
'Camaiore' concludes on a more simply sensual note, in lines
whose rhythmic fall exactly complements their diction:

> Falling hair fasten
>   Love to your breast
> By Florentine scentfall
>   Caressed.

Where 'Camaiore' was a poem of afternoon light, its successor 'Choriambics' is a poem of the night, more specifically of
the moment before dawn. The poet and his lover are 'wide-
eyed awake' while the children sleep

> safe in shared warmth,
> laid like sardines, secure
> From all hobgoblins and fears, terrors and ticks,
> giants and walking trees
> That bedtime stories have spun.

Security from fears is again the prerogative of innocence. For the two adults the desire for security can find expression only in the unrealistic desire to stay unmoving in this perfect spot and time, not to return to England and the world of 'envy' and 'caution':

> Beauty, star of my sight,
> Kiss me once more. Let us stay here
> now, while the first bird calls.
> In our flight far from the grey desolate days –
> acres of years misspent –
> We've discovered the best. Here let us rest,
> living complete content.

The 'grey desolate days' are those of previous unhappiness and discontent, as well as those of more northern climates, unblessed by sweet air of Tuscany. Their relationship hesitates at a moment of dawning but the desire to live in complete contentment is evidently unrealizable and unrealistic. The sleeping contentment of the children is in part created by the preceding 'terrors and ticks'. Any enduring happiness for the lovers is likely to be defined and shaped by surrounding trials. Untested, the idyll of the opening poems remains ambiguous—a model of 'the best' or a temporary escape from 'caution's catastrophe'? When the poet addresses his lover as 'Beauty, star of my sight' he locates their relationship in the tradition of Italian (and Italianate) love poetry, which the succeeding poems are to draw on more directly for their forms.[15] The 'truth' of that tradition is also to be tested by the painful 'realities' of life back in England.

The classical metres of 'Camaiore' and 'Choriambics' have, of course, sometimes been employed by earlier English poets, even if it cannot be said that they have ever become familiar elements in the English poetic tradition. The choriambics are the rarer metre. Malins mentions their use by Rupert Brooke (two poems of 1908 bear the titles 'Choriambics I' and 'II') as the only instance of the metre in modern English verse. In fact they are also to be found in the work of Robert Bridges (*e.g.* in the Chorus of Oceanides in Act One of *Demeter*). The metre is by no means wholly alien to the traditions of English verse. It underlies more than one nursery rhyme; there are several examples in Swinburne's work and Goethe's *Pandora* well illustrates their use in another Northern poetic tradition. Yet the sense remains that with the third poem of this sequence, 'Canzone', we are dealing with a form (rather than a metre) which exists more securely within the English tradition. That is not entirely to contradict the sentiments of Palgrave when he wrote of the canzone, describing it as 'that beautiful form, the nearest recompense for the loss of the Greek Ode-structure, of which English poetry, I know not why, has been strangely negligent'.[16] The employment of the Italian canzone form, pure and simple, has not been common in English verse. Imitation and adaptation of its formal virtues have, though, a long history. Palgrave's remarks were made apropos of Spenser's *Epithalamion*, perhaps the most exquisite of all English responses to the Italian form. In Milton's 'At a Solemn Music' and 'Upon the Circumcision' there are clear debts to the canzone, as there are in a number of the poems of William Drummond of Hawthornden. In more recent times, Ezra Pound's essays and translations stimulated poets such as Ronald Duncan to explore the possibilities of the form. The origins of the canzone were Provençal. The earliest Italian canzoni to survive date from the second or third decades of the thirteenth century; Dante first employed the form in the 1280's. As a major Italian form it was later to be used by such poets as Petrarch, Tasso, Chiabrera and Leopardi. As Edward Malins points out, it was the model of Dante that was uppermost in Warner's mind here in the 'Canzone' of the *Lucca Quartet*.

For the contemporary English reader of Dante's lyrics a standard work is the two volumes *Dante's Lyric Poetry* edited by K. Foster and P. Boyde, first published in 1967. It is probably no coincidence that this work's discussion of Dante's metric and versification should contain an analysis of precisely that one of Dante's canzoni which provides an exact formal parallel to the 'Canzone' of Warner's Italian sequence. The canzone consists of a number of stanzas (usually more than the two of Warner's poem, but not always so) of identical pattern. Dante's fullest discussion of the nature of the form is to be found in the *De Vulgari Eloquentia*. In origin the canzone was a lyrical form in the literal sense—it was sung. Far more often than not it was set to two distinct melodies. At least one of these melodies was repeated within the stanza. Translated into patterns of metre and rhyme the same basic structure held true even when, as in Dante, the canzoni were no longer necessarily set to music. That part of the stanza which was set to the first melody, Dante calls the *frons*; if this is repeated, the two parts are called *pedes*. The part of the stanza which is set to the second melody goes by a variety of names, most often the *sirima*. Each of these sections had a varying number of lines. The *pedes* usually had from three to six lines, the *sirimas* between five and twelve (in Dante's work, at any rate). Normally lines of either seven or eleven syllables were used. Rhyme-schemes were regarded as a major source of pleasure for the reader, and a major arena for the display of the poet's virtuosity. It is of the invention of rhyme-schemes that Dante is writing when he says in the *De Vulgari Eloquentia* that 'in this almost everyone takes the greatest licence, and . . . this is the principal source of the sweetness of an harmonious whole'.[17] Given Warner's evident delight, elsewhere in his verse, in the patterning of rhyme it is not surprising that he should have been attracted to such a form as the canzone. Foster and Boyde make clear the essential nature of the form by quoting and analyzing a stanza from poem no. 49 in their collection (a poem which has, incidentally, just two stanzas like the 'Canzone' of the *Lucca Quartet*). Its thirteen lines are divided into two *pedes* of 3 lines (with the order of rhymes changed) and a *sirima* of 7 lines:

E' si raccoglie ne li miei sospiri
un sono di pietate,
che va chiamando Morte tuttavia:

a lei si volser tutti i miei disiri,
quando la donna mia
fu giunta da la sua crudelitate;

perché 'l piacere de la sua bieltate
partendo sé da la nostra veduta,
divenne spiral bellezza grande,
che per lo cielo spande
luce d'amor, che li angeli saluta,
e lo intelletto loro alto, sottile
face maravigliar, sì v'è gentile.

Adopting the convention of a lower-case letter to indicate a
shorter line, this gives us a rhyme-scheme of *AbC; AcB; B,
DEeD, FF*. The reader will appreciate that this is precisely
the pattern of Warner's 'Canzone'. The second stanza of
Warner's poem will make the parallel clear;

You have returned to face the storm-wind's music
With heightened trepidation,
Branches of marriage falling in cold greeting.

What inner certainty drove you to choose it
A week from our first meeting
Turning all trials to wild exhilaration?

Spontaneous love's the father of creation.
When envy creeps up through our doors and shutters
Damning our sins, preaching anathemata
In hate of spring's cantata
Laughingly lived and sung past sneers and mutters,
Let us ignore caution's catastrophe
And breed proud children in shared ecstasy.

The affinities between Warner's poem and the theory and
practice of Dante are evident.

Just as 'Canzone' leaves behind the classical patterns of the
first two poems, so the location of the poem leaves behind
Lucca itself. Malins describes the transition thus:

By the third poem of *Lucca Quartet* the two weeks' 'complete content' is over, the lady has returned to face the 'storm wind's music' of her failing marriage, and the poet dejectedly muses like Coleridge upon 'Reality's dark dream' in his room at Oxford.[18]

'Choriambics' had proclaimed:

> We've discovered the best. Here let us rest,
> living complete content.

'Canzone' opens by repeating the word 'here', but with, as we have seen, a chillingly different reference. Its first stanza ends by wondering 'what is goodness if we lack the best?' Here, away from the 'wildwood contentment' of Tuscany, the poet finds himself surrounded by memorials of a vanished 'best'. The stilled chess-set speaks of 'self-mocking anger' and the postcards carried back from Florence cast an ironic light on the relationship celebrated in the previous two poems:

> Here sultry postcards, Carracci's Bacchante
> In tongue-tied exultation
> And the Urbino Venus caught in languor,
> Mother shocked stiff, scolding enough to hang her.

'Carracci's Bacchante' doubtless refers to the painting in the Uffizi in Florence which is more generally known as *Venus, a Satyr, and Two Cupids*. It is most conveniently reproduced in Donald Posner's study of the painter.[19] The picture probably dates from the late 1580s. The reclining Venus has her naked back to the viewer, two small children peer round her, and a satyr offers her a bowl richly laden with grapes. The Venus here has her head to the right of the canvas. The poem's second postcard is of Titian's so-called *Venus of Urbino*, also in the Uffizi, and painted some fifty years before the Carracci. Titian's naked Venus, also reclining of course, faces the viewer, and has her head to the left of the picture. The two paintings thus have a relationship to one another which, if not quite a matter of reversal, certainly encourages one to see each as a kind of mirror image of the other. Warner has interpreted Titian's painting not, as it is now usually interpreted, as symbolizing marital love, [20] but as an implied drama in which the two figures at the rear are seen as a mother (standing) and daughter (kneeling), the mother warning her daughter against (or chiding her for) the kind of sexual languor of which the Venus presents so powerful an emblem. While this interpretation is probably unsound in the light of recent iconographical studies, it is both apt and forceful in the context of Warner's sequence. The second stanza of 'Canzone' asserts the love of the poet and the girl against the criticism of society, and there is a clear reminiscence of the situation in Titian's painting. So, too, the *dramatis personae* of Carracci's picture provide a clear commentary on those of the Lucca sequence, the satyr an image of the poet as misrepresented by the malicious tongues of envy, or portrayed in 'damning . . . sneers and mutters'. Not for the first (or last) time in Warner's work there is created a sense of the achievements of love and art as well-nigh synonymous. The 'trophies' of the lovers' 'climbing zest' are images of Renaissance pictures; the relationship in Lucca is a 'spring cantata' both 'lived and sung'. The assertion that 'spontaneous love's the father of creation' employs to the full the ambiguities of the word 'creation'. It looks forward to Warner's play of Renaissance Florence, *Living Creation*, first produced almost exactly ten years after that visit to Tuscany which elicited the *Lucca Quartet*.

'Canzone', third poem of the sequence, has moved us to a point at which the idyll of the first two poems has come to an end. The idyllic is replaced by the 'dramatic'. Now the poet must plead 'let us ignore caution's catastrophe', where 'catastrophe' bears the sense both of 'a disastrous end . . . [a] calamitous fate', and of 'the change or revolution which produces the conclusion or final event of a dramatic piece'.[21] The increasing sense of the dramatic is reinforced by the fact that the fourth poem, 'Madrigal', actually takes the form of a dialogue. In 1967 Warner published a collection under the title *Madrigals*. Contained in it are a number of the poet's simplest, most 'singable' poems, and the term seems to be employed primarily to indicate this lyrical quality. In any stricter sense Warner's poem is a rather untypical madrigal;

since, however, a writer of madrigals such as Bembo could say, in the sixteenth century, that the madrigal was bound by no rules regarding number of lines or rhyme-scheme, the form is necessarily somewhat difficult of definition. Suffice it to say that nowhere in E.H. Fellowes' collection of English madrigal verse [22] is there any very close parallel for Warner's poem, though the presentation of dialogue within madrigals is by no means unknown.

In the first two poems of the sequence the governing atmosphere, as we have seen, is one of security and certainty. The poet's children play a key role in the creation of this atmosphere. In 'Camaiore':

> Calm and elation
> > Create this room.
> One child paints flowers
> > The other soon
> Will call from the dusty track
> > 'Wake up! Let's start!'

In 'Choriambics' the sleeping children are the embodiment of protected sleep:

> Next door
> Two soft brushed children asleep, safe in shared
> > warmth, laid like sardines, secure
> From all hobgoblins and fears, terrors and ticks,
> > giants and walking trees
> That bedtime stories have spun, read with a last
> > bloodcurdling tender squeeze.

In 'Canzone' the children are not present—though one is mentioned. The poet is alone. Preceding certainties turn to questions. The poet must analyse the significance of his position:

> Here are the trophies of our climbing zest
> But what is goodness if we lack the best?

He must also seek to understand the behaviour of the lover who has now left him:

> You have returned to face the storm-wind's music
> With heightened trepidation,
> Branches of marriage falling in cold greeting.
> What inner certainty drove you to choose it
> A week from our first meeting
> Turning all trials to wild exhilaration?

Here in 'Canzone' the poet can still summon up a ringing declaration of contentment's possibility, a reaffirmation of certainty and ecstasy:

> Spontaneous love's the father of creation.
> When envy creeps up through our doors and shutters
> Damning our sins, preaching anathemata
> In hate of spring's cantata
> Laughingly lived and sung past sneers and mutters,
> Let us ignore caution's catastrophe
> And breed proud children in shared ecstasy.

In 'Madrigal' the questions are even more frequent—and the interrogative becomes the most insistently recurrent mood in the final three poems of the sequence. Statement and affirmation are replaced by doubt and enquiry. Here in 'Madrigal' the poet is questioned by his children:

> 'Will she ring, will she come?' Children, what can I say?
> . . .
> 'Does she love, was she happy, wandering the world as ours?'

The questions in 'Canzone' prompted an assertive response. The poet had only himself to answer. Faced with his children's questions, no such assertion is possible—'Children, what can I say?'. 'Madrigal' is tenderly couched in terms adapted to the participants in its dialogue. The poet speaks in language and images suited to his young hearers. In some earlier poems (*e.g.* 'For a Child', 'For Georgina'), Warner had employed child-like images without descending to mere sentimentality. Here too the note is fittingly simple—'the adventures of playtime', 'sunshine is brief in a lifetime of showers', 'our magic carpet'. The poet's attitude is now radically different. The brevity of happiness is accepted:

> Children, sunshine is brief in a lifetime of showers.
> Our magic carpet was perfectest joy Fate can weave—
> If now unravelled, little ones, we must not grieve.

The poet's closing injunction to his children is surely ambiguous:

> Over the years such love will come your way.
> Outside now, darlings. Please don't look. Just turn
>   away.

Obviously the poet asks the children to leave him, not to gaze at his suffering. In conjunction with the poem's penultimate line, however, we may also take it as advice on how to react when their time of disappointed love comes: 'don't look. Just turn away'. For a poet in particular, drawn to emotional self-examination, such advice is especially difficult to follow. The children do not appear in the remaining two poems of the sequence; their final appearance here serves, amongst other things, to suggest that the experience out of which the sequence is written is a recurrent element in the pattern of human affairs.

The *Lucca Quartet* ends with two sonnets. Their particular rhyme-scheme (*abbacddceffegg*) is one that Warner has not used elsewhere in his sonnets. Though not a common variant of the form it has English precedents in, for example, Surrey ('I never saw you, madam, lay apart') and Drayton ('Sitting alone, Love bids me go and write'), or, more recently, Edwin Muir's powerful sonnet on Milton, 'Milton, his face set fair for Paradise'. It is odd that Edward Malins should call the second of these two closing sonnets a Shakespearian sonnet, though certainly the final rhyming couplet does function in a more or less Shakespearian fashion.

The first of the sonnets relates to a 'fresh meeting' between poet and lover. The questions continue, but the 'dialogue' is one in which we hear only the poet's questions, not the lover's answers:

> Is it a wonder that I love you so
> When everything about you is a greeting?
> In spite of your forced frown at our fresh meeting
> Your body, hands, eyes, cheeks, delight and glow.
> Is it so strange I simply do not care
> What is the cost, what transitory grief
> Must be endured, though surgery is brief,
> If your decisiveness cuts swift and clear?

Given the Tuscan background of the sequence, and the influence of Dante upon the 'Canzone', it is perhaps not fanciful to sense an echo, in the opening quatrain here, of the early chapters of the *Vita Nuova*. The second quatrain associates the parting of lovers with the imagery of medicine and surgery in a way that Warner was to make greater use of in *Morning Vespers*. The questions in this fifth poem of the Lucca sequence are ostensibly addressed to the poet's lover, but are effectively part of a soliloquy in sonnet form. Fittingly its final couplet re-employs key terms from earlier poems in the sequence:

> Guilt, subterfuge, despair are all you'll find
> If you decide to take the cautious way,
> Choose second-rate and waste the dawning day.

'The cautious way' is that recommended by the opponents of love in the closing lines of 'Canzone', in their envious warning of 'caution's catastrophe'. The alternative choice is 'the dawning day' of love. That dawn is the Tuscan dawn at the close of 'Choriambics'. It is also that dawn of love celebrated in *Spring Harvest*:

> On comes our day, our lifetime of delight
> Unhurt and marvellous as morning light.[23]

These questions, though syntactically addressed to the lover, seem more a matter of inner reflection for the poet. The sequence closes, however, with a sonnet which certainly addresses its questions—now even more numerous—to the lady.

A sequence which began in the Tuscan countryside has moved through an Oxford studded with memories of Flor-

ence and now reaches its conclusion (albeit one that contains
no final resolution) in the English countryside. The poet
offers his lover an 'emblem' illustrative, he suggests, of the
happy possibilities he believes still to exist for their love. The
final sonnet's episode of the mating hare and his doe is an
emblem both in the ordinary usage of the word and in its
specific literary sense—it is both a symbol and a 'silent
Parable' to borrow Francis Quarles' definition.[24] The poet's
questions lead his lover to the interpretation of the country
scene she has witnessed. The sonnet's opening words—'Was
it mere chance . . . ?'—are evidently intended to lead her to
the conclusion that far from being a matter of mere chance
her experience constituted a 'vision' with a definite meaning:

> Was it mere chance that brought the mating hare
> Almost to touching distance as you stood
> Still as a tree beside the sunlit wood
> Downwind of him, your beagle nowhere near?
> Were the white streaks along his whiskered cheeks
> Furrows, too, caused by solitary tears?
> Did his loose lope, his absence of all fears
> Delight you? All his muddy scattering freaks?
> Didn't you feel a happy naturalness
> When his doe crossed the harrow to his side?
> That all our Spring is blest, and has not died—
> That deep love triumphs over danger's stress?
>   Wasn't this vision in your saddest hours
>   An emblem, darling, of what might be ours?

Though the tone is, of course, very different, this hare and
his doe, in terms of their poetic function, are likely to remind
most readers of the inset of the courser and the jennet in
Venus and Adonis. As emblems of 'happy naturalness' they
offer both a reminder of a Tuscan spring and a possibility of
its renewal—'all our Spring is blest, and has not died'. The
carefully calculated degree of anthropomorphism in the
presentation of the hare effects a degree of identification
without excessive literalness. The hare does not literally have
cheeks streaked 'by solitary tears'—the lady is merely invited
to wonder whether she can trace in this naturalistically
observed animal a fancied resemblance to the tear-stained

face of the poet. Here and elsewhere in the poem wit and emotion exist in a precise balance. In another sense too the poem is a balanced conclusion to the sequence. It ends, characteristically, on a question, not an affirmation; it is, though, a question which rephrases the affirmations of the earlier poems in the sequence. It extends the possibility of happiness renewed, but does so with a tentativeness that comes close to acknowledging the likelihood that the opportunity may not be grasped.

CHAPTER 7

Morning Vespers

The title of *Morning Vespers* repeats a pattern found more than once in its author's works—the two-word phrase with punning and/or oxymoronic implications. Titles such as *Killing Time*, *Light Shadows* and *Meeting Ends* provide similar instances. *Morning Vespers* juxtaposes the beginning and end of daylight. The evening service of Vespers is named; the oxymoronic adjective with which Warner has provided it will surely make us think of its fellow in the Canonical Hours, the morning service of Lauds. Since 'in the Catholic Liturgy Lauds and Vespers have the same form'[1] a kind of oxymoronic parallelism is established. (Doubtless, too, we are right in hearing a punning undertone on 'mourning'. In *Lying Figures*, Laz transforms 'the bright and morning star' of *Revelation*, Chapter 22, into 'the blighted star of mourning'[2]). The plays which make up his *Requiem* series leave us in no doubt of the attraction Warner feels towards the use of the terminology and rhythms of the Liturgical sequence as a means both of perceiving order and of commenting upon disorder.

That love should be associated with light, and thus with morning, is both natural and traditional. The association is, of course, a frequent one in this author's work. In an earlier study I observed:

As in the neo-Platonists of the Italian Renaissance . . . the light of the sun is repeatedly used in Warner's plays as a symbol either of divine love or of that pseudo-divine love designated by the Biblical *agape*.[3]

Both the Platonic and Christian traditions lie behind one of Warner's finest statements of this central symbol in his work, Quark's love-song in Act One Scene Ten of *Killing Time*, which is included in the *Collected Poems*:

161

The universe spins on a shaft of light
        Whose name is love.
Flowers of the meadows folded up all night
        Spread for high strength above
Them, warming out their secrets till
Displayed for all to see each world's a daffodil.

Full-blown with morning, laughing to the sky
        With puckered lips
They kiss sun's mastery to catch his eye.
        No night-jar trips
Among the undergrowth between the stars,
For violets and primrose chain the bars.

I took a prism, dazzled as a king,
        And held it up.
Light shattered into all the flowers of spring.
        Kingcup
And stalked marsh-marigold, its spendthrift son,
Transfigured all around till night and day were one.

What vision have I seen? Flowers wheel like suns
        In daisy-chains of dance
Round daffodils, whose green-gold laughter stuns
        To ignorance
My day-dull thoughts. Then suddenly the clue
To all was clear. That source of light is you.[4]

There is much here that reappears, in a different context, in
Morning Vespers—the third stanza of Quark's lyric, for
example, is surely remembered in Poem VIII of *Morning
Vespers*. The beloved is recognized as the 'source of light'.
The recognition is, of course, one that is central to the
greatest Western traditions of love poetry. Charles Williams,
writing of the *Vita Nuova* and *Convivio*, observes that

It is a convention of love-poetry to speak of light emanating from
the person of the beloved . . . The forehead and the hand are
radiant; she disseminates glory. Or they do not, and she does not; if
it seems so, it does but seem. But no lover was ever content to allow
that it was but a seeming; rather it is to be that portion of the divine
light which, in the eternal creation of her in heaven, possesses her.
'The light that lightens every man that comes into the world' is
made visible through her by the will of grace, and by that alone. It
seems that no one yet discovered that light of glory in any woman or

any man by hunting for it; it seems that it may exist where it is not wanted.[5]

The beloved is the immediate source of light. In her is morning. If that source of light is removed, then morning fails to develop naturally into day. We move directly from morning to evening: morning vespers. It is such an experience which forms the subject matter of *Morning Vespers*. Like the lover of Donne's 'Nocturnall upon St. Lucies Day',[6] the poet here is moved to declare, effectively, that unlike the 'lesser sunne' (in the sky), his sun will not renew. Vespers functions in part as a seeking of protection against the oncoming night. These poems serve something of the same function.

Morning Vespers was first published in 1980 in a limited edition of 126 copies. The version included in the *Collected Poems* is not identical with this first edition. The order of the sequence has been changed. Referring to the poems by their first lines, the 1980 edition begins thus:

> 'Beloved friend, your faith has come to mean'
> 'Sadness salt-deeper than the sea'
> 'Blessed woman, wayward child'
> 'You came to me at nineteen'.

In the version included in the *Collected Poems*, the sequence opens with the same poems re-arranged as follows:

> 'Beloved friend, your faith has come to mean'
> 'Blessed woman, wayward child'
> 'You came to me at nineteen'
> 'Sadness salt-deeper than the sea'.

The remaining seven poems which complete the sequence appear in the same order in both editions. At least one textual revision has been made, as well as the above change in the order of poems. In 1980 the second stanza of 'Blessed woman, wayward child' read thus:

> Wayward woman, blessed child,
>   Have no further fears.
> Though winds of doubt turn inside out
>   I wipe away your tears

> Until uncertainty's dispelled,
>> And where a confused girl rebelled
> Our strong love strengthens, and is held
>> In greater arms than ours.

In the *Collected Poems* this stanza now appears as follows:

> Wayward woman, blessed child,
>> Have no further fears.
> Though winds of doubt turn inside out
>> I wipe away your tears
> Until uncertainty's dispelled,
>> And where a confused girl rebelled
> Our strong love strengthens, and is held
>> In arms now reconciled.

Though the revision is clearly an improvement in terms of rhyme, it may be doubted whether it is quite so satisfactory from a thematic point of view. 'Greater arms than ours' suggests the protective presence of God; 'arms now reconciled' suggests something more purely human. The balancing fourth line of the stanza is a clear Biblical echo. In *Isaiah* 25 is the promise that 'the Lord God will wipe away tears from off all faces'; *Revelation* 7 describes those who have suffered 'great tribulation' before the throne of God. We are told that 'God shall wipe away all tears from their eyes'.

Morning Vespers, in its first edition, carries two epigraphs (omitted from the *Collected Poems*). The first is taken from the First Epistle General of John:

If we love one another, God dwelleth in us, and his love is perfected in us. (I *John* 4.12)

The second is from 'How to Kill' by Keith Douglas:

> I am amused
> to see the centre of love diffused
> and the waves of love travel into vacancy.

The relevance of each can be seen if it is returned to its original context. The First Epistle of John has much to say about brotherhood and love:

Beloved, let us love one another: for love is of God; and every one
that loveth is born of God, and knoweth God.

He that loveth not knoweth not God; for God is love.

In this was manifested the love of God toward us, because that
God sent his only begotten Son into the world, that we might live
through him.

Herein is love, not that we loved God, but that he loved us, and
sent his Son to be the propitiation for our sins.

Beloved, if God so loved us, we ought also to love one another.

No man hath seen God at any time. If we love one another, God
dwelleth in us . . .

Herein is our love made perfect, that we may have boldness in
the day of judgment: because as he is, so are we in this world.

There is no fear in love; but perfect love casteth out fear: because
fear hath torment. He that feareth is not made perfect in love.[7]

John asserts that our capacity for love both reflects and
evidences our knowledge of God. So much is, in any case,
implicit in the kind of love-experience central to these
poems—what Charles Williams calls, with Dante in mind,
the Beatrician encounter.[8] It is such an idea which underlies,
for example, the marriage sonnet for Penny and Robin
Hodgkinson, written shortly after *Morning Vespers*:

> The looking-glass of long divided years
> Dissolves into a single wonderland
> Of harmony like music of the spheres
> Heard only when such spirits understand
> True love, as Bride and Bridegroom here, who meet
> Never to part, vowing love to suffice
> In matrimony, holy and complete—
> The crown of life and glimpse of Paradise.
> A silent crystal in a noisy world
> Shining in purity of selflessness
> Is such a moment, when two lives are pearled
> In one, as Earth and Heaven conjoin to bless
> > The highest aspiration that we know:
> > The love of God reflected here below.

In *Morning Vespers* that 'highest aspiration' is, finally, thwar-
ted. We shall see that in exploring the failure of that aspir-

ation the poems of the sequence often employ language and images to the significance of which the First Epistle of St. John should alert us.

The second epigraph is from one of the Second World War poems of Keith Douglas (like Warner a product of Christ's Hospital). In published form the poem is called 'How to Kill'. In at least one manuscript it carries the title 'The Sniper'.[9] In it 'a child turning into a man' learns his skill as a sniper. He takes aim at his target:

> I cry
> NOW. Death, like a familiar, hears
> and look, has made a man of dust
> of a man of flesh.This sorcery
> I do. Being damned, I am amused
> to see the centre of love diffused
> and the waves of love travel into vacancy.
> How easy it is to make a ghost.[10]

Perhaps not coincidentally one of the images here returns us to Dante. Douglas' image of a diffused 'circle' of love may remind us of the *Vita Nuova* once more. There, in one of the poet's dreams, Love describes himself and addresses the poet:

Ego tanquam centrum circuli, cui simili modo se habent circumferentiae partes; tu autem non sic.[11]

The two epigraphs stand in antithesis: the one an affirmation of the Divine nature of creative human love; the other a reminder of the human capacity to forget and abandon love, to destroy rather than create. It is that antithesis which is at the heart of *Morning Vespers*, reproducing more extensively the antithesis implicit in the title.

The sequence consists of eleven poems: eight sonnets and three songs. All carry dates, the earliest being dated 25th July 1978, the latest 27th June 1980. In terms of chronological order the midpoint (though, of course, it is not the midpoint in the span of time covered) is marked by no. VI, dated 30th December 1979. In a set of eleven poems, no. VI is also, of course, the central poem numerically. We may note that the date of the poem locates its composition not only at the very end of a year, but at the turning point between decades. Structurally, then, the poem bears considerable weight in terms of the sequence as a whole. Quite how it functions within the shape of the sequence needs to be further considered:

> The world turned upside-down has made us pause
> And gather up the wonder of our cause
> To give us breathing, meditation space.
> Yet sorrow's wisdom holds us by the hand,
> Teaches me treasure more your unique grace
> Poured out like Spring's pulse on the waiting land.
> Your early twenties can no more return,
> And yet, distilled in perpetuity,
> Our love continues, deepens, builds upon
> Such single-minded pure intensity
> Until, two thousand past, we both look back—
> Our children's children dazzling as the sun—
> In joy. Sweet Rose, though these last days seem black
> In this new decade we two will be one.

The poem's central position in the sequence is reinforced by a striking piece of formal wit. In terms of rhyme-scheme this is an inverted Shakespearian sonnet: a rhyming couplet *followed* by three quatrains. The turning upside-down (the reader's attention is directed towards the inversion by the opening line) operates, metaphorically, as the inverting of an hour-glass at the mid-point of the sequence.[12]

The opening poem of the sequence is a perfectly orthodox Shakespearian sonnet—establishing the form which will later be inverted and subjected to other variations of form. The opening poem is, in simple terms, the 'happiest' of the sequence. It defines and celebrates a unity in love. Its positive affirmations, like its form, delineate that 'world' which is later to be turned upside down. The opening lines take us back to the Johannine Epistle:

> Beloved friend, your faith has come to mean
> More to me now than I could once have dreamed.

'Beloved', especially in the immediate context of 'faith', sounds distinctly Biblical. Indeed, it is more than merely a vague evocation of Biblical atmosphere. It is a form of

address which occurs with particular frequency in the Epistles of John. The passage quoted earlier contains two such
instances in the space of only five verses. Here the address is
'beloved friend' and we may take the hint which this offers
and relate the language and imagery of this sequence to the
three poems for 'Koinonia' which appear on pages 184-6 of
the *Collected Poems* ('koinonia' being the Greek for 'friendship, partnership, absolute harmony'). Koinonia appears as
a character in *A Conception of Love*. Of more immediate
concern are the lyrics addressed to 'Koinonia', the name
becoming a poetic title for the poet's lady, much as, say,
Drayton addressed his sonnets to 'Idea'. Two of the poems to
Koinonia might almost be read as preludes to *Morning
Vespers*, though they have no formal connection with the
sequence. The first such lyric anticipates a number of
important ideas and images in *Morning Vespers*:

> She shone from a sea of faces
> A sun-danced wave of the bay,
> Others in orderly places,
> Her beauty in disarray,
> Their brows in concentration,
> Hers clear as a bell at night,
> Her skin as high as elation,
> Her cheeks my entire delight.
>
> I see a dream around you,
> You slip half in, half out.
> I reach to help surround you
> Above, between, about,
> With threads of golden lacework
> Woven in snowflake stars
> Until the dream grows tangible
> And you heal my face of scars.
>
> Ah, fresh as the milk of morning
> When the half-awake clouds are piled
> Welcomed as love is dawning,
> Woman no longer a child;
> Death is to me no stranger
> Although I wish he were:
> I'll lay you in a manger
> And cradle you with fur.

Here is the recognition of love understood as the arrival of
light in general, and morning in particular—both in the first
stanza and, most forcefully, in the first quatrain of stanza
three. That same quatrain's 'woman no longer a child'
anticipates the phrasing of the second poem of *Morning
Vespers*. Here, too, is the sense both of the poet as protector
of a younger girl, and of that girl as 'healer' of the older man's
wounds. This is a theme developed at some length in *Morning Vespers*. In 'A Song for Koinonia' the motif of the
discrepancy in age between the two is repeated and we also
have, though less concisely formulated than in the later
sequence, the juxtaposition of evening and morning:

> Come, say no more. There is no more to say.
> Long fields are shadowed now with end of play
> And laughter's thoughts diminish with the day.
>
> Flecked eggs no longer warm the sitting rooks
> And busy terms with tutors, lovers, books,
> Pass into history through backward looks.
>
> Though all has nearly gone, this will remain,
> This thought, this memory to ease my pain;
> That you have miracled the world's disdain.
>
> And in you Beauty finds she will not change
> Whatever cruel vicissitudes derange
> Or doctors, husbands, parents may arrange.
>
> Your goodness is incarnate in that glow
> Of gentleness that I lost long ago.
> And never thought to find again below.
>
> So may all years and countries be to you
> Blessings as tender as each life that's new
> With silent promise in the morning dew.

(There is much here that finds a further echo in the 'Epilogue' to *A Conception of Love*, which is not included in the
printed text of the play, but appears on page 192 of the
Collected Poems. One imagines that, if used in performance,
the lines would be given to Koinonia).

With these lyrics as our 'prologue', we must return to the
examination of the opening sonnets of *Morning Vespers*. The
first poem begins on a note of calm and contented retro-

spection. The past tenses delineate a relationship of growing discovery. Two literary allusions (though perhaps one is less certainly present than the other) serve to characterize the partners in this relationship of 'faith'. The poet speaks of the girl's personality as 'wild, yet serene, / Untamed, yet gentle'. Words such as these, appearing in a love-sonnet, prompt memories of Wyatt. They remind us of a poem such as 'Whoso list to hunt', the final couplet of which juxtaposes two of these terms:

> *Noli me tangere*, for Caesar's I am,
> And wild for to hold, though I seem tame

or of 'They flee from me', the first stanza of which brings together three of the same adjectives:

> They flee from me, that sometime did me seek
> With naked foot stalking in my chamber.
> I have seen them gentle, tame and meek
> That now are wild, and do not remember
> That sometime they put themself in danger
> To take bread at my hand; and now they range,
> Busily seeking with a continual change.

If I am right to sense such an allusion to Wyatt here in Poem I of *Morning Vespers* (Wyatt's influence upon some of Warner's other lyrics has already been illustrated in Chapter 1) we may see the echoes as constituting an affirmation both of the youthful vitality of the girl, and of the final impossibility of the poet's keeping her settled love. Words like 'untamed' and 'wild' retain here in Poem I the value of admiring compliment. With the echoes of Wyatt in mind they also offer an anticipation, even a warning, of the relationship's impermanence. This poet, like Wyatt, may find her a spirit impossible to hold. Such echoes of Wyatt are perhaps less certainly present than the clear presence in lines five and six of an allusion to the opening of the *Divine Comedy*. The poet talks of his

> dull stumbling through the wood
> Of this dark world

and the phrasing unmistakeably imitates the opening of the *Inferno*:

> Nel mezzo del cammin di nostra vita
> mi ritrovai per una selva oscura
> che la diritta via era smarrita.
>
> Ahi quanto a dir qual era è cosa dura
> esta selva selvaggia e aspra e forte
> che nel pensier rinova la paura![13]

In part the allusion establishes the contrast between the *dramatis personae*. Though here in *Morning Vespers* the poet says nothing of himself being 'nel mezzo del cammin' we may reasonably infer that he is, from the precision with which he adopts the other features of Dante's opening three lines. In the *Divine Comedy* the lines clarify Dante's age as thirty-five, midpoint of the Biblically decreed life-span of seventy years. On the evidence of the dates carried by the poems of *Morning Vespers*, their author must have been slightly older at the time of his first meeting with this 'beloved friend'—though not, perhaps, by so much as to fall outside the terms of one of Dante's other observations on the midpoint of human life:

Là dove sia lo punto summo di questo arco [de la vita] . . . è forte da sapere; ma ne li più io credo tra il trentesimo e quarentesimo anno, e io credo che ne li perfettamente naturati esso ne sia nel trentacinquesimo anno.[14]

In a neighbouring passage of the *Convivio* Dante talks of 'la selva erronea di questa vita'—a wandering wood in which one might, indeed, stumble. The 'dark world' of line 6 in the first poem of *Morning Vespers*, awaiting the 'illumination' of love, is violently figured in the third quatrain:

> Your love, unscathed, has risked through brothel streets,
> Searching me out between sheets of despair;
> Borne with my shadow-screams in wintry heats;
> Stepped between fighting razors with your care.

In one sense it is from the world of the *Requiem* plays that the poet is rescued by this meeting. The 'despair' of line 9 stands in specific antithesis to the 'faith' of line 1—the terms remind us, sending us back to the Epistle of John, that human love's power to redeem and save is very specifically a reflection of the redemptive love of Christ. Once again Dante, in the *Convivio*, provides a clear and helpful parallel. Charles Williams quotes and discusses some precisely relevant passages:

'Her beauty has power to renovate nature in those who behold her, which is a marvellous thing. And this confirms what has been said . . . that she is the helper of our faith'. . . 'She was created not only to make a good thing better, but also to turn a bad thing into good'. Things intolerable outside a state of love become blessed within: laughter and love convert for a moment the dark habitations within the soul to renewed gardens in Eden. The primal knowledge is restored, and something like pardon restores something like innocence.[15]

The girl's love (Poem III tells us that she was nineteen at the time of their first meeting) 'searches out' the poet. The phrase echoes the *Psalms* (e.g. 44.21; 139.23). The 'sheets of despair' conflate the bedsheets of loveless sex, or sleepless nights, with the papers on which the poet has poured out his despair—perhaps the pages of 'shadow-screams' which occupy some of the *Requiem* plays ('The best in this kind are but shadows') and where, in both *Meeting Ends* and *Lying Figures*, razors play a very important part in the battle between the sexes. The sonnet's final couplet, with its quasi-allegorical references to 'youth' and 'beauty', confounds traditional expectations of the young being instructed by their elders. Here it is the young girl who teaches the lesson of 'how to live' to a poet midway in 'the wood of this dark world'.

In the song which follows, the roles are partly reversed. Now it is primarily the poet who appears in the role of 'guardian':

> You who've shared your tender years,
>   Growing pains and fears, too,
> Trusting me in everything,
>   Knowing I'll protect.

The song's opening line develops the previous poem's sense of the girl's contradictory personality. Clearer still is the suggestion that this is due in large part to her being at the very moment of transition to full adulthood. The rhetorical figure which inverts the terms of the first line when they reappear in the first line of the second stanza establishes the point very economically:

Blessed woman, wayward child

becomes

Wayward woman, blessed child.

Turning, in a whole variety of senses, is at the heart of this sequence. Inversion we meet here as a rhetorical figure. In Poem VI we have inversion of form. In the second stanza of Poem II 'winds of doubt turn inside out'. Again in Poems IV and XI we shall see the verb playing an especially forceful role. In the sense of 'turning into', the process of growing from one stage of human life into another, it underlies much of the thought and emotion in these opening poems.

The third poem (using the numbering of the version in *Collected Poems*) is, in itself, a crucial turning point in the sequence's implicit narrative. It gives us information, such as the girl's age, that we were without in the first two poems. The poet's identity as an older man is, as it were, confirmed and extended by mention of his children. Above all, of course, the final sentence of the poem makes explicit what had, at the most, been only hinted at in the previous two poems: the relationship has been severed. What the poet has called, justly or unjustly, the girl's 'waywardness' is now discovered to have found expression in ways perhaps anticipated by the allusions to Wyatt in the first poem. The emotional force of this lyric perhaps exists in counterpoint to its talk of disruption. In the eight lines of each stanza the first four constitute a single uninterrupted sentence. In the second half of each stanza we also have a single sentence, the only difference in the two cases being the comma, not strictly necessary grammatically, which invites an unexpected pause before the final line of the poem. The emphasis on the final line is thus increased and the effect is to make us question the certainty of the poet's assertion there. The verb tenses in the poem work subtly. For the first twelve lines of the poem the past tense verbs may not appear to be anything more than the retrospection which characterized the first poem. There is, as we first read the lines, no reason to assume that verbs such as 'shared' and 'taught' refer to activities now completed and done with. With the switch to the present tense in lines 13 and 14 these past tenses earlier in the poem take on a different significance. The futures of the two final lines cannot, in such a context, sound quite so certain of fulfilment as the poet evidently hopes. The note of horror has been reintroduced into the poem (after the third quatrain and final couplet of Poem I had seemed to show it vanquished). The first stanza of the third poem—with its stress on 'shared' and on 'our'—had spoken of a more complete mutuality than was characteristic of either of the first two poems. Particularly poignant force is thus given to the disruptiveness of the second stanza.

Poem IV actually bears a date of composition two days earlier than that of no. III. In terms both of narrative and emotional sequence it is clearly better read after no. III. Here indeed is 'horror'—as experienced afresh by the poet. That horror is articulated through three interlocking patterns of imagery—drawn from the activities of war, medicine and law. The interaction of the languages of love and war is, of course, a recurrent feature in European love poetry. It is an interaction which is vividly active in the *Requiem* plays. Here in this fourth poem the pains of separation are identified with the life-destroying fires of war:

> Familiar agony returns
> Increasing till the will to live
> Diminishes in napalm burns.

'Returns' is another of the sequence's variations on 'turning'. The agony is 'familiar' because, for the poet, it is a return to the 'despair' of Poem I. The destructive impulses of 'war', once released, are not readily re-confined; rather, evil

> grows and spreads till less and less
> Can claims of peace be entertained.

Here 'claims' effects a link with the poem's legal imagery. In his suffering the poet's first reaction is to question the 'justice' of his 'punishment':

> What crime can so deserve such pain?

The vows of love have a different force from the contracts of the legal world, but in both contexts the 'perjured' can be 'overcome . . . with the perjurer's sin'. The emotional pain is forcefully evoked in the physical language of medicine. Wounds are stung with salt, 'each day's haemorrhaged again', and 'sold vows . . . scar another'. The poet-lover of Chaucer's *Book of the Duchess* insists that

> there is phisicien but oon
> That may me hele.[16]

F.N. Robinson notes that 'the comparison of the lady to a physician is a commonplace' and offers possible sources in Machaut.[17] Such a motif is here given expression in a particularly modern context:

> Sadness salt-deeper than the sea
> Stings the raw weeks till your touch heal.

The central stanzas of Poem IV offer an analysis of a quasi-legal moral system—akin to the 'iron law of right and wrong' referred to later in Poem X. Here in Poem IV a system of emotional retribution is elucidated in a manner that once again employs the idiom of 'turning' and 'returning':

> Each imposition we inflict
> On others at our own expense
> Strikes back its cursing interdict
> Till savage love claims precedence,
>
> And we, poor mortals that we are,
> Cringe as we feel our faults return,
> Knowing full well sold vows must scar
> Another, yet resent our turn.

These are pains, forms of 'justice', not readily healed:

> And where we thought a little wrong,
> A slight withdrawal, soon would heal,
> We find dead roots grown far too strong
> Till joy's impossible to feel.

The rejection of love sets in motion a process which neither poet nor girl may be able to reverse. The Second Prologue to *Moving Reflections* begins with the assertion that

> Those who reject love find love rejects them.

In the rejection of love resides the paradox of 'dead roots' grown strong. A waste land is created, and it becomes 'impossible to feel . . . joy'. Joy here surely carries something like the full weight it has in a Romantic poem such as Coleridge's *Dejection*:

> Joy, Lady! is the spirit and the power,
> Which wedding Nature to us gives in dower
>   A new Earth and new Heaven,
> Undreamt of by the sensual and the proud—
> Joy is the sweet voice, Joy the luminous cloud—
>   We in ourselves rejoice!
> And thence flows all that charms or ear or sight,
>   All melodies the echoes of that voice,
> All colours a suffusion from that light.

In the final stanza of Warner's poem the possibility is offered, the prayer is made, that in the renewal of the girl's 'blessing' that waste land might be avoided. The abbreviated last line of the final stanza echoes into a subsequent silence.

The silence is broken in Poem V, a sonnet which makes it clear that that prayer has not been answered:

> Eight winter weeks have dragged their weariness
> Across our lives since last we lay so warm
> Enfolded in each other's gentleness
> And petalled splendour of your naked form.

The title of the sequence invokes diurnal rhythms. Here, for the first time, the subject matter is located against the larger rhythm of the seasonal cycle. Although the first four poems carry dates they make no allusion to the time of year to which those dates refer. Here in Poem V the 'winter weeks' both reflect the poet's present state of mind and stand in stark antithesis to remembered warmth. Similarly, the darkness of winter is made more painful by the remembered 'splendour' of line 4. That that splendour should be described as 'petalled' anticipates coming patterns of imagery. Aptly enough in a poem in which the cycle of the seasons is of such importance, Poem V is structured around an opposition between growth and its denial. The eight weeks of winter have been preceded by

> two hundred weeks of shared delight,
> Of growth lived to the height of ecstasy,
> Loved by two children, blessed by God's own might
> In never-failing shared intensity,
> Have been our envied, legendary days.

The particular terms in which this sense of perfection is expressed—of unfailing growth, of days to be regarded as legendary—creates of this period of 'shared delight' a kind of personal version of the myth of the Golden Age. In the 'shared intensity' of those two hundred weeks the poet and his beloved have created and inhabited a time like that which Hesiod ascribes to the age of Chronos when 'the fruitful earth unforced bore them fruit abundantly and without stint'[18] or the Homeric garden of Alcinous with its orchard full of

> trees in bloom or weighted down for picking;
> pear trees, pomegranates, brilliant apples,
> luscious figs, and olives ripe and dark.
> Fruit never failed upon these trees: winter
> and summertime they bore.[19]

Now, however, those 'envied, legendary days' are no more:

> The orchard apples rot upon their boughs.
> Both lives hang stagnant till our wayward ways
> Return and join, fulfilled in love's own vows.

The fruit is unharvested—in December it rots. Two lives also hang stagnant, and the waywardness which, in Poem II characterized the girl, is now seen to be common to both poet and girl. The need for return, on more than a merely personal level, is asserted. The opening lines of this sonnet were the first in the sequence to make full acknowledgement of the passing of time, locating the events and emotions within the time-scheme of the world outside; in a related fashion the closing couplet of the poem first locates the sequence in a geographical setting:

> Never were two so well prepared to share
> One life of love than this tuned Oxford pair.

The mention of Oxford gives a particular resonance to the sequence's earlier talk of 'teaching' and, indeed, a particular appositeness to the imagery of church bells here.

The first two sonnets of the sequence, Poems I and V, have been regularly Shakespearian in form. Poem VI, however, as mentioned earlier, inverts that form, turning its rhyme-scheme on its head. How such an inversion functions as a medial point in the sequence has already been discussed. When a form, such as the sonnet, has well-developed associations with certain kinds of content and attitude, then manipulation of the form becomes a means, simultaneously, of commenting upon that attitude and content. The history of the sonnet provides us with some interesting examples. In Chapter Five I have already discussed, for example, Shakespeare's dramatic use of the sonnet in *Romeo and Juliet* on the occasion of the lovers' first exchange. There the Nurse's interruption of their dialogue of sonnets enacts in brief the destruction of love's aspirations which the play as a whole will see worked out at length. A more humorous, but similarly ironic, exploitation of similar associations underlies an inverted sonnet by Rupert Brooke:

> Hand trembling towards hand; the amazing lights
> Of heart and eye.They stood on supreme heights.
> Ah, the delirious weeks of honeymoon!
> Soon they returned, and after strange adventures,
> Settled at Balham by the end of June.
> Their money was in Can. Pacs. B. Debentures,
> And in Antofagastas. Still he went
> Cityward daily; still she did abide
> At home. And both were really quite content
> With work and social pleasures. Then they died.
> They left three children (besides George, who drank):
> The eldest Jane, who married Mr. Bell,
> William, the head-clerk in the County Bank,
> And Henry, a stock-broker, doing well.[20]

Here, by beginning with a celebration of honeymoon happiness, displacing the formal climax of the poem to its opening so as to do so, Brooke contrives a plodding and anti-climactic descent into banality. A form which speaks of aspiration has been inverted and become the vehicle for its opposite. Warner's irony, in his inverted sonnet, is more subdued and serves purposes of balance rather than satirical reversal. One effect here in Poem VI is to throw emphasis on the centre of the poem. The central lines of the central poem of the sequence, the narrowest point of the hour-glass, to use my earlier metaphor, enact the poem's balancing upon a turning-point between a happy remembered past and a future as yet uncertain:

> Your early twenties can no more return,
> And yet, distilled in perpetuity,
> Our love continues, deepens. . .

The moment of pause, of which the poem's first line speaks, is here acted out by its central lines. Again we are reminded of the date the poem bears, the turning of the year, the beginning, indeed of a new decade. The thought of the girl—though these central lines perhaps rebuke us for the continuing use of the term—is an affirmation of spring, even in deepest winter. There is much in the language of this sonnet which reminds us of Shakespeare's *Sonnets*. 'Distilled in perpetuity' relates to central images of the first eighteen of Shakespeare's sonnets, especially sonnets five and six. There the movement of time is opposed by the image of 'summer's distillation' and of 'flow'rs distilled'.[21] The first eighteen of Shakespeare's sonnets are, of course, those in which he seeks to persuade the Young Man to marry. Though for rather different reasons, the poet's purpose here in *Morning Vespers* is also a persuasion to marriage. The ironic affinity with Shakespeare's *Sonnets* is reinforced by the form of address which the poet adopts in the final lines of the poem: 'Sweet Rose'. *Morning Vespers* carries as dedication the words 'for Rosalind' and that offers one obvious and natural explanation for the phrasing here in Poem VI.[22] There is also, though, an unmistakeable reminiscence of the opening of

Shakespeare's *Sonnets*, especially in the form in which they appeared in the 1609 Quarto:

> From fairest creatures we desire increase,
> That thereby beauties *Rose* might never die.

That the poet's love should here be addressed as 'sweet Rose' does, of course, give a precise force to the 'distilled' of line 8. It picks up and defines the associations of the adjective 'petalled' applied to her in the previous poem. Above all, there is evoked one of the most perennial and powerful of all literary symbols. This is no place to begin an exploration of the tradition whereby 'the Rose has been for many centuries a symbol of spiritual love and supreme beauty'.[23] In Act One Scene Eight of *Living Creation* Simonetta was later to speak of the rose as 'the queen of flowers' which 'unfolds / The scented innocence of youth'. How the rose has most often functioned as a symbol in the literature of our own century has been very perceptively defined by Barbara Seward:

Our age, in despair of itself, sought the complex, intangible values that the Middle Ages had, and, in its attempt to express or discover a positive, possible hope, reemphasized the symbol of countless centuries of hope. In fact, the flower that since Isaiah had signified the fecundity promised to redeem the world's wilderness was the one unavoidable choice of writers seeking universal symbols through which to express their hope for redemption from the wastes of their lives or times.

For just as the wasteland can be said to be a prime symbol of our era, so the rose can be said to be its prime antithesis.[24]

Seward presumably refers to the opening verses of Chapter 35 of *Isaiah:*

The wilderness and the solitary place shall be glad for them; and the desert shall rejoice, and blossom as the rose.

It shall blossom abundantly, and rejoice even with joy and singing: the glory of Lebanon shall be given unto it, the excellency of Carmel and Sharon, they shall see the glory of the Lord, and the excellency of our God.

The 'waste land' here redeemed is produced by the sequence of events with which Chapter 24 of *Isaiah* opens:

Behold, the Lord maketh the earth empty, and maketh it waste, and turneth it upside down, and scattereth abroad the inhabitants thereof.

We are close here to the kind of language with which the sixth poem of *Morning Vespers* opens, with its talk of 'the world turned upside-down'. The literary device of the world turned upside down, the *mundus inversus*, is an old and favourite one, as Ernst Curtius has shown.[25] It is most often used for comic or satirical purposes, but can occasionally serve to express the horror of a mind robbed of all comfort and certainty—Curtius quotes a striking piece by the French Baroque poet Théophile de Viau. There is no comedy here in *Morning Vespers*, as the world is turned upside down, and what Curtius calls 'the twilight of a distracted mind',[26] in describing the poem by Théophile, is only held in abeyance by the sense that the poem represents a moment of stasis at the beginning of a new span of time.

If not positively 'distracted', the mind revealed in Poem VII is, at any rate, one inhabiting a waste land, in need of the redemptive power of the rose. Visiting a Paris formerly visited in the company of his love, the poet finds myths and hopes 'turned dust upon the tongue', encounters a Paris now 'wanly desolate' and must endure a life now felt to be a 'worthless waste'. Previously love had defined a relationship with the world which was one of possession and creativity. The Left Bank's streets were 'so effortlessly ours'. The windows were, metaphorically, canvases upon which they could create 'new myths and hopes'. Now the locations of former love—'gallery, clothes-shop and monument'—serve only to reinforce the sense of loss and absence:

> agony
> Bleaker than bodily pain, harsher than grief
> To counter, lemon in the eye of pride.

The couplet conjoins a sense of this landscape as waste land with a sense of its origins in the loss of that trust, that faith, which the whole sequence began with in the opening lines of Poem I. Now the poet finds

> life without your love a worthless waste
> When all our deepest vows are so defaced.

'Defaced' is a word with a powerful physical resonance—it takes us back to some of the images of Poem IV; in the context of a word such as 'worthless' it also perhaps has overtones of coinage defaced—the coinage, as it were, of love's exchange. We must also recognize, though, that it is another word which takes part of its force from its use in the opening movement of Shakespeare's *Sonnets*. Sonnets 5 and 6, already referred to in connection with the 'distilled' of Poem VI of *Morning Vespers*, again provide the context; the opening of Shakespeare's sixth sonnet juxtaposes the two terms:

> Then let not winter's ragged hand deface
> In thee thy summer ere thou be distilled.

After the inversions of Poem VI, Poem VII of *Morning Vespers* re-establishes the orthodox Shakespearian sonnet. The norm does not, though, remain long unchallenged. Indeed it is the last conventional sonnet in the sequence. From this point onwards the expected and traditional patterns, with all their associations, seem to be deemed inappropriate for the poet's emotions.

Poem VIII does not at first glance appear to be a sonnet at all, though it clearly has fourteen lines:

> When I was eight I took a burning-glass
> No larger than a pebble sliced in half
> And concentrated all the summer's sun
> Ten thousand times its strength upon one spot,
> Glowing, until the edge of some dry leaf
> Fanned into smouldering till sparks caught fire.
> Such energy, I knew, could also blast
> Spider's leg, ant, or beetle. This strange thought
> Widened the ring of light and softened strength,
> Touching the small boy to humility.
> Much later, now, I find this God-like power
> Hides in a grown man's all-embracing love,
> Rides over all vicissitudes to leap,
> Clutch, pierce, and focus two lives in one flame.

In fact, the rhymes are now initial rather than terminal, placed in the first syllable of each line. Analyzed in those terms the poem produces the rhyme-scheme *abcabcdeeddeed*. Once more a kind of inversion has taken place, since this, after all, is the pattern of a normal Italian sestet *followed* by a regular Italian octave. (Taking the normal Italian sonnet pattern of *abbaabbacdecde* as our point of reference Poem VIII might be said to use a rhyme-scheme of *cdecdeabbaabba*). Perception of the form is made somewhat easier by the marked pause after 'fire' at the end of the sestet. If there is a *volta* here it is, naturally and properly in an inverted Italian sonnet, to be found at this point. The sequence as a whole has as one of its concerns 'reversed emotions' (Poem XI). Formal reversal and inversion become means of expressing such a sense of a 'world turned upside down'. In Poem VIII the poet goes much further back in his memories than in any of the previous poems. His own childhood is recalled, and in recognizing affinities between childhood and adult years he touches once more on themes suggested previously in connection with the 'blessed woman, wayward child' of the sequence. Relatedly, the light which was of such importance in earlier poems now takes on a new force and direction. The identification of love and light underlies the whole sequence. Earlier, light appeared as an unqualified good. In Poem VIII things are not so simple. Light is energy. Energy is not an unquestionable moral good. The young experimentalist of the poet's childhood discovers the destructive power of the light concentrated with great intensity on one spot. Both the dry leaf and the living creature can be 'blasted' by it. 'Blast' in line 7 is a word that might as readily refer to the blighting of a rose as to the destructions of war. 'Intensity' had earlier been used as a term of celebration:

> Loved by two children, blessed by God's own might
> In never-failing shared intensity,
> Have been our envied legendary days. (V)

> Our love continues, deepens, builds upon
> Such single-minded pure intensity. (VI)

In this eighth poem, however, intensity's dangers are recognized, at least in retrospect. The destructive power recognized prompts a relaxation in the eight-year-old's use of the 'burning-glass':

> This strange thought
> Widened the ring of light and softened strength.

The sequence's epigraph from Keith Douglas surely has a bearing here. The final four lines of the poem register the poet's recognition of the common ground between his childhood 'game' and his present situation. What is not perhaps explicitly recognised is that the adult, riding

> over all vicissitudes to leap,
> Clutch, pierce, and focus two lives in one flame

may not be able to raise the burning-glass as the eight-year-old did, may not be able to 'widen . . . the ring of light'. Unable to do so, both he and the woman he loves are likely to be blasted. The power may be 'God-like'; its possessors may, though, lack Divine wisdom. The poet finds in a childhood activity a mirror-image of his present condition. Yet the difference is evident in the verbs which characterize each experience. Against the relatively quiet, almost scientific language of the sonnet's opening, stands the fearsome energy of the last two lines, with their five powerful verbs. The child may, indeed, be wiser than the man.

Poem IX offers another variation on sonnet form— another attempt to relate experience to inherited idiom. Here half-rhyme sometimes replaces full rhyme, and end-rhyme and initial rhyme are both employed. Italicization of the rhyme fellows is perhaps the clearest way to show the rhyme-scheme:

> *Your* hand in mine, we watched a sunbeam strike
> *The* dancing dust in Lavenham's old church
> *Soar*ing and falling all the scented, sung
> *E*vensong in a joy-shaft on our love
> *Till*, setting as we fulfilled down the hill
> *Back* to The Swan, to live what we had felt,
> The dusk enfolded in its soft em*brace*
> While the last marigold transformed your *face*,

> *Kill*ing all trace of any sorrows past,
> *Track*ing a stairway from your smile to heaven.
> *Now* darkness falls indeed, and no beams dance.
> *Hand*s reach, but only find dust on your heart.
> *Prou*d tenderness must wait with patient faith
> *And* watching through the long hours of each night.

The pattern, thus, is of three quatrains, the central one interrupted by the couplet, again displaced from its 'proper' place in the Shakespearian sonnet.

The last moment of union, or near union, is here in Poem IX. Hand in hand the lovers watch the dust vivified by light, the waste land ('myths and hopes turned dust upon the tongue') momentarily transfigured by a shaft of light, reminding one of Quark's love song, in which

> The universe spins on a shaft of light
> Whose name is love.

This moment of transfiguration is witnessed at sung Evensong in a country church. We are reminded of the 'vespers' of the sequence's title (though Evensong and Vespers are not, of course, identical). There is the further sense of a vigil performed, in hope, in the final lines of the poem (compare 'The Statues'). The centrality of the 'displaced' couplet offers a guide to one of the poem's key patterns. The first and second 'halves' of the poem—the first six and the last six lines—are, to quote the poem's own seventh line, 'enfolded' symmetrically upon its centre. Lines 1 and 14 offer a kind of mirror image of one another:

> Your hand in mine, we *watched a sun*beam strike

being reflected in

> And *watching* through the long hours of each *night*.

The repeated verbs are coupled with symmetrically opposed nouns—light opposes darkness. Lines 2-4, with their images of light falling and dust dancing, are counterpointed by the matching negatives of lines 11 and 12. Now it is darkness that falls and 'no beams dance'. Now the dust is of emotional death:

> Hands reach, but only find dust on your heart.

The first six lines of the sonnet close with a movement of descent:

> Till, setting as we fulfilled down the hill
> Back to The Swan, to live what we had felt.

In this enfolding symmetry it is natural that the lines which balance them, lines 9 and 10, should affirm an ascending movement:

> Killing all trace of any sorrows past,
> Tracking a stairway from your smile to heaven.

The poem ends, however, with the fall of darkness—the sunlight of the opening quatrain is the last that we shall meet in the sequence. The lovers may be hand in hand at the poem's opening; by its final quatrain hands reach out and find only dust.

Poem X has the same rhyme scheme as no. VIII. It too is an inverted Italian sonnet, but unlike the earlier poem its rhymes are not all placed at the beginning of the line. Indeed the poem has a regular pattern of alternating initial and terminal rhymes. Perception of this is made easier by the fact that the syntactical structure respects the divisions implied by the units of rhyme. This is perhaps clearer if we italicize, once more, the rhyme fellows, and if we separate the poem into its distinguishable units:

> The iron law of right and wrong has *claimed*
> *Its* penalty for sacred love blasphemed
> As we both knew it would, exactly *timed*.
>
> *Maimed*, I survive. The other man you loved,
> Your father, the sad sacrifice, comm*its*,
> Re*fined*, his soul to beauty of our best.
>
> His death on your Damascus road can *bring*
> *Good* out of evil, if humility
> Like Paul's accepts rebuke as holy *food*
> *Sting*ing to heal and turn round into God.
>
> Years back we two were set apart. A *ring*
> *Would* be our aspiration's longed delight,
> Now a command. Wrath's awe is under*stood*.
> *King*dom or chaos is your lifelong choice.

The 'narrative' has moved on an important stage. Earlier we heard of the poet as a father; now we hear of the woman's father. Her father has died. The poet, distracted, interprets the death as the fulfilment of the 'iron law' which punishes their failure to bring their love to a proper and completed union. This is the 'penalty for sacred love blasphemed'. The experience is, not altogether happily, compared to Paul's experience on the road to Damascus. In her pain she is confronted with the necessity for choice, and with the possibility of bringing 'good out of evil'. The medical and legal imagery which in Poem IV articulated the poet's unhappiness is now active in the context of her suffering. 'Stinging' and 'heal' in line 10 are words we have met in earlier poems of the sequence, as of course we have repeatedly encountered 'turn'. The closing line of the poem offers the 'lifelong choice' of kingdom or chaos. Both are words with a theological dimension, befitting both the specific diction of this sonnet and the constant interpenetration of 'secular' and 'divine' love which is such a hallmark of the sequence as a whole. A primary force of each word, though, comes from the traditions of love poetry. The 'kingdom' of love-union is familiar to us, for example, from such poems by Donne as 'The Anniversarie', with its lovers 'who Prince enough in one another be' and its ringing assertion that

> Here upon earth, we'are Kings, and none but we
> Can be such Kings, nor of such subjects be.

'Chaos', in this particular context, reminds us of a crucial moment in *Othello* (a passage previously echoed in *Meeting Ends*),[27] Othello's preliminary observation upon Desdemona:

> Excellent wretch, perdition catch my soul,
> But I do love thee, and when I love thee not,
> Chaos is come again.[28]

There is an ironic relevance in the lines. Where Othello's fear is that he might come not to love Desdemona, the poet-lover of *Morning Vespers* has to come to terms with his fear that his 'excellent wretch' will no longer love him, that her heart will 'turn away' (XI). Her choice is not only for herself; for the poet, too, chaos will 'come again' should she choose not to share a kingdom.

The final poem of the sequence, while not finally acknowledging defeat, is written out of that chaos. Its conclusion, a final couplet in its expected place, such as we have not had since Poem VII, has a clear relationship to the conclusion of Poem IV. That poem ended

> Bless, while our hearts can still be one,
> And let love win.

The final lines of the sequence express the same plea:

> Our four-year home is nine-months tempest-tossed.
> Rose, let not dearest loveliness be lost.

The phrasing of this last line again echoes the *Sonnets* of Shakespeare. The 'loveliness' in danger of being lost is not only the experience the two lovers have shared. It is also that 'unthrifty loveliness' of which Shakespeare writes in the fourth sonnet. One theme of the first group of sonnets is the begetting of children. So, too, in Poem III of *Morning Vespers* we read

> You made my children love you
> And shared our private joys
> And lying on our pillow
> Whispered you'd breed me boys.

That hope seems now to have vanished. There is a painful irony in the way Poem XI delineates precisely the length of their separation—'nine-months' love-denial' and 'nine-months tempest-tossed'. Fittingly, in the final poem of the sequence, Poem XI picks up many other words and motifs from earlier poems. Words like 'blessing' (line 2), 'learns' (3), 'child' (10), 'wildly' (12) and 'Rose' (14) have all been discussed in terms of their importance in preceding poems. That 'nine-months' love-denial' should have destroyed a 'Paradise' is explicit statement of that motif of the Golden Age which was traced in the imagery of Poem V. 'The scorched-earth landscape' of line 8 is anticipated by the

destructive fire of the burning-glass in Poem VIII. Poem IV's
fear was that

> Evil cannot be self-contained
> But grows and spreads till less and less
> Can claims of peace be entertained.

Here in Poem XI 'evil spreads like cancer through your
days'. Poem I's juxtaposition of 'faith' and 'despair' is echoed
here in lines 10 and 12. The 'blessed woman, wayward child'
of Poem II is here a 'child of reversed emotions'. The
opening lines of the poem, with the word 'turn' reiterated yet
once more, explore the nature of the reversal that has
happened. The third quatrain of the poem affirms the possibility of a further reversal, a 'proving' of love out of wild
disintegration, a reassertion of love's order and meaning
drawn from the 'chaos' which closed Poem X. There is a
sense in which the form of this final poem serves in part to
enact this possibility. It was earlier suggested that the Shakespearian sonnet provided, within this sequence, as elsewhere
in English poetry, a model of the harmony and balance
aspired to in the union of love. In the second part of *Morning
Vespers* the form is only briefly present (in Poem VII).
Elsewhere, as 'joy's most cherished vow / wildly disinte-
grates', this formal ideal is stood on its head and turned
inside out. Poems VI, VIII, IX and X have offered a whole
catalogue of sonnet variants. Only with Poem XI do we come
close to the re-establishment of the Shakespearian model,
with all that that can be seen to imply. The form is not
altogether re-affirmed; that would be false to the sequence's
subject-matter. Rather, just as the hoped-for marriage
remains out of reach, just as the 'dearest loveliness' remains
unfulfilled, so too the Shakespearian sonnet remains a formal
ideal not re-attained. As printed, Poem XI's appearance on
the page more closely resembles the Shakespearian model
than is the case with its immediate predecessors. It has, at
any rate, a clear final couplet. Examination of the poem will
show that the quatrain structure is there and that the syntactical and logical structures of the poem respect it. The
rhymes are italicized below:

> The deepest sadness is when one heart *turns*
> *Away*, first having willed, with blessing's self
> Over the years the other's love, and *learns*
> To‑*prey* upon those joys it nourished most.
> Now evil spreads like cancer through your *days*,
> *And* nine-months' love-denial has destroyed
> The Paradise where now a donkey *brays*
> *Grand* in its scorched-earth landscape of complaint.
> Yet those whom you loved most still love you *now*,
> *Child* of reversed emotions, near despair.
> Love is most proved when joy's most cherished *vow*
> *Wild*ly disintegrates, yet faith holds on.
> > Our four-year home is nine-months tempest-*tossed*.
> > Rose, let not dearest loveliness be *lost*.

Different though his diction is, the poet of *Morning Vespers*
would surely have shared the sentiments of one anonymous
madrigalist:

> I always loved to call my lady Rose,
> For in her cheeks roses do sweetly glose;
> And from her lips she such sweet odours threw,
> As roses do 'gainst Phoebus' morning view.
> But when I thought to pull't, hope was bereft me,
> My Rose was gone, and nought but prickles left me.[29]

More directly, both Shakespearian Rose and Shakespearian
form are invoked in this final poem. With the end of the
sequence, however, both invocations reverberate only into
silence. Vespers and the sense of valediction dominate the
close of the sequence as morning and light's new beginning
had dominated its opening. Such non-dramatic sonnets as
Warner has written since *Morning Vespers* are far less
committed to the exploration of the dimensions and flexibility of the inherited form. The experiments which began with
Experimental Sonnets, some fifteen years earlier, find their
culmination, for the time being at least, in *Morning Vespers*.
Formal innovation is here, as I have tried to show, altogether
inseparable from the pressures of content. Each has visibly
shaped the other. Warner would not, perhaps, agree with
Donne, that

I thought, if I could draw my paines,
Through Rimes vexation, I should them allay,
Griefe brought to numbers cannot be so fierce,
For, he tames it, that fetters it in verse.[30]

What is clear, however, is that the complex 'vexations' of
Morning Vespers, whether or not they served to 'allay' the
poet's grief, were of central importance in ensuring that the
love with which they were concerned was 'distilled in [the]
perpetuity' (VI) of verse.

CHAPTER 8

Spring Harvest

Spring Harvest is distinguished from its author's other two
sequences of love-poetry by its lack of narrative content.
Both *Morning Vespers* and the *Lucca Quartet* are structured
around implied narratives. Both deal, in varying degrees,
with the experience of loss and separation. *Spring Harvest*
tells no story. It celebrates union, affirms the ecstasy of love;
the poems explore that ecstasy's capacity to heighten and
transform the lover's perception of the world around,
'making sacramental each soft day'(IV).

The sequence contains some of Warner's most richly
sensuous poetry. It consists of one brief lyric and six sonnets.
All of the sonnets acrostically spell out messages of love.
Fittingly the sequence—a spring sequence, after all—begins
with the metaphorical melting of winter's prime symbol:

> May the snow upon your lids
> Sleep till melted into dreams.

It ends with a definition (though, of course, there is a sense in
which the sequence as a whole constitutes such a definition)
of the 'harvest' which this timeless spring has, paradoxically,
produced:

> Spring joy, this glorious summer-scented world
> Of ours, of dappled light's security
> Flooding our daily leaves, driving them, swirled,
> Galvanized into stripped fecundity
> Of soul and body, is the highest reach
> Devotion knows, for each is all to each.

The very opening stanza of the sequence, of which the initial
lines were quoted above, immediately locates human love
within a religious context, in a way entirely typical of
Warner:

192

> Answered loving, which redeems
> Everything through Heaven and Earth.

When first published in 1981[1] *Spring Harvest* carried the following epigraph:

> God is love,
> and those who live in love live in God;
> and God lives in them.
>   I John 4.16

What follows is, in large part, an excited vision of the kind of 'redeemed' world spoken of in the sequence's opening stanza. Each stanza of this opening poem begins in a related fashion:

> May the snow upon your lids . . .

> In my eyes you see you are
> All that wildest hopes can wish . . .

> Even so your altering eyes
> Never less than full of love . . .

Eyes and light are dominant images and themes in the succeeding poems. The first sonnet beautifully evokes the growing light of day, its acts of clarification and restoration, seeing in them the pattern of love's commencement:

> Sometimes a summer's day begins in mist
> And light's expectancy unwraps the trees
> Raising the grass to green from amethyst
> And whitening soft bird-song melodies.
> Heart-lifting certainty the gleam will spread
> Irradiates each nerve and every leaf
> Across day's blue dominion when the shed
> Darkness dissolves and splendour conquers grief.
> Opening eyes see all creation waits.
> Richness arrives, outlined in early dawn.
> Everywhere certainty anticipates
> Youth's wild fulfilment as our love is born.
>   On comes our day, our lifetime of delight
>   Unhurt and marvellous as morning light.

In the fifth poem of the sequence Sarah (we know the beloved's name from the acrostic of Poem II and the direct

address of IV) is addressed in terms which re-affirm her role
as the bringer of dawn on her arrival in the poet's life:

> Morning and new-born star so frolicsome,
> You are the dayspring from which pure light starts.

In the third quatrain of the same poem we are reminded of
that light and certainty which 'irradiate each nerve and every
leaf' (II); now the imagery recurs in lines which distinctly
echo Donne's 'The Good-morrow' and the traditions which
lie behind it:

> As we lie here we are two worlds made one,
> Risen to irradiate and complete the other.

In that act of completion resides an act of creation. As each
dawn creates the world afresh, so the new discovery of love is
a creative act:

> Music is in your blood and in my heart
> As we compose our lifetime's masterpiece.
> You have the gift, the high, creative art,
> Growing in strength, through ecstasy to peace,
> Of making sacramental each soft day;
> Drawing your finest flowers from my dull weeds;
> Bringing out shapes and patterns as you play
> Love's complex symphony of words and deeds:
> Even to make our most fantastic dreams,
> Spontaneous hopes and proud, high-darting fires
> Swell into sunrise as your beauty's beams
> Yield into fact our fantasies' desires.
>> Oh Sarah, you bring joy to birth, and prove
>> Under your modesty, creating love.

Creation and its emergence from darkness and mist is again
the theme of the sixth poem, though with its setting in
Venice the language here is predominantly that of architecture and the visual arts ('etch'), rather than music:

> Mastery lightens the sky as Venice rises
> Yellow-gold, knowing, complete on the waves of her sickle
> Lagoon, with San Marco, her palaces, squares and surprises
> Over the Grand Canal, where fresh blood can still trickle

Viewed from the stone-humped Rialto. Now, this clear
    morning,
Enchantment touches endearment with nakedness sleeping –
Innocence fallen from Heaven, our world freshly dawning
Scattering darkness for ever in mutual safe-keeping,
Wonder incarnate, more precious than all this proud city
Imagined it flaunted when Genoa, broken, defeated,
Trashed here the boast of her wealth. Serenissima's pity
Holds back no gift from her children whose prayers have
    entreated
    Marriage of city and ocean, bridegroom caressed.
    Etch your light, Venice, to bless the soft head on my breast.

The poet celebrates a wealth greater than the mercantile
riches of Venice, a war more important than the conflicts of
Venice and Genoa, since

> Love is larger than life, stronger than death,
> Opulent without material needs,
> Victorious because it cannot lose. (VII)

Poem VI's allusion to the Venetian ceremony of the Doge's
ritual marriage to the Adriatic is not merely a piece of
descriptive ornament. It both echoes and enlarges the human
union at the centre of the poems (the third poem acrostically
makes a proposal of marriage). It makes explicit the
sequence's most characteristic gesture—of the fusing and
harmonizing of the elements in a fecund sensuousness. The
poems have a greater than average density of hyphenated
compounds, the grammatical enactment of this gesture. The
third poem alone contains five such compounds—'wide-
blown innocence . . . milk-flushed skin . . . life-force on the
briar . . . rose-blushed and open in magnificence . . . earth-
born new life'. The poem as a whole shows how such
compounds play an important part in the celebration of a
kind of marriage of the elements, in which, for the poet, the
woman plays a central role:

> When you disclose your beauties to the air
> In tenderness of wide-blown innocence,
> Like April roses when great thunder's near –
> Lightning above us waking more intense
> Your milk-flushed skin, firm in its stripped pretence,

Or overhead the wrath of mountains bless
Us with cataclysmic violence
Making thick rain applaud our wild excess –
All nature hesitates in spread suspense
Revelling in the life-force on the briar
Rose-blushed and open in magnificence.
Your elemental thrust of air and fire
    Meeting in storm and lightning will create
    Earth-born new life that leaps through Heaven's
    gate.

Perennia made much use of the doctrine of the four elements.
Here in the last few lines of this sonnet they meet in imagery
which speaks forcefully of the sequence's concern with
fecundity and birth. The poem as a whole takes its particular
quality from its precise juxtaposition of the tender and the
violent, evoking sexual energies in a powerful, if indirect,
fashion. The 'new life that leaps through Heaven's gate',
though it does not exclude human birth, refers principally to
the heightened perception, the 'redeemed' world, that this
meeting makes possible.

Poem IV has a related final couplet:

Oh Sarah, you bring joy to birth, and prove
Under your modesty, creating love

while V ends with a couplet affirming, if not birth, at any rate
a closely related kind of re-creation:

Ah, my sole joy, and joy of all my soul,
Hold in your hands and heart a man made whole.

That wholeness is intimately linked with the idea of innocence. Waking with his mistress to a Venetian morning:

Now, this clear morning
Enchantment touches endearment with nakedness sleeping –
Innocence fallen from Heaven, our world freshly dawning
Scattering darkness for ever in mutual safe-keeping,
Wonder incarnate

or delighting in her beauty:

> Ravishing are your breasts, your sea-soft skin,
> Lovely as lightning are your answering eyes.
> Innocent wantonnesses, silk beams, spin
> New threads to brim our endless ecstasies[2]

the prevailing affirmation is of innocence and renewal:

> Gone are the sighs that greyed a setting sun.

In discussing some of Warner's earlier poetry Suheil Bushrui appropriated Yeats's description of Spenser as 'the poet of the delighted senses'.[3] That same essay by Yeats contains other sentiments which one might, in turn, apply to the Warner of *Spring Harvest*: 'he seemed always to feel through the eyes . . . he delighted in sensuous beauty . . . with perfect delight'.[4] Synaesthetic imagery is frequent, touch and sight mingled inseparably:

> Milk spilt from the furthest star
> On a beam that wise men kiss
> Bursts into a prism's range
> Of glory that can never change (I)

or sound and light—'whitening soft bird-song melodies' (II). Modulations of colour are recorded with precise sensitivity:

> light's expectancy unwraps the trees
> Raising the grass to green from amethyst.

Literal and metaphorical are registered in modes where 'feeling with the eyes' joins with an excited alertness of the other senses:

> Out of a grey sky came your wind of spring
> Under the buds, stirring birth with sun's breath . . .

> Spring joy, this glorious summer-scented world
> Of ours, of dappled light's security
> Flooding our daily leaves . . .

It is the expression of radiant light which remains central, however. The 'beam' of the first poem reappears in the sequence's fourth poem:

> your beauty's beams
> Yield into fact our fantasies' desires

and in the fifth poem's 'silk beams'. The lady is fittingly
adorned with 'diamonds and opals' (V), her eyes are a fire to

> Burn the sacrifice where dies
> All save rarest joy.

In their love is the power to make 'proud, high-darting fires /
Swell into sunrise'. The fifth poem of the sequence opens
with a direct address to the lady:

> Morning and new-born star so frolicsome,
> You are the dayspring from which pure love starts.

The modern reader is most likely to be familiar with the word
dayspring from its use in the Gospel of St. Luke:

> And thou, child, shalt be called the prophet of the Highest: for
> thou shalt go before the face of the Lord to prepare his ways;
> To give knowledge of salvation unto his people by the remission
> of their sins,
> Through the tender mercy of our God; whereby the dayspring
> from on high hath visited us,
> To give light to them that sit in darkness and in the shadow of
> death, to guide our feet into the way of peace.[5]

(The lines also contain a suggestion of the 'bright and
morning star' of *Revelation*). The lady is seen (literally) as
analogous to Christ, in her role as a bringer of light and love
to 'them that sit in darkness'. It is, once again, poetry of that
'Beatrician experience' examined earlier in our discussion of
Morning Vespers. The lady is a new day, a new spring (the
archaic 'dayspring' fuses the two); 'her beauty has power to
renovate nature in those who behold her'.[6] It is natural and
fitting that the seeds of spring should find fulfilment in
harvest. The 'unfruitful works of darkness'[7] can be left
behind:

> For ye were sometimes darkness, but now are ye light in the
> Lord: walk as children of light:
> For the fruit of the Spirit is in all goodness and righteousness and
> truth.[8]

We have noted the epigraph which *Spring Harvest* carried in
its 1981 publication. There we found the poet quoting from

Chapter Four of the First Epistle of John. In connection with this sequence it would be just as apt to make quotation from the first Chapter of the same Epistle:

This then is the message which we have heard of him, and declare unto you, that God is light, and in him is no darkness at all.[9]

We have already seen this same Biblical text providing one of the epigraphs for *Morning Vespers*, and it is with the composition of this very same Epistle that one of the most memorable scenes of *Moving Reflections* was later to deal.[10] In the words of one Biblical commentator:

the Johannine writings present love . . . as the fulfilment and the one authentic seal of all Christian life.[11]

Love and light are as inseparable in Warner's poems and plays as they are in the Johannine writings, one of the profoundest sources of their characteristic imagery. In many of Warner's works we are witnesses to a world in which, in the words of Gonad:

Emptiness enfolds. Darkness encroaches on the light, and in lightness we dare not comprehend.[12]

In *Spring Harvest*, though, the light is triumphant and absolute. Amongst Warner's lyrical verse this sequence is the most sustained and explicit articulation of the experience of

> delight
> Unhurt and marvellous as morning light.

Here, in these poems, is rich evidence of what Warner had earlier called

> The spirit's diet of love's harvestry[13]

the truth that

> Love is larger than life, stronger than death,
> Opulent without material needs,
> Victorious because it cannot lose,
> Enriching and ennobling all the creeds
> Ignorant man constructs but cannot use.

CHAPTER 9

Persons and Places

Francis Warner's *Collected Poems* are prefaced by some 'Introductory Stanzas':

> I give a tongue to my accustomed streets,
> The buildings two slow rivers wind among;
> Cambridge's sun-touched world of youth and song
> That mellow Oxford's majesty completes.
>
> For I have known them each day of the year,
> Each paving slab and overarching bridge,
> Each daffodil that yellow-peers its ridge
> To wave at King's, or royalist-gentle Clare.
>
> The bitterest wrench of winter's harshest claw
> Experienced—graves dug with roadmen's drills,
> Taking the pauper from his concrete floor,
> Obese professor with religious frills.
>
> For these two holy cities set apart
> In meditation undeterred by time
> Have been the shaping parents of my art,
> Shown me their truth, and truth her paradigm:
>
> Two market towns where scholars come to search
> In bell-blest courts among old libraries
> For secrets of the enzyme or the Church
> Through paradoxical intricacies.
>
> Here in St. Peter's, high among the spires,
> With New Year's footfall crunching on the snow,
> I pay a tribute of the debt I owe
> Before my calendar of days expires.

Much of Warner's poetry is, indeed, located in a firm sense of place, and in a response to the poet's friends and family. His own background in Oxford and Cambridge, his years as Fellow in English Literature at St. Peter's College, Oxford, are reflected in his writing, though not in ways that exclude

200

the non-academic reader. In fact Warner's schooldays are the subject of one early poem, 'Christ's Hospital Remembered'. The simple quatrains register his own early aspirations to freedom and poetry and remind one of that school's extraordinary tradition of poets—which includes George Peele, Coleridge, Lamb, Leigh Hunt, Edmund Blunden and Keith Douglas.[1] It is a different association, with Cambridge, which provides the title for 'Byron's Pool'. This refers to the weir above Grantchester, in which Byron, while a student at Cambridge, was in the habit of swimming with his friend Edward Noel Lang.[2] Warner's poem is a nightpiece in blank verse, an evocation of the sounds, smells and movements in the thickly-wooded surroundings of the weirpool. Quietly observant, the poet penetrates the illusion of nocturnal stillness and finds that

> Nothing is still: the whole wood breathes and feels;
> A water-vole runs through the undergrowth
> And drops in the stream; a noisy pigeon calls
> His four-fold, clownish cry . . .
> A hawthorn tree breaks its spiked reflection
> In the swirling river, as it leans from the bank
> And sways its twisted trunk.

The central section of the poem has about it effects of light and fecundity which perhaps owe something to Warner's love for the work of Samuel Palmer as well as to his own sensitivity to the interplay of the natural and the human:

> High overhead
> Rustle of branches merges with the rush
> Of water on the weir; and to the west
> Streaks of fantastic sunset hover still
> Over the cottages of Grantchester,
> While by the church beyond the cornfield
> The moon is full and low over the barns
> That store the harness, sugar-beet, and grain.

In the final section, as dusk is succeeded by greater darkness, the handling of the iambic pentameter is especially impressive, sensitive in its precise notation of the actual and the fluidity of its phrasing, without ever betraying the reader's sense of the formality of the metre:

> Darkness grows, and still my ears are full
> With multitudes of sounds. Slowly the smell
> Of mist creeps from the fields. Two new-hatched owls
> Call, and there comes a hedgehog scuffling twigs,
> Oblivious of me and all around him.
> On flows a swan, with cygnets like herself,
> But brown; on, past the weir. Bats play in the air,
> Moths flirt with the river; a fish dives up
> For a gnat, and leaves circles of water rippling
> Outwards and outwards till they fade in weeds.

'Byron's Pool', written in the present tense, is concerned to record the texture and density of the particular. Another poem from the same initial collection (*Early Poems*, 1964), 'Kinvara', undertakes a rather different task. We move from blank verse to lyric quatrains rhymed *abcb* (*abab* in stanza 5); the present tense is exchanged for the future. 'Byron's Pool', for all the absence of other human figures, was essentially a poem of a humanized and agricultural landscape. 'Kinvara' (which is on the coast of Galway) deals, instead, with a wilder, less human landscape. As Alan Bold has noted[3] the poem echoes both Hopkins ('Heaven-Haven') and Yeats ('The Lake Isle of Innisfree'). The effect, though, is not merely one of pastiche; Warner's poem is unlike either of these poems rhythmically; the overt literary echoes function as part of the poem's meaning, its recognition that even the election of the unsocialized wild is, after Romanticism, a socially conditioned choice, a product of education. That does nothing to rob the poem of its qualities of music and lyricism:

> I shall go where the swan soars,
> Where the wind and the rain are born,
> Where the coral lies on the bed of the sea,
> Where the badger hides from the storm. . .
>
> I shall watch my footprints fill
> As the tide seeps in the sand:
> Watch the sun on the wide horizon
> Set, from the darkening land.

> I shall learn what the cormorant knows
> When, far beyond our sight,
> He finds the thrill of a leaf that blows
> In a gust on a stormy night.

'Castle Leslie' is another Irish poem, but certainly not of the wild and elemental kind. The poem begins in celebration of a scene at the home of the biographer Anita Leslie, Castle Leslie, County Monaghan. Here in a country-house setting is a thoroughly civilized nature. If 'Kinvara' reminded one of 'The Lake Isle of Innisfree' then 'Castle Leslie' is strongly reminiscent of some of Yeats's great country-house poems. Here, above all, the concern is not with wildness, but with the 'courtesy of nature':

> My eyes are full, and I can see no more.
> These sloping lawns, sweeping to the lake,
> That rowing-boat that laps against the shore;
> The walks, the cedars, chestnut trees that turn
> From green to golden-russet, turn and burn
> Out of the sunrise, deep into my soul
> Until, filled with tranquillity, they make
> This courtesy of nature mist the whole.

The individual mind and the natural world are entirely in harmony, a symmetry which finds its emblems at the beginning of the second stanza, when

> Gently the morning rain falls on the water
> Tuning the whole to some mysterious key,
> While merrily carefree dances Anita's daughter
> Down to her pony, shaking her hair in laughter.

This laughing girl anticipates Warner's poems on his own daughters, as the poem moves from the natural world to the social, to her anticipated marriage many years later

> When, grown into a bride, she hides no truth
> From nature, but in happy ecstasy
> Builds her life-love from memories of youth.

The properly social is itself an expression of the natural, and takes its nourishment from it. The final two stanzas of 'Castle Leslie' are the poet's consideration of how he too might find in this experience a future source of 'tranquil restoration . . . mid the din of towns and cities'. It is, indeed, a concern that the poem shares with Wordsworth's 'Tintern Abbey', though of course it has none of the philosophical complexity and range of Wordsworth's poem. The one is a lyric, the other an irregular Ode. 'The Lake Isle of Innisfree' is another poem which seems to have felt the same Wordsworthian influence. The third stanza of Yeats' lyric announces

> I will arise and go now, for always night and day
> I hear lake water lapping with low sounds by the shore;
> While I stand on the roadway, or on the pavements grey,
> I hear it in the deep heart's core.

Warner's final stanzas belong unmistakably in the line of descent from Wordsworth's great poem:

> How shall I, in a busy London street
> Walking amongst the traffic and flashing lights
> And all the worrying hustle that will greet
> Me when I leave, how shall I re-create
> This healing peacefulness and natural state
> Of mind, that breathes so seldom in the swirl
> Of mercenary rush, and garish sights?
> How there evoke this lake and laughing girl?

The answer is found in a conscious exercise of memory, consequent upon the belief that 'the soul must store its riches'; all the aspects of the scene are to be focused in a single image—that of a swan upon the lake. A technique of memory is also a technique of the poetic imagination—as it so often is in Romantic poetry:

> The soul must store its riches; feed upon
> Moments of love and quiet such as these;
> Mould them into one image: mine a swan
> Floating upon the lake in this soft breeze;
> And as the morning sun streams through the trees
> Upon a swan, wherever I may be,
> All will come back; the laughter, lake, the rain,
> This overflowing, peace-grown memory.

We have so far considered only examples of Warner's early work. In some later poems of place the range is greater, the themes less 'romantically' personal.

'Beirut, April 1983' is a poem of indignant compassion. It is written in the stanza of Donne's 'Nocturnall upon St. Lucies Day' (save that the third and fourth lines are here expanded to ten syllables) and the bleakness of that remarkable poem finds a partial echo here. In other respects the poem has affinities with the war poetry of Blunden and Sassoon, of which Warner has more than once written with admiration,[4] or with the work of such Arab poets as Mahmoud Darwish and Sa'di Yusuf, prompted by the sufferings of Beirut.[5] The poem is a monologue in the persona of a western journalist in Beirut (though based on the poet's own experiences in that city):

> Why do they bring me to the battlefields?
> Haven't I spent enough time close to death?
> Haven't we thrown away that shibboleth,
> 'The public needs to know'? Here, nothing shields;
> This is not breakfast food,
> But unbelievable at home. How could
> I tell the sickening smell of widowhood
> Without a gross betrayal of all trust?
> How can we look on war without disgust?

The poem's first stanza has the staccato rhythm of the journalist's notebook, annotations of horror, clipped and devoid of comment or judgement:

> Muezzin at dawn, three-thirty, jerks me awake:
> Metallic, interminable. Overhead,
> So low I see its pilot from my bed,
> A lone, dark bomber crawls north for a break.
> Black-eyed for sleep, and hot,
> I doze. Cock-crow. One double rifle-shot:
> *Put-put.* Again. No more. Dogs bark, cringe, trot,
> As I look out across the burning tyres
> As muezzin ceases, and the night expires.

There is more to the poet/journalist's thoughts, however, than the bare recording of death. In the destruction of

Beirut, its giving over to violence is an emblem of the larger devastation of human possibilities. Shelley wrote of 'the paradise of Lebanon'.[6] Warner himself had written some thirteen years before of the Lebanese prophet and poet Kahlil Gibran and of the Gibran Museum at Bisharri:

> If, in this ancient land of soaring hills
> And spreading cedars, I have food for tears,
> It is perhaps that nowhere else so fills
> The traveller's heart with ease from all his cares.[7]

Now there are other causes for tears, the paradise lies devastated. In its suffering there is that which ought to prompt more than disgust; its cry is for peace, and through the pain of others such peace might be restored, paradise regained:

> This place was Paradise on earth. Now great
> Metal containers stacked like sugar-cubes
> Form half-safe sprint-ways in between the feuds,
> Down to the ships, up to the hotel gate.
>   High children snipe, for sweets.
> Yet, to this desolation of burned streets,
> This anguished cry: 'What is it that defeats
> Evil like ours?' we must respond, with pain,
> To bring to Lebanon its peace again.

In the *Collected Poems* 'Beirut, April 1983' forms a kind of diptych with the sonnet 'King's College Chapel, Cambridge'. The 'desolation of burned streets' and the 'torn slums' stand in antithesis to 'the held cascade of vaulting stone'. In the balanced grandeur of King's College Chapel is a 'demand . . . that no more blood be shed'. The building speaks of the purposes of its founder—Henry VI—amidst the Wars of the Roses:

> See! Every soaring window's highest lights
> Demand, undimmed, that no more blood be shed.
> The spacious grandeur of this house of God,
> Dreamed by a saint, heals internecine blows:
> Where seventh Henry's filial steps have trod
> Beaufort portcullis joins the Tudor rose.

Even the greatest of architectural achievements has about it an essential fragility; that which depends upon balance may all too readily be the victim of the loss of balance. So may that of which it stands as a symbol. The poem closes with a prayer: 'Lord, let not England fall again in two'.

The social sense, the sense of civilization, of which such poems speak, is reflected in Warner's poems on individuals, on persons rather than places. Of course the distinction need not be a very sharp one. The two—personal relationship strengthened by a sense of shared place, pleasure in place intensified by its being a setting for love and friendship— come together in the 'Sonnet Inscribed in a Copy of Andrew Young's *The Poet and the Landscape*':

> Come, take this book with me when winter winds
> Blow boisterous through the crucifixion trees
> And tread again those pathways in our minds,
> Our summer's foliage of memories.
> Why, we have set the sun on Helpston church,
> Sought out the resting-place of weary Crabbe,
> Searched in the roof of Diss, where hawks would perch,
> Seen where King Charles and Rochester would drab.
> Ah, many ways we've wandered, you and I,
> Treading the varied haunts of poetry—
> From where Ben Bulben merges mist with sky
> To Blunden's Suffolk, mill-board reverie.
> Each place we visit's ours, because your mind
> Makes the past live till life itself seems kind.

The figure of Edmund Blunden appears more than once in Warner's works—a mentor and exemplar, another poet with a deep love of the traditions of English poetry. Warner's work has a degree of experimentalism absent from that of the older poet, but there is much in Warner's poetry that derives directly from that pre-modernist mainstream represented in Blunden. In the same year—1965—that his own *Experimental Sonnets* were published, Warner edited a selection of unpublished poems by Blunden. In the prefatory note to this volume Blunden wrote of Warner as 'a poet whose perception I value as I do his friendship'.[8] *Experimental Sonnets* illustrates some of the ways in which Warner has sought to

extend poetic tradition; the editing of Blunden illustrates
Warner's delight in that tradition itself. Edmund Blunden
stands as a marker for one of the poles between which
Warner's own poetry exists and moves, in another sonnet
called 'The Imperious Ones':

> The imperious ones—Picasso, Bacon, Moore,
> Lifted above themselves by certainty,
> Exhilarating self-belief so sure
> That objects bend to personality,
> Proud God-usurpers, dam the darting stream,
> Moulding out strength from leaves of daily life,
> With X-ray vision of a killer-beam
> Burning fresh outlines with a surgeon's knife.
> What self-renewing confidence you have!
> Renaissance emperors from a broken past.
> What arrow of daring there in all you gave
> For us who stumble now the gate is fast!
>   Humbled, I praise; yet turn, I must confess,
>   To Beckett's truth and Blunden's gentleness.

The attraction to 'Blunden's gentleness' had already produced a poem such as 'Bells', headed 'For Edmund', and
very much in Blunden's own manner; it was later to produce
poems like the lyrics from *A Conception of Love*, 'What is it in
your walk, your face, your eyes' and 'May the healing angel
touch'.[9] The admiration of 'Beckett's truth' is reflected at
every turn in the *Requiem* plays. (The 'Renaissance emperors' of 'The Imperious Ones' sound like an anticipation of
Living Creation). Another, earlier poem on poetry and
friendship, 'Candlesmoke', celebrates poets and scholars for
whose work (and personality) Warner feels a particular
affinity. The poem closes with a powerful and exquisite
characterization of the poetry of Kathleen Raine,

> purest poet of this company
> Priestess of ecstasy and natural pain:
> The lonely sea-bird cries in Kathleen Raine.[10]

Raine's work has certainly had its influence on Warner's, and
Warner was associated with Kathleen Raine's brilliant scholarly work on Blake.[11]

Others of Warner's 'Lyrics, Public and Private' pay tribute to academic colleagues, *e.g.* the sonnets 'When, on the farther shore in time to come' and 'For Robert and Elizabeth Burchfield'. The artist Josephine Skinner, whose work includes a portrait bronze of Warner, is celebrated in a splendid pastoral anticipation of a new Golden Age:

> When goat-foot gods and naked woodnymphs peer
> Once more
> Dancing a new world's spring
> And our sad doubts are dusted all away,
> Then, when old buzzing love is sure
> And has no sting
> And old age smells as sweet as apples stored,
> Silenus and his sons
> Will search about to find one sunbeam more
> And hesitate their dance
> Till sweet Jo join them on that harvest floor.

Two poems for Richard Burton and Elizabeth Taylor ('Elysium' and 'Richard, Quinquagenarian') in their use of acrostic (in one case a double acrostic) and in their fanciful hyperbole (which makes their affirmations no less honest) are contemporary versions of Renaissance panegyric. The Renaissance poet took it as one of his tasks to celebrate those who made incarnate 'the myths by which we live', those of his contemporaries of whom it could be said that they made

> life a work of art
> Endowing myth with joy, and joy with care.

In the recognition that 'Love is life's drama, poetry its land', Warner can close the sonnet. 'Elysium', which was inscribed in a presentation copy of Sir Walter Ralegh's *History of the World* given to Elizabeth Taylor, ends with a witty adaptation of famous words from the *History*:

> O eloquent and just and mighty Death!
> Neglect for once your kiss of such sweet breath.

Amongst Warner's poems of person and place, the most rewarding work is perhaps to be found in a series of nine poems to, or about, the poet's three daughters. (One of

these, 'Rubaiyat' has already been discussed in Chapter 4).
Eight of the poems appear in the *Collected Poems*. The
exception is 'Lullaby', which was first published in the
periodical *Acumen* in April 1987.[12] The earliest of these
poems, 'For Georgina', celebrates the youthful vitality and
freedom of spirit of a three-year-old girl:

> Laughing little buttercup
>   Sunbeam of the meadows
> Ear of wheat among the corn
>   Fledgeling of the hedgerows
>
> Mimic of the open air
>   Seeking the way the wind went
> Stern to escape, swift to return
>   Fearlessly dependent
>
> May you ever hide and skip
>   By Cherwell or by Granta
> Innocent as you are now
>   My goldenhaired enchanter.

The simple quatrains and the single, breathless, almost
unpunctuated sentence capture very well the child's own
energy. The initial series of appositive phrases have about
them an appropriately childlike innocence, appealing as they
do to archetypal features of the English country scene—
flowers, sun, wheat and bird, as well as to the air and wind
themselves. From the mid-point of the poem, however, a
certain ambiguity becomes more apparent. If not a paradox,
the phrase 'fearlessly dependent' has, at any rate, the quality
of surprise about it, effectively recognizing both strength
and weakness. Despite her seeming lack of fear the child is
still dependent upon the protection of her father; or perhaps
we should simply take the phrase to mean that she has no
fears about being dependent on her father. Either way, the
phrase sets up complexities not present in the poem's opening lines. The final stanza balances nicely between a joy in the
three-year-old's innocent simplicity and an awareness of the
adult world which she must, eventually, enter. To invoke
Oxford and Cambridge ('By Cherwell or by Granta') has its

charm but the wish that she should 'ever hide and skip' by
their rivers can, obviously, be no more than a playful possibility. The Universities have their customs and ceremonies
and

> How but in custom and in ceremony
> Are innocence and beauty born?[13]

Yet their 'innocence' is not that of the child. To grow and to
mature, and yet to retain one's innocence, now to find
expression in activities other than skipping and hiding, is the
problem that will inevitably confront the poet's daughter, as
it confronts all in their turn. The poet can hope for her that
she will 'ever' be as innocent as she is now, but she cannot be
innocent in the way she is now. He celebrates her three-year-
old charms as a 'goldenhaired enchanter' and the phrase is
delightful. Yet it is disturbingly reminiscent of a very different kind of enchantment. The world of Renaissance
poetry is thickly populated with 'goldenhaired enchanters'.
Two examples must suffice here. The first is literally an
enchanter—the sorceress Alcina in Ariosto's *Orlando
Furioso*, described thus in Harington's Elizabethan translation:

> A shape whose like in wax 'twere hard to frame
> Or to express by skill of painters rare.
> Her hair was long and yellow to the same,
> As might with wire of beaten gold compare.[14]

The second is one of many that might be chosen from the
Petrarchan poetry of the period. This is Sonnet 37 of Spenser's *Amoretti*:

> What guyle is this, that those her golden tresses,
>   She doth attyre under a net of gold:
>   and with sly skill so cunningly them dresses,
>   that which is gold or heare, may scarse be told?
> Is it that mens frayle eyes, which gaze too bold,
>   she may entangle in that golden snare:
>   and being caught may craftily enfold,
>   theyr weaker harts, which are not wel aware?

> Take heed therefore, myne eyes, how ye doe stare
> henceforth too rashly on that guilefull net,
> in which if ever ye entrapped are,
> out of her bands ye by no meanes shall get.
> Fondnesse it were for any being free
> to covet fetters, though they golden bee.[15]

To praise the three-year-old girl as a 'goldenhaired enchanter' is to do justice to her innocent beauty; it is also to suggest some of the prospects of adulthood. As with 'Little T.C.' in her 'prospect of flowers', innocence and its setting suggest the very complexities which will later challenge them—education and passion.

'For Lucy: aged four' is a related, though perhaps simpler, poem. Again in quatrains, it once more begins with a series of appositional descriptive phrases:

> Spontaneous protector,
> Fierce guard against the world,
> Unerring lie-detector.

Here the stress falls upon the child's role as protector of her father. Dependence here, if not exactly reversed, is at least mutual. In her 'warm certainty of duty' the four-year-old sees through falsities which may deceive her more experienced father. The paradox is that her own beauty is transparent, offering no deceptions and being precisely what it seems. In the poem 'For Georgina' it was the child herself who danced; now, in the twinned poem 'For Lucy', it is the poet who is moved to dance, metaphorically at least:

> Such transparent beauty
> Dances your father's heart.

Father writes of daughter that 'warm certainty of duty' is her 'unquestioned art'. The innocent and 'natural' child provides a model of art. It is a pattern to which later poems in the series will return.

Immediately before 'For Lucy' in the *Collected Poems* are printed 'Daughters' and 'With Georgie on the Ramparts of Jerusalem'. 'With Georgie' is another quatrain poem. Recounting a trip to Jerusalem made by father and daughter,

it locates their affection in the context of 'Christ's life-time'.
The child's youth is placed against the background of events
both timeless and far back in time. As is the case with the
other quatrain poems, the language here is simple, the
syntax, and the relationship between syntax and verse-form,
wholly straightforward. This is, in the best sense, a poetry
for children as well as about children:

> Among the trees where Jesus wept
> At night we two have walked,
> On stones where his grey donkey stepped
> We've climbed, and sat and talked;
>
> And high over the Golden Gate
> Looked down and watched the sun
> Set, till the stars showed it was late
> As often He had done.

In such a context the father's blessing upon his daughter
takes on a particular force:

> Small daughter, on these sun-drenched walls
> So many hands have piled
> I bless you where Christ's life-time calls
> My darling firstborn child.

The phrasing here—'my darling firstborn child'—sets off
fittingly Biblical echoes (*e.g. Matthew* 1.25, *Luke* 2.7). What
had earlier seemed mere topographical colour takes on a
greater significance:

> Under King Herod's massive tower
> Within the citadel
> We've seen the Sultan's turret flower
> With dreams, and light, and bell.

The father's protective concern for his daughter, his blessing
of her, has particular force with his reminder of Herod who
'sent forth, and slew all the children that were in Bethlehem,
and in all the coasts thereof' (*Matthew* 2.16). It needs no great
imagination to be aware that Herod has his modern successors.

'Daughters' is more complex in language and form than
the poems we have so far discussed. Those poems all have the

quality of addresses, real or implicit, by father to daughter. 'Daughters' is an inner monologue; for the first time, too, the relationship between the daughters is considered. The poem is a touching account of father and daughters living in loving warmth (the poem's first image is of 'flame'), the world shut out; sleep and play, the poet believes, will prepare these children for the harsher world outside. Innocence itself may be insufficient for that world, but what is learned in innocence is a source of later strength:

> Firm, tiny flame, asleep upon my pillow,
> Your infant hands half-clenched beside your ears,
> Spiders-webs brushed, and forehead clean as dawn,
>   Sleep tightly on among my books.
>   These early years
> Shared by us three high in these college rooms—
>   The oak fast-closed,
> Your doll's house near and toys spread all around—
> Will give you courage when flat day's steel grip
>   Seems unopposed
> And danger masquerades on a green lawn.
>   May what's here born
>   In our security
>   Breed a profound
>   Curious certainty
> That you are safe beyond all that consumes.

In the relationship of the two sisters is an image of all the complexities of nature and nurture, instinct and education. The older sister teaches that which she herself has not been taught:

> Sister shows sister masteries untaught
> Till scattered hours lie strewn from dancing palms—
>   Quarrelling, laughing looks,
>   Grotesque, mind-toppling tales,
>   Each taking turn as cooks,
> Making wolf-shadows as the log-fire fails,
> And if, in riding on my back, one slip,
> Or I mistake, the other's quick to follow
> Protect, warn, scold. Two girls: a lark, a swallow.

In imaginative play—'making wolf-shadows' and telling 'mind-toppling tales'—the girls both prepare themselves for the world beyond 'the oak fast closed' and exercise their own instinctive creativity. Their activities become a poem-within-the-poem, emblem of what their poet-father does in the writing of these very words. In 'College Rooms' this same effect is even more pronounced:

> Lucy in the great armchair
> With her loose and golden hair
> Writes a poem late at night:
> Only stars give any light,
> All the world is shadow-land
> While her firmly moving hand
> Builds on the page her dream of dreams,
> Imagination's silk that seems
> Clothing for the saddest mind,
> A shelter where all life is kind.

The hand no longer makes 'wolf-shadows' in the dark, but in a starlit 'shadow-land' writes poems, poems spun from 'imagination's silk' and providing 'clothing for the saddest mind'. The phrases might as readily be applied to the poet's own activity in the composition of the poem in which they occur. The effect is akin to a drawing such as Escher's *Drawing Hands*. The self-referential circularity of a poem like 'College Rooms' does nothing to invalidate its statements. It seems, rather, to enact them.

The 'Letter to Lucy' dates from some years later, and is the first of these poems which does not presuppose close physical proximity of father and daughter(s). In the previous poems the writer has been either a participant in the games of the children or a close and immediately present observer and guardian of the children. It is with the fact of physical separation that this later poem begins. That physical separation functions, in part, as a symbol of the change in relationship between father and daughter, now that that daughter is no longer a child. Lucy, recipient of this verse letter, is now sixteen. Her own adult life is about to begin and the poem reflects, and prompts her to reflect, both on her birth and on her future:

Though I am far, and you remain behind,
Untouched bloom of my heart, breeze stilled to gold,
Gentle in beauty, excellent in mind,
Our sixteen years' companionship will hold
Up the bright edifice of adult years
Ahead. The garden of your loving play
Will flower in rich profusion free of fears,
Happy and fertile as a field in May.

And I, high in the sky, lifted and fresh
(England's green quilt seems very far away),
Exult that you, my poetry made flesh,
Will live beyond my petty judgement-day
To find new worlds, of faith, of lust to live,
Strong in a love that far outlasts the tomb,
Forged through your childhood, now your own to give
Your man, your children, to the crack of doom.

What stormy night did you come into the world?
What brush with stillness preluded your breath?
What marvel, heartbeat, through that storm that hurled
Its thunder round the sky and promised death!
Out of the darkness comes a flickering light,
A tiny daughter hesitates to live –
Life falters; wins. My gratitude that night
Spreads down the years, compelling me to give

You blessing from above the Memphis clouds
Touching the sun, like Icarus, in blue
Carefree, entire in happiness that crowds
In on me as I wing home back to you.
Soon we shall be in Rembrandt's home, perhaps;
See where Anne Frank's life innocence was lost –
Our million joys have covered many maps.
Ah, may you never more be tempest-tost.

The images with which the poem opens ('untouched bloom',
'breeze stilled to gold') are reminiscent of the earliest poems
of this group, such as 'For Georgina'. The sixteen-year-old
Lucy retains the qualities of childhood; her father looks back
to sixteen years of 'companionship' (the word already implies
a relationship of equals) and anticipates that the loving
context—'the garden'—of his daughter's childhood will

allow her to take her place happily in a larger world. The 'untouched bloom' must come to flower:

> The garden of your loving play
> Will flower in rich profusion free of fears,
> Happy and fertile as a field in May.

Warner, writing his verse letter in an aeroplane high above America, looks down like a latter-day Troilus in the 'eighthe sphere' upon 'this litel spot of erthe'. Where Troilus sees only a 'wreeched world', this airborne observer is 'lifted and fresh' and can 'exult'. He exults that his daughter will be 'strong in love', that she 'will live beyond [his] petty judgement-day / To find new worlds'. Her capacity for love has been 'forged' in her childhood and is now hers to give. In her is crystallized the poet's sense of the power of love and of human continuity. To call her his 'poetry made flesh' is to affirm an important analogy. The phrase is a kind of submerged pun on the word 'maker'. Ben Jonson calls his son 'Ben Jonson his best piece of poetry',[16] recognizing the analogy between procreation and artistic creation. Warner's adaptation of Jonson's phrase adds a third term to the analogy. In doing so he does nothing that the Renaissance has not done before him. George Puttenham's *Arte of English Poesie* opens thus:

A Poet is as much to say as a maker. And our English name well conformes with the Greek word, for of ποιεῖν, to make, they call a maker *Poeta*. Such as (by way of resemblance and reverently) we may say of God; who without any travell to his divine imagination made all the world of nought, nor also by any paterne or mould, as the Platonicks with their Idees do phantastically suppose. Even so the very Poet makes and contrives out of his owne braine both the verse and matter of his poeme.[17]

Warner invokes the tradition by his deliberate allusion to Biblical phraseology (e.g. *Romans* 8.3., *Hebrews* 10.20, and above all *John* 1.14). His phrasing thus affirms an analogy between procreation, artistic creativity, and the Divine Creation. It is an analogy explored in more than one of Warner's plays. Here his daughter is his 'poetry made flesh' insofar as her character makes incarnate the highest aspirations of his poetry. 'Created' by her father, she has the power to re-create him. The language in which the poem affirms love's power over time has, not perhaps surprisingly, a distinct Shake-spearian ring to it. To write of a 'love that far outlasts the tomb' and which will endure 'to the crack of doom' is inescapably to invoke Shakespeare's *Sonnets*. The second of these phrases is strongly reminiscent of Sonnet 116, with its asseveration that

> Love's not Time's fool, though rosy lips and cheeks
> Within his bending sickle's compass come;
> Love alters not with his brief hours and weeks,
> But bears it out even to the edge of doom.

The voyager of Shakespeare's sonnet, in his 'wandering bark', finds in love

> an ever-fixed mark
> That looks on tempests and is never shaken.

That voyager's place is taken, in 'Letter to Lucy', by the twentieth-century air traveller. He too celebrates love's power and can express the wish, for one who has learned to love, that she 'may . . . never more be tempest-tost'. The poem's final phrase—'tempest-tost'—is, indeed, another Shakespearian reminiscence, since the phrase is to be found in both *Macbeth* and *Romeo and Juliet*.[18] The Shakespearian echoes of the second stanza prepare us for a third stanza which seems to lead us directly into a world closely akin to that of Shakespeare's Last Plays:

> What stormy night did you come into the world?
> What brush with stillness preluded your breath?
> What marvel, heartbeat, through that storm that hurled
> Its thunder round the sky and promised death!
> Out of the darkness comes a flickering light,
> A tiny daughter hesitates to live –
> Life falters; wins.

This birth is powerfully reminiscent of *Pericles*—that most 'tempest-tost' of Shakespeare's plays. In particular, of course, it echoes the episode (and significance) of Marina's

birth at sea in the first scene of Act III. There too a father
addresses a daughter—this time an infant:

> Now, mild may be thy life!
> For a more blusterous birth had never babe;
> Quiet and gentle thy conditions! for
> Thou art the rudeliest welcome to this world
> That e'er was prince's child. Happy what follows!
> Thou hast as chiding a nativity
> As fire, air, water, earth, and heaven can make
> To herald thee from the womb.[19]

(It is probably not coincidental that *Pericles* should be a play
in which 'the action takes about sixteen years'[20]). The third
stanza of 'Letter to Lucy' has a significance closely related to
some of the themes of *Pericles*—the enduring and redemptive power of love, especially between father and daughter.
In the birth is the identity of love and creation—light
surviving amid darkness (this is, of course, a pattern of
imagery very frequent in Warner's plays) and peace emerging from tumult. In the fourth stanza are images which do
something to qualify the poem's positive affirmations. To
describe himself as 'touching the sun, like Icarus' as the
aircraft flies high above Memphis, is to turn the poet into a
son rather than a father and to set up somewhat disturbing
associations. Evidently he intends, reunited with his
daughter, to visit Amsterdam. The places to which he refers
in anticipating this trip together are not merely touristic
details. Anne Frank exists as the tragic inverse of all that the
writer wishes for his daughter. Anne Frank's 'life-innocence
was lost'; for her there was no 'flowering in profusion'.
Instead there were, in the words of Andrew Motion's fine
poem 'Anne Frank Huis', 'years of whispering and lone-
liness' before she died aged just sixteen (again). To visit that
house is, Motion observes, to see that

> What hope
> she had for ordinary love and interest
> survives her here, displayed above the bed
>
> as pictures of her family; some actors;
> fashions chosen by Princess Elizabeth.[21]

Rembrandt's House in the Breestraat saw nothing so dreadful as the fate of Anne Frank.[22] Yet Rembrandt's own life was scarcely marked by happy parenthood. His first two daughters, both given the name Cornelia, were born in 1638 and 1640; the first lived for three weeks, the second for two. His first son had been born in 1635 and lived for no more than two months. When another son, Titus, was born in 1641 it led to the death of his mother, Saskia, not long afterwards. Titus was to die in 1668, shortly after his own marriage. He left his widow to bear a daughter. Rembrandt himself did have a daughter, by Hendrickje Stoffels. She too was named Cornelia. Born in 1654 she was almost sixteen when her father died. There is, though, much that is poignant in the fact that, as Anthony Bailey writes:

The last picture he worked on, found unfinished on his easel, was a *Simeon in the Temple*, for one of the van Cattenborch brothers, a painting of an old man holding a baby.[23]

The allusions of the final stanza do not render invalid the positive affirmations of the 'Letter to Lucy'; rather, by their awareness of a fallen world, a world of darkness which has need of every moment of 'flickering light', they ensure that the poem avoids any sense of facile optimism. It is a striking poem, its texture far more complex than at first appears.

'First Sound' is the final poem in Warner's *Collected Poems* of 1985. The poem bears the date 25th September 1984, and was written in anticipation of the birth of the poet's third child. It is built out of the interconnections between those three kinds of creation and creativity which have been discussed above. The pregnant mother is at home in England; the writer-father is in Florence (Warner's *Living Creation*, set in Florence, was first performed in March 1985). To be in Florence and to think of a birth is to be reminded afresh of what the word 'Renaissance' means. Warner's poem opens, as others of his poems to his daughters had done, with the imagery of spring and flowers:

> My everlasting springtime breeds
> A flower new-born
> Though not yet ready with bold needs
> To claim its dawn
> Under the sky veins of great nature's dome;
> Yet the wild heartbeat has been heard at home.

The date in September which the poem bears was that of a new moon. Several kinds of renewal and new beginning interact in the language of the poem:

> Behind me rises the all-ripening sun
> And the new moon's nine circles have begun.

Though the month may be September yet the moment extends a spring-like promise of new life. The sense of personal renewal is evident in the account of a dawn awakening in the second and third stanzas:

> Touched by daylight, I throw the sheet
> As cockcrow calls.
> Quick with excitement in bare feet
> I climb down walls
> Where olives thicken on their bark-damp trees,
> And thank life-giving God upon my knees.
> Here all around flower and leaf
> Lift with the light.[24]

These, of course, are the very images in terms of which the Florentine Renaissance saw itself, perhaps not surprisingly in a city whose name—Florenza—signifies a city built in a flowery meadow. Petrarch's famous lines in his *Africa*, addressed to the poem itself, envisage an approaching time (the poem was written in 1338) of dawning light and new generations:

> At tibi fortassis, si—quod mens sperat et optat –
> Es post me victura diu, meliora supersunt
> Secula: non omnes veniet Letheus in annos
> Iste sopor! Poterunt discussis forte tenebris
> Ad purum priscumque iubar remeare nepotes.[25]

Images of light, of spring and flower, became a familiar way of expressing the sense of a new age. As Peter Burke puts it:

Petrarch's successors shared his enthusiasm for antiquity but not his pessimism about the present, so came to divide history into three periods instead of two: Antiquity, a period of decline, and the new age, called with luxuriant abundance of metaphors an age of light after darkness, spring after winter, awakening after sleep, recall, restoration, renovation, revival (in the literal sense of raising the dead to life), rebirth (or renaissance).[26]

Erwin Panofsky has pointed out that such metaphors are Biblical or Patristic in origin.[27] Warner's use of these same metaphors in the articulation of his personal situation draws meaning from both their Christian and their historical employment. Once again, different (but related) kinds of creation interact in the central motifs of the poem. The Florentine Renaissance enters the poem directly in the third stanza:

> Relief
> Opens my sight
> To Brunelleschi's dome, half-found through mist.

In the first stanza we have had the line

> Under the sky veins of great nature's dome.

There is surely an echo of that great poem of renewal and approaching birth, the Fourth Eclogue of Virgil. There (in line 50) is the sky's dome:

> aspice conuexo nutantem pondere mundum.

In the image of the dome Warner's poem brings together the hope and anticipation of Virgil's poem; the richly 'domed' stomach of a mother-to-be; and one of the great buildings of the Florentine Renaissance. Brunelleschi has often been called the first Renaissance architect, and his dome for the Santa Maria del Fiore (the cathedral church) in Florence is one of his most remarkable achievements, innovative and daring. Vasari's comments communicate something of the admiration it provoked (and continues to provoke):

It may be safely asserted that the ancients never raised their buildings so high or incurred such great risks in contending with

the skies as this building appears to, for it rises to such a height that
the mountains about Florence look like its fellows.[28]

Warner's poem stands in wonder before three new forms of
life—an unborn child, a fecund natural world, and the
masterpieces of art. All of them speak of the triumph of life,
of the refusal to submit meekly to time and death:

> This stream over Etruscan stones
> Will still be here
> When the as-yet-unborn condones
> Grandchildren's cheer.
> Though grey hairs come one day, yet earth will still
> Praise new life won on Fiesole's hill.

Similar concerns underlie the beautiful 'Lullaby', in
sapphics, written later for the newly-born child anticipated
in 'First Sound'. In a characteristic touch, the poem inverts
the traditional concerns of the genre. It says more about
waking than sleeping.

> Breathing softly, wrapped in a shawl of daylight,
> Trusting blossom loveliness brought to being,
> Too small yet to lift up your head or turn round,
> I will stay with you
>
> On till you, too, cradle your new-born, marvel
> Life has once more laughed at the sun clock's motto,
> You, too, feel the triumph of first light's tide turn
> Bringing the future.
>
> Changing colours riot across the darkness.
> Keep those wisp-fringed fluttering thoughts in stillness,
> Dreaming gently nothing can ever harm you
> Safe in my keeping.
>
> Now you stir, but movement is life's own promise.
> I must wake your mother who sleeps so little,
> Tiny echo; she has the milk to give our
> Wide-eyed Miranda.[29]

Here too is the capacity for wonder; that this third and
youngest daughter should be given the name Miranda has an
obvious aptness. She symbolizes the power of creativity (in
all its forms and aspects) to find in the world a braveness and

a newness which ensure that life can 'laugh . . . at the sun clock's motto'.[30] The sun-dial motto frequently has its own laconic wisdom to offer:

> Tempus obit mors venit
>
> Ut umbra sic vita
>
> Life's but a shadow
> Man's but dust;
> This diall says
> Dy all we must.[31]

While Warner's work is never without a related sense of morality and mortality, it also seeks an affirmation of values in life and creation, in 'living creation', which transcend the austerity of such sentiments. The world is found worthy of more than contempt. The poems to and about persons and places, especially those about the poet's daughters, establish some of those values; the two verse plays, with which the remaining chapters of this study will be concerned, give fuller expression to them.

CHAPTER 10

Moving Reflections

Francis Warner's three most recent plays—*Light Shadows*, *Moving Reflections* and *Living Creation*—are all very individual, but are unified by a common thematic concern. That concern might, in necessarily simplified terms, be defined as the interaction of Classical and Christian. In an earlier study of *Light Shadows*[1] I wrote of it as a 'philosophical banquet', a play organized around the intellectual and emotional debate between the philosophical and religious ideas represented by such characters as Petronius, Philo, Josephus, Lucan, Seneca and St. Paul. *Light Shadows* organizes its debate along quasi-musical lines. The same might be said of *Moving Reflections*, though there are important differences too. The prose of the earlier play gives place, here in *Moving Reflections*, to the blank verse of the great English tradition of verse drama. Structurally there are both similarities and differences between the two plays. Scene Nine of *Light Shadows* is built upon a permutational, fugal structure.[2] A similarly tight permutational pattern underlies Act One Scene Nine of *Moving Reflections*. The scene contains four speakers: Philo, Mary Clopas, Mary Virgin, and John. Each speaks six times. The twenty-four speeches of the scene are disposed according to a cyclical pattern which will perhaps be clearest if set out in numerical form. If we designate the characters as follows: Philo 1, Mary Clopas 2, Mary Virgin 3, and John 4, then the sequence can be represented thus:

1234 2341 3412 4123 1234 2341

The patterns of *Moving Reflections* have a resonance absent from those of *Light Shadows*. *Light Shadows* consists of thirteen scenes, all set, in the words of the text, in 'an open space in Nero's court'.[3] The thirteen scenes are presented in a single undivided sequence. *Moving Reflections* is made up of twenty-four scenes. This time, however, these scenes are divided into two acts, each of twelve scenes, thus effecting a large structural symmetry. If one examines the dramatist's own description of the play's locations, then this sense of symmetrical design is further enhanced:

Act One is set on Capri, and in Jerusalem, at the time of the Crucifixion.

Act Two is set near Ephesus, and in Smyrna, seventy years after Act One.[4]

One precedent for such a dramatic pattern is obviously provided by the late plays of Shakespeare. Perhaps even more relevant, however, is the consideration that this is an essentially Hebraic world with which the dramatist is dealing. The central aesthetic principle of Hebrew poetry in the Biblical period is symmetry—not of feet, as in Greek poetry, but of units of meaning. Robert Lowth, in his *Lectures on Hebrew Poetry*,[5] gave the name *parallelismus membrorum* to this most characteristic feature of the Hebrew poetry of the Bible, and his stylistic studies were developed by later scholars such as John Jebb in his *Sacred Literature* of 1820. Examples are not far to seek on every hand in the verse of the Old Testament. From *Ecclesiastes*

To every thing there is a season, and a time to every purpose under the heaven:
A time to be born, and a time to die; a time to plant, and a time to pluck up that which is planted;
A time to kill, and a time to heal; a time to break down, and a time to build up;
A time to weep, and a time to laugh; a time to mourn, and a time to dance;
A time to cast away stones, and a time to gather stones together; a time to embrace, and a time to refrain from embracing;
A time to get, and a time to lose; a time to keep, and a time to cast away;
A time to rend, and a time to sew; a time to keep silence, and a time to speak;
A time to love, and a time to hate; a time of war, and a time of peace.[6]

Or from the *Psalms*

My heart is smitten, and withered like grass; so that I forget to eat my bread.
By reason of the voice of my groaning my bones cleave to my skin.
I am like the pelican of the wilderness: I am like an owl of the desert.[7]

The influence of such symmetrical structures upon Warner's verse in *Moving Reflections* is evident if one considers lines such as the following from a moving speech by Mary Magdalene, which opens Act One Scene Three:

Jerusalem, built on two hills, surrounded with honey walls,
You have become a criminal; your dress drags in the dirt.
In the souk little children sigh standing in open places.
Does it mean nothing to you who pass by? Has there ever been
    anguish like mine?
Our too-much-loved city degraded; our music and laughter
    silenced.
Even the sun is eclipsed. An earthquake has shattered the Temple.
Was this the perfection of cities, the joy of the whole earth?
Now women abort on benches and there is no-one to help.
The cats and dogs will be eaten. The sucking child's tongue turns
    black.
We drink our own water: there is nothing to fill our breasts.
My dancing is lost to grief, my long hair matted with sorrow.
Oh God, oh God, come and help me! The joy of my heart has died.

The lines are reminiscent of the opening chapter of *Lamentations*, but what is perhaps more striking is that they are lines in which the essentially Hebraic pattern of parallelism is superimposed upon the quintessentially Greek metrical pattern of the hexameter. It enacts in small the kind of cultural fusion with which the play as a whole is concerned.

Moving Reflections is characterized by other symmetries and parallelisms which exist beyond the level of phrasing. We have already observed the symmetrical disposition of the play's twenty-four scenes. Some relationships between scenes are established by striking parallelisms. For example, the risen Christ's encounter with Mary Magdalene, immediately after the speech we have just examined:

CHRIST   Mary.
MAGDALENE   (*Turning to him*) Rabbuni! (*Drops on knees about to clasp his feet*)
CHRIST   You may not touch me now, because I have not yet ascended.

is echoed, though without direct verbal imitation, in Mary Magdalene's later meeting with the Emperor Tiberius. The relevant passage closes Act One:

TIBERIUS   The Senate shall
                Receive with this imperial letter word
                That Caesar votes in favour of your Jesus:
                And my grey anger will admit no light
                Against accusers of the Christians.
MAGDALENE   If you, Tiberius, were just a man
                I'd hug you.
TIBERIUS   No. You make me weep. In fifty
                Years no tears have stained my cheeks! Go
                    home.
                Go from this room! The master of the world
                Bows to your Christ.

In another sense the conclusion to Act One stands, fittingly, in parallel with the conclusion of Act Two. Both are moments which, in their very different fashions, mark 'the glory of [the] spreading word'.

Within individual scenes too, parallelism is a recurrent feature of *Moving Reflections*. The opening scene will provide us with one clear and telling example. The play's opening soliloquy by Tiberius reaches its climax (and conclusion) in lines adapted from the Fourth of Virgil's *Eclogues*:

                And yet strange opal words
        Sung by our gravest singer, who taught me
        When I was young, Virgil: he said that Time,
        Pregnant, was bringing to birth a new Apollo,
        And all past centuries of hated wars
        Will cease, the night of horror end with dawn.
        Creation dances in expectancy.

Lion and ox will play in peace; foxgloves,
Smiling acanthus, ivy, Egyptian lilies,
Will shape themselves his petal-pillowed cradle.
Where is this god, forecast when I was born?

The most obviously relevant lines in Virgil are the following:

iam nova progenies caelo demittitur alto.
tu modo nascenti puero, quo ferrea primum
desinet ac toto surget gens aurea mundo,
casta fave Lucina: tuus iam regnat Apollo . . .

te duce, [addressed to Pollio] si qua manent sceleris
    vestigia nostri,
inrita perpetua solvent formidine terras . . .

At tibi prima, puer, nullo munuscula cultu
errantis hederas passim cum baccare tellus
mixtaque ridenti colocasia fundet acantho.
ipsae lacte domum referent distenta capellae
ubera, nec magnos metuent armenta leones;
ipsa tibi blandos fundent cunabula flores.[8]

This fourth Eclogue of Virgil has, of course, traditionally been known as the 'Messianic Eclogue'. Lactantius and Augustine were amongst the first to see in it a prophecy of the birth of Christ. (One might note, incidentally, that no less a person than the Emperor Constantine made a translation of it into Greek hexameters!). Scholarship has long debated whether Virgil's poem is explicable entirely in terms of native Roman tradition, or whether we must posit the influence of Jewish literature; or whether, indeed, Virgil himself had received a pre-vision of the birth of Christ. Warner need not enter into the lists of this particular debate. What matters for him is the dramatic effect to be achieved by the way in which the second speech of the play, by Philo, who has overheard at least the end of Tiberius' speech, works its way towards a parallel conclusion, based this time on the Biblical verses of *Isaiah*. The sense of shared traditions and sensibilities, beneath obvious differences, is heightened still further by the way in which Philo's adaptation of *Isaiah* (Chapter Eleven) is prefaced by allusions to the Greek lyrical poets:

In Alexandria I teach the Law
Of Moses, and we Jews, too, love the Greek
Poets as you do—Meleager's Cos,
Theocritus, and sweet Callimachus:
'Delos, wind-swept and battered by the sea,'
Is not unlike your island sanctuary.
We honour, too, your tutor and your friend,
Virgil; and have a prophecy that says
A boy is born whose goodness will be known,
For God has given him strength and thoughtfulness.
The wolf and new-born lamb will share their straw
In friendship, and this little child will lead
The calf and lion, as he shepherds home
All tear-stained cheeks of the far-scattered ones
From the four corners of a world at peace.
None will destroy, or hurt, for, as the sea
Blankets its coral bed to the far ice,
So all mankind will leave its night of vice.

Warner's interest is not in a scholarly thesis as to source and influence. Both prophecies, as they are here (very beautifully) paraphrased and developed, are part of a larger pattern of dramatic irony which will declare itself forcefully in the following scene. Roman and Jew alike discourse upon the prophecies of their own tradition; both do so in the midst of their blindness to the fulfilment of those very prophecies; the Crucifixion happens in the very next scene of the play. A similar dramatic irony supervises their discussion of the term 'logos'.

The 'logos' seems first to have appeared in the work of Heraclitus, amongst Greek philosophers, as the rational principle governing the universe (though such a form of words can only be an approximation to Heraclitus' subtle— and obscure—ideas). In the work of the Stoics

Logos was the principle of all rationality in the universe, and as such it was identified with God and with the source of all activity . . . As active principle it was *logos spermatikos*, or seminal reason, which worked on passive matter to generate the world, and in its plural form as seminal reasons, it functioned as the universals which Plato and Aristotle had attempted to account for by their respective doctrines of transcendent and immanent forms.[9]

This is the burden of Tiberius' declaration, coupled with his recognition that the word had taken on a new force in Jewish Hellenism:

> Philo, we both are scholars, you the greater.
> This Greek word 'Logos', which our Stoics call
> The reasoning principle that creates matter,
> Its coded pattern, immanent in all—
> You use the word in a far different sense
> In Alexandria.

Philo was not the earliest Jewish thinker to appropriate the term. It occurs, for example, in the work of Aristobulus of Paneas (*fl. c.* 160 B.C.), as the voice of the Lord, constituting a kind of natural law, by means of which the universe operates.[10] The most systematic and influential employment of the term is found, however, in the voluminous works of Philo himself. We must content ourselves with the summary contained in one standard work of reference:

Logos is central to Philo's thought. It is the chief power of God; it unites His strength and His goodness, and hence it is the rational term which connects opposites, another meaning of the Greek word. In this function, logos brings God to man and man to God. It is the representative of the Governor to His subjects: and its position is intermediate between created things and the uncreated . . . Logos is a copy (Gr. *eikon*) of God . . . through which the world was made, . . . and human intelligence is a copy of it . . . Philo applies the term logos, or the holy logos, to Scripture itself, i.e., the Law . . . It is not a person, according to Philo, nor is it an intermediary between God and man, although it is identified with the biblical angel of the Lord . . . Rather, it is sometimes the same as wisdom, . . . because it is the most inclusive expression of the thoughts and ideas of God, which in turn are identified with the Law, or the Torah, with the pattern of all creation, and with the law that directs and maintains all things.[11]

It is against such a background that we must locate Philo's elucidation of his position here in the dialogue with Tiberius:

> For us the Logos is not in the world
> At all, but far beyond it, perfect form
> Of our imperfect possibilities
> There realized fresh from the mind of God.
> Think how a beam of light is not its source,
> Nor is it that which it reveals to sight,
> And yet without light nothing is perceived.
> God is the fountain from which water flows
> To nourish earthly life. To us the Logos
> Is water, light, and wisdom.

For Philo it is an impossibility that the Logos could ever be embodied in a human individual:

> The urge to know God is the gift of God,
> *That* is his revelation to us here.
> The Logos never could be one frail man;
> Only in metaphor is it God's son.

These two passages from the words of Philo, both from the first scene of the play, are separated by other significant words and events. Tiberius speculates upon the possibility that 'once in Time' the prophecies of Virgil and Isaiah might, indeed, find human incarnation, so that

> That go-between became embodied in
> Not light, nor water, but one living man?
> And, as I loved my Drusus, God loved him;
> And he died, murdered, as my Drusus was.
> Can you imagine, though no Emperor,
> As I am, what the creator of the world,
> The archetype of which I am the copy,
> Might feel; might do?

Such fearful speculations are interrupted, or perhaps one should say commented upon, by the sound of thunder and of a rainless storm wind. Tiberius reports

> I feel the earth quake, but can't understand!
> . . . Look! the sky's eclipsed!

The irony is fierce. Their conversation takes place at the very moment of the Crucifixion, when 'from the sixth hour there was darkness over all the land unto the ninth hour . . . and

the earth did quake'.[12] In their ignorance of the significance
of this very moment 'in Time' (Philo promises to journey to
Palestine and then return bringing 'whatever little news' is
his to bring), and in the limitation (from a Christian
viewpoint) of their concept of the divine, their speculations
necessarily lead them to a state of 'spiritual fear'. There is
further grim irony in Tiberius' bleak and terrible imaginings
of what might happen should God lose a beloved Son:

> God would become a Stoic, and the Logos
> From now on would indeed become the code
> Inherent in all matter; nothing else:
> A formula soon to be found by man,
> Who being evil to the very core
> Will turn it on itself, the secret found
> And harnessed will become the plaything, boast
> Of power politics, and one sick day
> Some petty Caesar will blow up the earth.

The formula has been found, and the day of nuclear weapons
has long been with us. That we shall, indeed, 'blow up the
earth' seems all too possible. If we would explain the course
of events not by God having become a Stoic, but by man
having turned away from God, then we may locate that
difference too in the limitations of Tiberius' conception of
the divine. The whole first scene, as well as clarifying some of
the central historical and intellectual concerns of the play,
has established telling similarities between a Roman and a
Jew, an Emperor and a Scholar, who, for all their differences, share an awareness (albeit undeveloped) of the kind
of spiritual possibility which the life and death of Christ
uniquely embodies. One of the major movements of Act One
is to register the awakening of Tiberius and Philo, their
liberation from 'spiritual fear'.

Both figures are presented very sympathetically by
Warner. Tiberius has not, of course, always been viewed
very sympathetically, to put it mildly. Tacitus is very hostile
to him, viewing Tiberius as tyrannical and hypocritical,
cunning and sensual, gradually revealing the full horror of
his vicious nature as the years passed. For many Christian

interpreters, influenced by Tacitus and Suetonius, the very fact that the Crucifixion should have happened during the reign of Tiberius was further confirmation of his wickedness. The anonymous dramatist of the fifteenth-century 'Digby Plays' presents, in the play of *Mary Magdalene*, a Tiberius who might almost be said to out-Herod Herod:

> I woll it be knowyn to al the world unyversal,
> That of heven and hell chyff rewlar am I,
> to wos Magnyfycens non stondyt egall,
> for I am soveren of al soverens subjugal
> On-to myn empere, beyng in-comparable,
> tyberyus sesar, wos power is potencyall.
> I am the blod ryall most of soverente;
> of all emperowers and kynges my birth is best,
> & all regeouns obey my myty volunte;
> lyfe and lem and goodes, all be at my request:
> so of all soverens, my magnyfycens most mytyest
> May nat be a-gayn-sayd of frend nor of foo;
> But all abydyn Iugment and rewle of my lyst.[13]

More sympathetic judgements were made by some rather earlier writers. Some of the most interesting and significant are to be found in the work of Jewish writers such as Josephus and Philo. Philo observes of Tiberius that he

Was a man of very profound prudence, and the most able of all the men of his court at perceiving the hidden intentions of any man, and who was as pre-eminent in intelligence and acuteness as he was in good fortune.[14]

Most modern judgements of Tiberius have found in him, in the words of David Stockton, a man 'dour and introspective, poisoned by unhappy private experience, with more than a touch of melancholia and insecurity'.[15] Yet such judgements need not deflect attention from the recognition of his considerable virtues and accomplishments as an administrator. Finding in him a man of absolutely honest intentions who lacked tact and an understanding of the necessities of political popularity, Albino Garzetti presents a balanced picture of his final years on Capri:

There was a resurgence of fatalism (Stoic fatalism?) in him, and his life, henceforth divided between painful alternatives, passed in gloomy abandonment to uncertainty and inaction and in frenzied bursts of energy. These attitudes were for the most part not understood. 'If I know what I should write to you at this time, senators, or how to write it, or what I should not write, may the gods destroy me, and with a crueller fate than the one I feel overtaking me day by day!' That is how he began a letter to the Senate in 32, in which he rejected as ridiculous the accusation against Cotta Messalinus.[16]

Tacitus comments:

His crimes and wickedness had rebounded to torment himself. How truly the wisest of men used to assert that the souls of despots, if revealed, would show wounds and mutilations—weals left on the spirit, like lash-marks on a body, by cruelty, lust and malevolence. Neither Tiberius' autocracy nor isolation could save him from confessing the internal torments which were his retribution.[17]

When Warner, in Act One Scene Eleven, incorporates the same sentences from Tiberius' letter to the Senate, it is not as the expression of any revulsion at a supposed life of 'unrestrained crime and infamy'.[18] Warner's Tiberius is well aware of what rumour says of him:

> Am I transformed, deranged by total power,
> As men say? No. Saddened. My solitude
> They misconstrue debauchery.

The struggle for articulation which Tacitus and Warner quote is part of a larger search for meaning; it belongs logically (and emotionally) with Tiberius' words in the play's opening exchange between Philo and the Emperor. Warner's Tiberius is a man of great accomplishment, efficient and firmly principled. The same soliloquy in Act One Scene Eleven shows him (in defiance of chronological exactitude) reacting to the excesses of the Roman actors and to the bizarre activities of Decius Mundus. Tiberius refuses to entertain the foolish flatteries extended to him, refuses all offers of divine honours.[19] Tacitus reports Tiberius' insistence to the Senate:

As for myself, senators, I emphasize to you that I am human, performing human tasks, and content to occupy the first place among men.

but characteristically observes that many ascribed this refusal of veneration to 'degeneracy, on the grounds that the best men aimed highest'.[20] Warner's Tiberius seeks a truer sense of the divine than 'the fawning gifts of flattery' can provide. His words to the Senate, which we have seen Garzetti quoting, are part of a precisely calculated dramatic effect when they reappear in Warner's text:

TIBERIUS　　　　　　　Compromise, commodity,
　　　　　　　　　　　Those twin gold eagles of the Roman State
　　　　　　　　　　　Are not enough. (*Writing*) 'If I knew what to
　　　　　　　　　　　　　write,
　　　　　　　　　　　To you at this time, or what not to write,
　　　　　　　　　　　Senators, may heaven plunge me in
　　　　　　　　　　　Worse ruin than I feel now overwhelms
　　　　　　　　　　　Me every day . . . ' (*Writes*)

SCENE TWELVE

MAGDALENE　　　　　　　　　　Caesar?
TIBERIUS　　　　　　　　　　　　　　Are you a ghost?
MAGDALENE　　No. Just a girl too terrified to speak.

At the very moment when Tiberius comes to the realization, and inarticulate expression, of the final insufficiency of the philosophy by which he has lived, there appears to him the figure of Mary Magdalene.

Warner has here allowed his dramatic imagination to work upon the implications of the apocryphal *Letters* of Tiberius and Pilate, where we find Tiberius writing:

I have been exceedingly distressed at the reports that have reached me: a woman, a disciple of Jesus, has been here, called Mary Magdalene . . . and has told of all his wonderful cures. How could you permit him to be crucified? If you did not receive him as a God, you might at least have honoured him as a physician.[21]

The Tiberius of Warner's play is a noble and thoughtful (perhaps melancholic) figure; though now old (in his seventies) he has an openness and honest self-knowledge which

make very plausible the picture of him presented by certain
of the Apocryphal New Testament texts.[22]

In Act One Scene Three of *Moving Reflections* Mary
Magdalene, in an episode very firmly modelled on *John*
(Chap. 20), had been approached unawares by the Risen
Christ, and had mistaken him for a gardener. Here now in,
presumably, the garden of the Villa Jovis, the situation finds
a kind of mirror image. Tiberius is approached, unawares,
by Mary Magdalene and he, initially, imagines her to be a
ghost. The many legendary Lives of Mary Magdalene frequently present her as an agent in the spreading of
Christianity. So the 'Digby' play of *Mary Magdalene*, to
which reference was made earlier, shows her as responsible
for the conversion of the 'King of Marcylle'. The episode is
perhaps a distant dramatic progenitor of Warner's scene
between Tiberius and Mary. This requires no detailed
analysis, being both simple and eloquent. Mary Magdalene's
straightforward certainty that she has seen God comes upon
Tiberius at the very moment at which he is most open to an
affirmation of the genuinely divine. She has for him a
message of 'joy . . . certainty and love'. Its impact is all the
more forceful for Tiberius' recognition in Mary of an image
of his Vispania. From their different directions, Tiberius
and Mary Magdalene approach the cave, peopled and empty:

TIBERIUS   We live, as Plato taught, our earthly life
                Inside a fire-lit cave, in which we see
                Only the shadows of reality,
                Moving reflections, prisoned in our flesh.
                Only beyond death can we reach the air
                And see, leaving perplexity behind,
                The sun itself, the goodness we have sought
                In vain below.
MAGDALENE   Jesus was in that cave,
                Buried, sealed in, a Roman guard on watch.
                And yet he broke, like pannag through the soil,
                Out of death's dark dominion![23]

It is release from his cave that Magdalene offers Tiberius,
with her message of Christ's liberation from his. Tiberius has
the wisdom and maturity to accept his release. The Tiberius

of the 'Digby' plays may have regarded himself as 'chyff rewlar . . . of heven and hell'; Warner's Tiberius knows and recognizes the necessity of this moment when

> The master of the world
> Bows to your Christ.

Philo's search 'to know God' is plotted more gradually, over a number of scenes. The details of his growth to knowledge are dependent upon what Warner conceives to be the nature of his relationship with John. The Greek of St. John's Gospel, and of the First Epistle, is both somewhat technical and rather restricted in vocabulary. It reads, that is, like the Greek of a man who has learned the language at University, say, rather than through the rough and tumble of daily usage. (There is a non-academic strain to the Greek of these writings too; that we shall discuss later). The idea of John as a student may, perhaps, seem a little odd. The most familiar image of him is as a fisherman—both Matthew (4.21) and Mark (1.19) appear to present him thus. But if one looks more closely at the relevant verses of Mark another possibility is suggested:

> Jesus came into Galilee, preaching the gospel of the kingdom of God.
> And saying, The time is fulfilled, and the kingdom of God is at hand: repent ye, and believe the gospel.
> Now as he walked by the sea of Galilee, he saw Simon and Andrew his brother casting a net into the sea: for they were fishers.
> And Jesus said unto them, Come ye after me, and I will make you to become fishers of men.
> And straightway they forsook their nets, and followed him.
> And when he had gone a little farther thence, he saw James the son of Zebedee, and John his brother, who also were in the ship mending their nets.
> And straightway he called them: and they left their father Zebedee in the ship with the hired servants, and went after him.
> (Mark.1.14-20)

Simon and Andrew are unambiguously described as fishermen. The same is not said of James and John. It is noticeable that their father, Zebedee, is in a position to employ 'hired servants' to work in his vessel. Is it entirely fanciful to imagine James and John as, say, helping out on their father's vessel during a break in their studies? They are not 'fishers' like Simon and Andrew, but undergraduates given a vacation job by their father![24]

If one insists on seeing John as a humble fisherman, then one problem immediately presents itself. That the author of the opening verses of the Gospel was familiar both with the traditions of Greek philosophy and with the thought of Philo of Alexandria and other Jewish thinkers would be hard to deny. Who would be more likely to possess such a familiarity, and be able to employ it with supreme literary tact, a fisherman from Galilee, or a young man from Galilee whose father was not without the money to pay for his education at University? The second is, at any rate, an attractive hypothesis. A natural development of such a hypothesis would be to imagine John as a student in Alexandria, the centre of Jewish Hellenism, studying with Philo himself. St. Augustine recognized the sources of John's language in the neo-Platonist tradition. Augustine, in the *Confessions*, explains how he read

certain books of the Platonists translated from the Greek into Latin. And therein I found, not indeed these precise words, but precisely the same truth fortified with many and divers arguments, that 'in the beginning was the Word, and the Word was with God, and the Word was God, and the same was in the beginning with God; all things were made by Him, and without Him was nothing made that was made; in Him is life, and the life was the light of men, and the light shineth in darkness, and the darkness comprehended it not'. Further, that the soul of man, though it bears witness to the light, is not itself that light, but God, the Word of God, is the true light that lighteth every man that cometh into the world. And that 'He was in the world, and the world was made by Him, and the world knew him not' but that 'He came unto his own, and His own received Him not; but as many as received Him, to them gave He power to become the sons of God, even to them that believe on His name, '—this I could not find there.

Also I found there that God the Word 'was born, not of flesh, nor of blood, nor of the will of man, nor of the will of the flesh, but of God'. But that 'the Word was made flesh and dwelt among us', this I found not there.[25]

Such an intellectual affinity is given most economical and effective dramatic expression by the simple expedient of making Philo John's tutor. It is as such that John first refers to Philo in Act One Scene Six, in his account, as his wounds are tended by the Virgin Mary, of the treatment he and Peter had received at the hands of the Sanhedrin. Philo's sympathy is clear, and so too is the possibility that he will come to 'understand'. John can only regret that Christ and Philo did not meet. In Scene Seven of this first Act, Philo does meet the Virgin Mary. It is significant that at the moment when the 'Aramaic Temple Priests' are busy about the stoning of Stephen, Philo chooses to be with John and Mary. His identity with their cause becomes more and more pronounced. In Scene Nine, he is an active participant in the very moment of John's composition of the opening verses of the Gospel. The scene is a theatrical enactment, a making literal and spectacular, of a scholarly hypothesis. It is not the first occasion on which the play has presented to us the image of John in the midst of composition. For the first we must return to Scene Six.

John's relationship with Philo is presented by the dramatist as one formative influence upon his thinking, and upon the articulation of his thought. That such an influence existed has often been suggested by Biblical scholars, though not in so direct and human a form as Warner's play gives to it. More startling, perhaps, is Warner's suggestion as to another, counterpoising, influence upon John—that of the Virgin Mary. The nature of their relationship is touchingly (and humorously) apparent in Scene Six. In important respects it is prepared for in Scene Two, the scene of the Crucifixion. Tradition has interpreted verses 26 and 27 of Chapter 19 of St. John's Gospel as having reference to John himself:

When Jesus therefore saw his mother, and the disciple standing by, whom he loved, he saith unto his mother, Woman, behold thy son!

Then saith he to the disciple, Behold thy mother! And from
that hour that disciple took her unto his own home.

Warner's Scene Two is based upon the traditional interpretation of these verses:

JESUS   Mother, accept your son. Son, take your
                 mother.
JOHN   I will. (*To* MARY) You've seen enough; can
                 bear no more.
                 (*Leading her away. To* MAGDALENE *and*
                 MARY CLOPAS)
                 The final moments will be unbearable
                 For her. I'll take her home, and then come
                 back.[26]

In Scene Six John, tended to by Mary, questions her gently
as to her earlier life. The passage must be quoted at some
length:

JOHN   (*In pain*) Ah! Dearest Mother, thank you . . .
                 Mary, you married so young; tell me, when
                 Did you learn Greek?
MARY VIRGIN   (*Laughs*) John! Not too young.
                 Trembling
                 Just on the brink of womanhood, before
                 I had lost blood. Yes, I was twelve years old,
                 According to our normal Jewish custom,
                 When I was given by my beloved father
                 To quiet Joseph as his future bride.
JOHN   And then?
MARY VIRGIN   And then? Yes, it was that same year
                 Jesus was born . . .
                 You asked when I learned Greek? Once we were
                 married,
                 Joseph and I took our baby away to Egypt
                 Because of Herod's mad infanticide
                 In Bethlehem and villages around.
                 Once we had settled (as you will have found
                 Now you're an undergraduate yourself
                 In Egypt's Alexandria) no-one could speak
                 Our native Aramaic. To buy a melon,
                 Or make new friends with other teenage
                 mothers,

Greek was the only language. Yes, the soldiers
Speak Latin, but Greek is the common talk.
Even your tutor, Philo—and you are lucky
To have him as your tutor—our greatest scholar
Of Jewish law and God's philosophy,
Can read no Hebrew.

In the *Mishnah*—the collection of binding precepts which is the basis of the Talmud, and is a summary of the oral law—we have an immensely valuable guide to the customs and practices of orthodox Judaism during the period of Mary's youth. (The *Mishnah* was probably compiled during the second century A.D., but it records the customary practice of an earlier time.) In the section of the *Mishnah* devoted to 'Kiddushin' (Betrothals), we are told that

A man may betroth a woman either by his own act or by that of his agent; and a woman may become betrothed either by her own act or by that of her agent. A man may give his daughter in betrothal while she is still in her girlhood either by his own act or by that of his agent.[27]

Now it is interesting that in the first Chapter of Matthew we should read the following:

Now the birth of Jesus Christ was on this wise: When as his mother Mary was espoused to Joseph, before they came together, she was found with child of the Holy Ghost.
Then Joseph her husband, being a just man, and not willing to make her a publick example, was minded to put her away privily.
(Matthew 1.18-19)

The 'just' Joseph presumably had in mind an arrangement that could be made with her father privately, rather than a separation involving the public bills of divorce ('Gittin'). In that section of the *Mishnah* known as the 'Ketuboth' it is explained that a father has the right to set aside his daughter's marriage vows, so long as she remains *na'arah*.[28] This word signifies a girl between the ages of twelve and twelve and a half.[29] The 'Ketuboth', which is the section of the *Mishnah* concerned with marriage deeds, seems throughout to presume that this is the age at which a father will arrange for his daughter's betrothal. The Greek of the New Testament is of no help here since its term 'parthenos' has no necessary implications as to age. The orthodox customs of Judaism would have ensured that the most likely course of events would have been for Mary to have been espoused to Joseph by her father during the first six months of her thirteenth year. It is on such an assumption that Warner has proceeded in *Moving Reflections*.[30] Mary's native language would have been Aramaic; her religious upbringing would have given her some knowledge of Hebrew. If we are right to assume her marriage in her thirteenth year, then it follows that she became a mother before her fourteenth birthday. Warner's picture of her as a teenage mother acquiring a working knowledge of colloquial Greek is an attractive one.

If we grant Warner's hypotheses about both Mary and John—and there seems no reason why we should not accept them as, at the least, viable dramatic premises—then it becomes clear that Philo was not likely to be the only influence upon the Greek of John's Gospel and Epistle. Alongside the formal and learned Greek of Philo was the more colloquial and far less formal Greek of Mary. The remainder of Scene Six brilliantly illustrates the interaction between Mary's direct language and simple thought, and the relative stiffness of language and earnest undergraduate intensity of John:

JOHN	Here's a start: (*Reads in rhetorical manner*) 'That which was from the beginning, which we have heard, which we have seen with our eyes, which we have looked upon, and our hands have handled, of the Word of Life . . . '
MARY VIRGIN	Why don't you just say 'We tell you what we have seen and heard'?
JOHN	Ah, yes. That's better. (*Pause*) Right! I'll start with that.
MARY VIRGIN	God is light, and in him is no darkness at all.
JOHN	Yes, but now to the point. 'If we say we are his and walk in darkness, we lie'.
MARY VIRGIN	I should have thought the point was that if we Acknowledge our sins, he will forgive us?

JOHN   Absolutely!
                       'If we say we've not sinned we make God a liar'.
MARY VIRGIN Must you? This is what he used to say:
                       'He that loves his brother lives in light and
                       won't stumble'.
JOHN   That's not enough! We must put the other side –
                       And a reference . . .

The whole scene (and there is a good deal more in the same vein) is a delightful embodiment of a critical perception about the First Epistle of John. Warner has discerned the presence of two layers in the Greek. One 'voice' is straightforward both in language and in doctrine, often affectionate in tone. To quote some verses from the Authorised Version's translation of the Epistle:

> My little children, these things write I unto you, that ye sin not. And if any man sin, we have an advocate with the Father, Jesus Christ the righteous. (2.1)
> Beloved, let us love one another: for love is of God; and every one that loveth is born of God, and knoweth God. (4.7)
> Little children, keep yourselves from idols. Amen. (5.21)

The other 'voice' is far more given to tortuous theological speculation and analysis, as well as to a greater fierceness of tone. Again, some verses from the Authorised Version:

> Whosoever hateth his brother is a murderer; and ye know that no murderer hath eternal life abiding in him.
> Hereby perceive we the love of God, because he laid down his life for us: and we ought to lay down our lives for the brethren.
> But whosoever hath this world's good, and seeth his brother have need, and shutteth up his bowels of compassion from him, how dwelleth the love of God in him? (3.15-17)
> If any man sees his brother sin a sin which is not unto death, he shall ask, and he shall give him life for them that sin not unto death. There is a sin unto death: I do not say that he shall pray for it.
> All unrighteousness is sin: and there is a sin not unto death. (5.16-17)

Scene Nine, the musical-permutational form of which has already been noted, extends to the opening verses of the Gospel the same sense of a joining together and interacting of

voices. There are four voices this time. To those of John and
Mary are added those of Philo and Mary Clopas. (She is
known to us from the Gospel's account of the Crucifixion:

> Now there stood by the cross of Jesus his mother, and his mother's
> sister, Mary the wife of Cleophas, and Mary Magdalene. (19.25))

The text with which we are familiar emerges from the patter-
ned dialogue of Scene Nine with a sense both of spontaneity
and inevitability:

MARY VIRGIN   Philo, teach us words
            As cousin John, our Baptist; give us manna
            Clean, clear, transparent for our aching minds.
JOHN   In the beginning was the Word. (*Writing*)
PHILO   With God,
            And of God. And the world was made by him.
MARY CLOPAS In him is life; his life the light of men.
JOHN   Shining in darkness darkness cannot grasp.

The composition of the Gospel, and the First Epistle, and
the emotional and intellectual context within which that
composition took place, is one major theme of Act One of
Moving Reflections. Another (and one that becomes even more
prominent in Act Two) is martyrdom. We may take as our
starting point a speech by the Virgin Mary in Act One Scene
Seven:

> The almond blossom, January pink
> And white, comes long before its pointed leaves,
> And later still the dark nut white with oil.
> Our wind anemone's own crimson blush
> Touches our eyes each year after the first
> And early rain, weeks before Passover.
> John, John. A sword will pierce your own heart, too.
> But, from the blood that fell from Jesus' side,
> And from the wounds your suffering has borne,
> The purple life soon to leave Stephen's veins
> And those of crowds of joyful witnesses
> As yet to come, in countries still unborn,
> There will rise up, beyond our Jewish race,
> Above the wealth of Greece and reach of Rome,
> A new humanity beloved of Christ.
> We are its birth, its spring.

Mary's words recognize (and proclaim) in Christ's death a pattern to be repeated in the death of each new martyr. Christ, in the words of Irenaeus, was the 'Master of Martyrdom':

By a sure instinct the Church discerned in the death of the martyr the repetition, not the less real because faint, of the central Sacrifice of Calvary. 'As we behold the martyrs', writes Origen, 'coming forth from every Church to be brought before the tribunal, we see in each the Lord Himself condemned'. So Irenaeus speaks of the martyrs as 'endeavouring to follow in the footsteps of Christ', and of St. Stephen as 'imitating in all things the Master of Martyrdom'.[31]

In *Moving Reflections* the death of St. Stephen, protomartyr, follows almost immediately upon Mary's words. Scene Eight begins with the High Priest's reaction to Stephen's great discourse recorded in *Acts* 7.2-53. Some verses of that discourse are paraphrased by the High Priest. Verse 48, for example:

> 'The Most High does not live in temples built
> With human hands . . . ' What insolence!

Just as we hear that discourse only in terms of the High Priest's reactions to it, so Stephen's martyrdom itself is presented indirectly, as observed by Mary Clopas and reported to the Virgin Mary, John and Philo. The Biblical account in *Acts* 7. 54-60 provides the obvious basis for the scene:

When they heard these things, they were cut to the heart, and they gnashed on him with their teeth.

But he, being full of the Holy Ghost, looked up stedfastly into heaven, and saw the glory of God, and Jesus standing on the right hand of God.

And said, Behold, I see the heavens opened, and the Son of man standing on the right hand of God.

Then they cried out with a loud voice, and stopped their ears, and ran upon him with one accord,

And cast him out of the city, and stoned him: and the witnesses laid down their clothes at a young man's feet, whose name was Saul.

And they stoned Stephen, calling upon God, and saying, Lord Jesus, receive my spirit.

And he kneeled down, and cried with a loud voice, Lord, lay not this sin to their charge. And when he had said this, he fell asleep.

In Warner's adaptation of these verses Mary Clopas functions almost in the manner of a *nuntius* in Senecan drama:

HIGH PRIEST   You, who despise our ritual purity,
    Would mock our customs, tear our Temple
        down,
    Shall die by stones beside this city wall.
    A cheer from the crowd.
    Enter MARY CLOPAS. *She climbs high to look
    out of window.*

MARY CLOPAS   The witnesses are throwing the first stones
    But they are falling short. Oh God, God save
        him!
    They're using builders' rubble. He's on his
        knees,
    He's turned this way, near me. Yes! I can hear!
    He's telling us: 'I see high Heaven open!'
    He's smiling, looking up; his face transfigured.
    'I can see Heaven open now on high,
    The Son of Man standing on the right hand
    Of God.' They put their fingers in their ears
    And savage him with rocks.
    (*Great shout from crowd. Then silence*)

JOHN   Why are they silent?
MARY CLOPAS   He's dead. No. No! He's not! What is he
        saying?
    He commends his soul to God as your son did,
    And asks forgiveness for his murderers.
MARY VIRGIN   It's over?
MARY CLOPAS   Yes.
    (*They pray silently*).

In Act One of *Moving Reflections* the two witnesses of scripture and martyrdom have both been vividly presented. The Prologue to Act Two, serving its purpose of transition, looks both backward and forward.

Act One had closed with Tiberius declaring that he would 'vote' for Jesus. The Prologue to Act Two narrates the sequel:

> Tiberius, agèd and torn apart
> By bursts of frenzied inactivity –
> The wishes of Augustus still his law –
> Heard that the cringing Senate had rejected
> His great proposal for the Christians
> (You'll find it all there in Tertullian)
> Because they had not stamped their own approval
> On the agenda first.

The passage's source, indeed, is in Tertullian's *Apologeticus*, Chapter Five. The same chapter goes on to give an outline account of the Roman persecution of the Christians:

> Consult your histories; you will there find that Nero was the first who assailed with the imperial sword the Christian sect, making progress then especially at Rome. But we glory in having our condemnation hallowed by the hostility of such a wretch . . . Domitian, too, a man of Nero's type in cruelty, tried his hand at persecution; but as he had something of the human in him, he soon put an end to what he had begun.[32]

The events of Act Two take place around the year 100.[33] John's death approaches. His presence frames and unites the events of Act Two. The Prologue announces its contents clearly enough. We are to see John's Gospel brought to completion, and

> fresh men of God
> Strengthened by beasts and fires of martyrdom.

Trajan is now Emperor. John 'completes his Gospel in a desert cave'—the motif of the cave recurs for a third significant time. Scene One is a soliloquy for the aged John as he strives with 'rough pens / And only parchment skins' to complete the composition of the final Gospel. John has a unique importance—he is the one remaining eye-witness to the events of Christ's life, the last human link:

> All Jesus' closest friends are taken back
> To God, save only me, last one on earth
> Who shared his human thoughts and prayers; my Christ
> With laughter, tears, and blessing on his lips;
> Who skimped his meals, and would neglect his sleep.

> When I am loved into eternal life
> The last surviving link will be extinct –
> Though only in the flesh! The Church moves on
> As resurrected body of our Lord!
> Now, on my hundredth birthday, I will spend
> All the thin heat this body burns, to write.

As he works upon the text of his Gospel (this same soliloquy contains a version of verses 23-29 of the first Chapter) he is attended by Alke and Burrhus. Both are known to us from the *Epistles* of Ignatius. In the first of these, 'To the Ephesians', Ignatius refers to 'my fellow-servant Burrhus, who by the will of God is your deacon blessed in all things'.[34] In the last of them, 'To St. Polycarp', he closes 'I salute Alce, a name very dear to me. Fare ye well in the Lord'.[35] The opening scenes of Act Two are taken up with dialogue between John, Alke and Burrhus. With the kind of symmetry we have come to expect in this play, it is no surprise to find that the closing scenes of the play again present these three in conversation. Now John can declare

> My work on earth is nearly done.
> Burrhus, if any part of this our Gospel
> On which I have been working seems unfinished,
> You, who know all my literary thoughts,
> And Alke, you who know what I would write,
> Complete and tidy it.

These scenes frame a central section of Act Two which narrates three episodes of martyrdom and persecution, in all of which John plays a part. The three episodes concern Ignatius, Flavia Domitilla and Polycarp. Let us consider them in this order.

Alke introduces word of persecutions in Antioch and the arrest of Ignatius in the closing words of Scene Two. Burrhus takes up the tale at the beginning of Scene Three. Ignatius was the second Bishop of Antioch (according to Origen; Eusebius says he was the third). Burrhus refers to him as

> 'God's Fiery One', Ignatius of Antioch,
> Theophorus as he's so often called.

'God's Fiery One' is, of course, a play on the name (and character) of Ignatius.[36] Each of the *Epistles* begins with the formula 'Ignatius, who is also Theophorus'. As the *Oxford Dictionary of the Christian Church* points out this may signify either θεοφόρος 'bearer of God', or perhaps θεόφορος, 'borne by God'.[37] If we take it in the latter sense then the name may well refer to the tradition that Ignatius was the very child referred to in *Matthew* 18.1-6 when 'Jesus called a little child unto him, and set him in the midst of them [the disciples]'. Certainly John, in Scene Eight of this second Act of *Moving Reflections*, refers to this episode when he addresses Ignatius as

> God-carried Ignatius, you
> Whom as a babe Jesus held in his arms.

While Bishop in Antioch Ignatius was sentenced to death and was sent, under guard of ten soldiers, to Rome to be cast to the wild beasts in the public games. The famous *Epistles* were written during the course of this journey. The journey was halted for a time at Smyrna. While there Ignatius wrote letters to the Churches of Ephesus, Magnesia, Tralles and Rome. He was later taken to Troas, and from there wrote letters to the Churches of Philadelphia and Smyrna, as well as a valediction to Polycarp. While at Smyrna we know him to have been visited by Polycarp and other local Christians. That John should also have visited him on this occasion, as he is made to do in *Moving Reflections*, is probably the dramatist's invention. The *Epistles* of Ignatius constitute fascinating evidence of a Christian martyr's attitude as he made the long journey to his death, from Asia Minor to Rome. One modern scholar says of the letters that they 'display a state of exaltation bordering on mania',[38] but this seems to ignore the rhetorical purpose of the letters. Certainly Ignatius is passionately eager for the reward of martyrdom. The fourth *Epistle* is to the Church at Rome, begging them to do nothing which might deprive him of martyrdom. Warner's Ignatius is given many words and sentiments taken directly from the *Epistles*, so that he is allowed, as it were, to speak in his own words. One example of this indebtedness to the language of the *Epistles* must suffice. Scene Eight contains the following powerful lines, as Ignatius converses with John:

> I am God's wheat, ground fine between the teeth
> Of wild beasts to become pure bread for Christ.
> I want no more of what these men call life,
> For I would rather die than rule the earth.
> John, what is this I feel? What is this weird
> Joy the arena beasts bring out in me?
> I hope they will leap on, and tear, and not
> Hang back, as some do, in their fear of man.
> If so, I'll coax, entice them, violently,
> If necessary to feed on my flesh.
> Now I begin to feel myself our Lord's.
> May nothing come between me and my God.
> Come fire, nailed crucifixion, savage beasts,
> Pain wrenching out my bones, hacking of limbs,
> Crushing my entire body head to foot,
> The gladiator's butchery, come all
> The devil can provide, only give me
> A chance to win through to my Jesus Christ.

Almost every phrase here has its source in the *Epistles*. Some passages from Bishop Lightfoot's translation of the *Epistles* should make clear the closeness of the relationship:

Let me be given to the wild beasts, for through them I can attain unto God. I am God's wheat, and I am ground by the teeth of wild beasts that I may be found pure bread [of Christ].

It is good for me to die for Jesus Christ rather than to reign over the farthest bounds of the earth.

May I have joy of the beasts that have been prepared for me; and I pray that I may find them prompt; nay I will entice them that they may devour me promptly, not as they have done to some, refusing to touch them through fear. Yea though of themselves they should not be willing while I am ready, I myself will force them to it.

Now am I beginning to be a disciple. May naught of things visible and things invisible envy me; that I may attain unto Jesus Christ. Come fire and cross and grapplings with wild beasts, [cuttings and manglings], wrenching of bones, hacking of limbs, crushings of my whole body, come cruel tortures of the devil to assail me. Only be it mine to attain unto Jesus Christ.[39]

For all the intensity of such wishes the Ignatius of *Moving Reflections* is not merely a man in the grip of a mania. Indeed, his exchanges with Polycarp in Scene Four of this second Act show him to be well aware of the dangers of 'spiritual pride' implicit in his 'impetuous ambition'. The *Epistles* themselves, outside their more 'sensational' passages, are not the work of a man entirely self-absorbed in his own desire for martyrdom. They also exhibit a profound pastoral concern for the fate of the Church he leaves behind. The Ignatius of Warner's play asks Burrhus and Polycarp to

> Pray for my church bereft in Antioch;
> Pray for the souls of all who suffer pain;
> And Polycarp, pray we may meet again
> In the great heart of Christ's eternity.

The historical Ignatius had enough detachment to be able to make an ironic comment upon his captors:

From Syria even unto Rome I fight with wild beasts, by land and sea, by night and by day, being bound amidst ten leopards, even a company of soldiers, who only wax worse when they are kindly treated.[40]

It is with an adaptation of this remark that Scene Four of the second act of *Moving Reflections* opens. In the play the narrative of Ignatius is interwoven with that of Flavia Domitilla.

Flavia Domitilla was a matron of the Roman Imperial family, who became a Christian. Her mother was the daughter of the Emperor Vespasian. She herself married Titus Flavius Clemens, a first cousin of Domitian. Domitian put Clemens to death on a charge of atheism (there is some considerable uncertainty as to whether Clemens was actually a Christian) and, on the same charge, banished Flavia Domitilla to the island of Pandateria in the Tyrrhenian Sea. On her property, on the Via Ardeatina outside Rome, was the 'Coemeterium Domitillae', which became an early place of Christian burial. Much of this information finds its way into *Moving Reflections*. She is first mentioned by Burrhus in Scene Five of Act Two. John meets with her in Scene Six and talks of the

> fine double-crypted catacomb
> Bright with the frescoes of devoted ones

in which she 'harbour[s] . . . our Christian family'. That
Flavia Domitilla should have found her way to Smyrna and
encountered both John and Pliny there does not, so far as I
am aware, have any historical foundation. The dramatic
incidents are, though, wholly representative of the historical
and intellectual realities of the period. Pliny is, in John's
words, 'a thoughtful man . . . not cruel'. John cites in his
favour the story of Pliny's generous care for Zosimus, his
freedman—a story based on one of Pliny's own letters to
Valerius Paulinus.[41] (Another letter provides the source for
his speech to Domitilla in Act Two Scene Seven in which he
relates his uncle's death in the eruption of Vesuvius).[42] Pliny
is the quintessential patrician, sceptical and, in his fashion,
tolerant. In the 'private examination' of Domitilla he has no
serious interest in the pursuit of the truth. His concern is that
he should obtain from Domitilla lip-service to the conventions of patrician society:

PLINY   Now, Domitilla; take care what you say,
                For no-one will convict you, but yourself.
                Be wise, say nothing. Just observe the norms
                Of sweet decorum and of common sense.
                Let moderation be our guide in all,
                And courtesy to our loved Emperor.
DOMITILLA   What must I do?
PLINY   Now, Domitilla, we
                Should think a moment of why I am here.
                We are patricians; I, as well as you.
                We know the guardian of the Roman laws
                And constitution, guarantor of peace
                Throughout the world, Caesar, must hold the
                    hearts
                And minds of all; and all he asks of us,
                The educated ruling class, is nominal
                Allegiance. Mere good form unites us all,
                And makes cohesive this great sprawling mass
                We call the Empire.
DOMITILLA   Yes, I gladly give
                To Caesar what is his.

PLINY   Good! Then that's settled.
The saving common sense of the true Roman.
And now—come. Will you dine with me?

The invitation to dinner makes clear the level at which Pliny
assumes the whole discussion to be conducted. It is Domitilla who, by reference to their mutual acquaintance Quinti-
lian, insists that the truth must be spoken, not glossed over:

> He would say
> In Cato's words, 'A good man, skilled in speaking,
> Does not disguise the truth but looks for it'.
> Pliny, I am a Christian.

Domitilla has none of the frenzy of Ignatius. Yet her
determination is as absolute, the price she is prepared to pay
every bit as great. Her imitation of the 'Master of Martyrdom' is evident in the quiet certainty of her words:

> I will not change.
> To Caesar I give Caesar's, but to Christ
> Alone I give the honour due to God.

Pliny is distressed that by her declaration she should 'have
lost a first-class dinner'!

Pliny is central to a further important scene—Scene Ten.
This takes place after the arrest of Polycarp. Although, as we
shall see, Warner adds distinctive touches of his own (mainly
in the pursuit of dramatic unity) the scene is essentially a
conflation of materials from two sources: firstly, the letters
exchanged between Pliny and Trajan and, secondly, the
document usually known as *The Letter of the Smyrnæans on
the Martyrdom of St. Polycarp*. As Governor of Bithynia, at a
date around 112, Pliny wrote to Trajan asking for advice on
how to proceed in the prosecution of Christians. He has not,
he says, previously been present at an examination of
Christians. What kind of punishments should normally be
meted out to them? On what grounds should an investigation
be commenced? How rigorously should it be pursued? Is he
to make any special allowance for youth? Should pardons be
granted to those who recant? Is the very name of Christian a
sufficient cause for punishment, or should he seek evidence

of specific criminal acts? He describes the procedure he has so far adopted:

For the moment this is the line I have taken with all persons brought before me on the charge of being Christians. I have asked them in person if they are Christians, and if they admit it, I repeat the question a second and third time, with a warning of the punishment awaiting them. If they persist, I order them to be led away for execution . . . An anonymous pamphlet has been circulated which contains the names of a number of accused persons. Amongst these I considered that I should dismiss any who denied that they were or ever had been Christians when they had repeated after me a formula of invocation to the gods and had made offerings of wine and incense to your statue (which I had ordered to be brought into court for this purpose along with the images of the gods), and furthermore had reviled the name of Christ: none of which things, I understand, any genuine Christian can be induced to do.[43]

He has, he explains, made an attempt

to extract the truth by torture from two slave-women, whom they call deaconesses. I found nothing but a degenerate sort of cult carried to extravagant lengths.[44]

From Trajan Pliny received the following reply:

You have followed the right course of procedure, my dear Pliny, in your examination of the cases of persons charged with being Christians, for it is impossible to lay down a general rule to a fixed formula. These people must not be hunted out; if they are brought before you and the charge against them is proved, they must be punished, but in the case of anyone who denies that he is a Christian, and makes it clear that he is not by offering prayers to our gods, he is to be pardoned as a result of his repentance however suspect his past conduct may be. But pamphlets circulated anonymously must play no part in any accusation. They create the worst sort of precedent and are quite out of keeping with the spirit of our age.[45]

In these letters we have the source for the procedure Pliny adopts in the case of Domitilla. We also have the source for Pliny's initial conversation with Polycarp in Scene Ten.

These materials from the letters exchanged between Pliny

and Trajan are combined in Scene Ten with other materials from a very different source. The 'trial' of Polycarp which occupies the remainder of the scene is very closely based upon a fascinating document probably composed very shortly after the death of Polycarp. This is a letter addressed by the Church of Smyrna to the Church of Philomelium. It contains a narrative of the arrest and martyrdom of Polycarp. Polycarp, it relates, was arrested at a farm outside the city. When he was brought into the city

he was met by Herod the captain of police and his father Nicetes, who . . . tried to prevail upon him . . . saying, 'Why what harm is there in saying, Caesar is Lord, and offering incense', with more to this effect, 'and saving thyself?' . . . When they persisted, he said, 'I am not going to do what ye counsel me'. . . . [he was] taken to the stadium; there being such a tumult in the stadium that no man's voice could be so much as heard. But as Polycarp entered into the stadium, a voice came to him from heaven; 'Be strong, Polycarp, and play the man'. . . . The proconsul . . . tried to persuade him to a denial saying . . . 'Swear by the genius of Caesar; repent and say, Away with the atheists'. Then Polycarp with solemn countenance looked upon the whole multitude of lawless heathen that were in the stadium, and waved his hand to them; and groaning and looking up to heaven he said, 'Away with the atheists'. But when the magistrate pressed him hard and said, 'Swear the oath, and I will release thee; revile the Christ', Polycarp said, 'Fourscore and six years have I been His servant, and He hath done me no wrong. How then can I blaspheme my King who saved me? . . . If thou supposest vainly that I will swear by the genius of Caesar, as thou sayest, and feignest that thou art ignorant who I am, hear thou plainly, I am a Christian. But if thou wouldest learn the doctrine of Christianity, assign a day and give me a hearing'. The proconsul said; 'Prevail upon the people'. But Polycarp said; 'As for thyself, I should have held thee worthy of discourse; for we have been taught to render, as is meet, to princes and authorities appointed by God such honour as does us no harm; but as for these, I do not hold them worthy, that I should defend myself before them'.[46]

Almost all of this is represented in the text of *Moving Reflections*. What follows in Scene Ten is similarly close to the text of the *Letter of the Smyrnæans*: the threat of the beasts and Polycarp's immovability before such a threat; the threat

of the fire and Polycarp's rejoinder as to the fires of eternal
punishment; the fact that he cannot be given to the lions
because the games are officially over; all these are details
taken from the *Letter* and reproduced in *Moving Reflections*.
So too is the crowd's shouting that he should be burned alive.
Only Pliny's final speech of the scene has no obvious model
in the *Letter*. Of course Pliny's presence itself represents a
considerable change to Warner's sources. That he should be
employed here by the dramatist is clearly a means of unifying
the scenes involving Domitilla and Polycarp. It also provides
a means of giving a personal and dramatic identity to Roman
attitudes towards the Christians. Warner has taken over
from the *Letter* the name of Nicetes, but the Nicetes of
Moving Reflections is individualized in a way quite absent
from the *Letter*. Warner has noted from that *Letter* that
Nicetes was, remarkably, the older brother of John's
companion Alke. His bitterness against the Christians
(which contrasts with Pliny's urbanity) clearly stems in large
part from his personal grievance—he sees the Christians as
disrupters of the virtues of Roman family life. He is eager to
make the oft repeated charge that the Christians 'cannibalize
bread with human flesh'. Herodes is no longer the Chief of
Police but the (apparently) young son of Nicetes. He is
evidently to be brought up in the cruder traditions of Roman
Stoicism:

> There is no finer testing of a boy
> Than showing him the gladiators' games
> (Yes. As I take my own son Herodes)
> And training him to be unmoved by blood.

This ethos is part of a grimly ironic moment when Warner
transfers from the heavenly voice the injunction to 'play the
man' and gives it, instead, to Nicetes. In his mouth it
bespeaks the crassest kind of incomprehension. Scene Ten
closes with the command for Polycarp's death. The manner
of that death is recounted by Alke in Scene Eleven. Once
again Warner bases his account very closely upon the text of
the *Letter*. Alke's speech is exactly modelled upon para-
graphs 12-16 of the Smyrnæan Church's account of Poly-

carp's death. One small passage will illustrate the manner in which Warner has made use of his source. Paragraph 15 of the *Letter* reads as follows:

When he had offered up the Amen and finished his prayer, the firemen lighted the fire. And, a mighty flame flashing forth, we to whom it was given to see, saw a marvel, yea and we were preserved that we might relate what happened to the rest. The fire, making the appearance of a vault, like the sail of a vessel filled by the wind, made a wall round about the body of the martyr; and it was there in the midst, not like flesh burning, but like [a loaf in the oven or like] gold and silver refined in a furnace. For we perceived such a fragrant smell, as if it were the wafted odour of frankincense or some other precious spice.[47]

By some abbreviation and omission, some re-ordering of material and some discreet addition—above all by a radical simplification of syntax—Warner produces from this paragraph a piece of vivid narrative verse:

> He prayed—I could not hear now—then the flames
> Blazed up. But God was kind. The hasty faggots
> Encircling him drew air up in the centre
> And no flames burned him. Like a vaulted chamber,
> Or a ship's sail filled out with wind, the fire
> Curved round. It was a miracle. A sweet
> Scent rose up from the woodsmoke. Flames died down
> And he was still unharmed.

Polycarp, in John's words, has won 'the crown of immortality'. He is the third of Act Two's Christian victims. John's own death is very close—though his is not the death of martyrdom.

The life of the historical Apostle John has been the subject of much scholarly debate. We need not, fortunately, enter into the details of the controversy. Suffice it to say that Warner has followed the tradition recorded for us in the *Church History* of Eusebius, who cites the testimony of Irenaeus and Clement of Alexandria to the effect that John lived in Ephesus 'until the time of Trajan'.[48] It is on such a premise that Warner has constructed his play and it is one that has enabled him to make of John a figure unifying many of the major events and personalities in the early history of Asian Christianity. John, in *Moving Reflections*, is what Irenaeus calls him—'a true witness of the tradition of the apostles'.[49] Irenaeus, as a boy, listened to Polycarp. The tradition was continuous: from John, to Polycarp, to Irenaeus. Mere longevity was not enough for some believers. Verses in the final chapter of St. John's Gospel were sometimes wrongly interpreted as evidence that John would be immortal:

> Peter seeing him [John] saith to Jesus, Lord, and what shall this man do?
> Jesus saith unto him, If I will that he tarry till I come, what is that to thee? follow thou me.

John himself offers correction to the misinterpretation of Christ's words, in phrasing which makes it clear that such misinterpretation had gained wide circulation:

> Then went this saying abroad among the brethren, that that disciple should not die; yet Jesus said not unto him, He shall not die; but, If I will that he tarry till I come, what is that to thee?
> *(John* 21.21-23)

Even Alke has fallen into this error. This is how Scene Two of the second Act of *Moving Reflections* begins:

ALKE   My Father in God, they say you'll live for ever!
JOHN   No! That's a gross distortion of the truth!
              Because I'm old enough to be a legend
              That does not give me immortality
              In any earthly sense: nor would I want it.
              I long to be united now with God.
              When Peter said to Jesus 'What of John?'
              Jesus replied—these are his actual words:
              'If I will that he stays here till I come,
              Why, what is that to you?' He said it kindly
              To emphasize Peter would follow him –
              One day upon a cross, as we found, later:
              Martyred, with our great Paul, by Nero's will.

John is not to be a martyr. When he calls for fire, in the speech immediately before the passage just quoted, it is not the fire of martyrdom he requests, not the miraculous fire of Polycarp's death. It is, rather, fire that will melt his congealed ink, so that the Gospel may be finished. His testimony is there, his witness is in his words. His death is to bear further witness in a fashion other than that of martyrdom.

After the violence of the persecutions and martyrdoms which have featured so prominently in this second half of the play, it is on a quieter, but no less triumphant, note that *Moving Reflections* ends, with the death of John himself. We have a beautiful account of John's death in the text known as *The Acts of John*. This account is the source for the general conception of the last scene of the play. The Verus of the *Acts* is the Burrhus of *Moving Reflections*:

He said to Verus, 'Take some men with you, with two baskets and shovels, and follow me.' And Verus without delay did what was ordered by John the servant of God. So the blessed John came out of the house and walked outside the gates, having told the greater number that they should leave him; and when he came to a tomb of a brother of ours, he said to the young men, 'Dig, my sons'. And they dug. And he was more insistent with them, and said, 'The digging must go deeper'. And while they were digging he spoke to them the word of God, and encouraged those that had come from the house with him, edifying them and preparing them for the greatness of God, and praying for each one of us . . . [and] saying . . . 'Lord, now that I have fulfilled the charge which I was entrusted by thee count me worthy of thy rest and grant me my end in thee, which is inexpressible and unutterable salvation' . . . And having sealed himself in every part . . . he said '(Be) thou with me, Lord Jesus Christ'; and he lay down in the trench where he had spread out his clothes; and he said to us, 'Peace (be) with you, my brethren', and gave up his spirit rejoicing.[50]

John's final two speeches in *Moving Reflections*, and their associated stage directions, constitute a faithful theatrical adaptation of this account. (Warner has, of course, been highly selective in his use of the *Acts*. The narrative of John's death contains much more material not represented in the text of the play, or in my abbreviated quotation above.) The text of *Moving Reflections* closes with a long stage direction which must be quoted in full:

JOHN *climbs into coffin. It is raised up and carried out by four male figures.* MARY VIRGIN, *in full white bridal dress, and holding a single lit candle, follows, some way behind coffin, alone. Music for this procession (during which the lights dim down to only the candle) Allegri's Miserere (Psalm 51) for Tenebrae, beginning with the second half of verse one: 'According to the multitude of thy mercies . . .' and closing at the end of verse six, or verse ten. The soaring voice of the solo boy should be heard in pitch darkness, after the candle held by the bride has departed.*

Tenebrae is the name (it means 'darkness') given to the Matins and Lauds of the last three days of Holy Week. The customary ceremony involves the extinguishing, one by one during the service, of the lights in the Church. Traditionally, a set of fifteen candles 'fitted on to a "hearse" '[51] were put out in turn, after each of the Psalms and, finally, after the Benedictus. The service ends with the recitation, in full darkness, of Psalm 51. The final moments of *Moving Reflections* are clearly a theatrical adaptation of this service. The lights are dimmed; the coffin and the candle are on stage; the Miserere is sung. Psalm 51 is a petition for forgiveness and regeneration:

Wash me throughly from mine iniquity, and cleanse me from my sin. (verse 2)
Create in me a clean heart, O God; and renew a right spirit within me. (verse 10)

The service of Tenebrae is a symbolic re-enactment of the death of Christ and the descent into Hell; the presence of the Virgin Mary, following the coffin, confirms the relationship between her Son and her 'son' John. That she should be wearing 'full white bridal dress' is an eloquent testimony to the Church's role as the bride of Christ. The 'soaring voice of the solo boy' speaks of a greater ascent. The earthly remains of John may sink into the ground, but his spirit already ascends. With its unmistakable allusions to the services of the church, this final movement of *Moving Reflections* makes of the audience in the theatre (the play was first performed in St. Giles' Cathedral in Edinburgh, and is perhaps best suited to church performance) witnesses, as they sit in the closing darkness, of the light's survival. The candle is one of the most insistent of symbols in Warner's earlier plays. Nowhere else, though, has it greater power and poignancy than here, final silent testimony of the play's affirmation that, in the famous words of John's Gospel itself, 'the light shineth in darkness; and the darkness comprehended it not'.

CHAPTER 11

Living Creation

In many of Francis Warner's lyrical poems the note of Christian neo-Platonism is a prominent one. It receives lucid and lyrical expression in the Blake-like stanzas of 'For a Child':

> I saw a squirrel on a tree,
> And he laughing said to me
> 'Funny human, tell me why
> You are so afraid to die?'
>
> 'Little squirrel, ' I replied,
> 'Many, many folk have died;
> Yet not one's come back to me
> Proving immortality.'
>
> 'Timid mortal,' said my friend,
> 'Do you think that death's the end?
> Know the acorn, when it dies,
> Doubts an oak-tree will arise:
>
> '"How could such a mighty tree
> Spring from nut so small as me?"
> For the acorn does not know
> Where it grew, or what will grow.
>
> 'If you cultivate your shell
> And starve the kernel in its cell,
> When the earth gives you her bed,
> Your true part is maggoted.
>
> 'You are sleeping in this life
> In a shadow world of strife;
> Yet when the dream grows old and lame
> You will wake to life again.'
>
> 'Thank you, gentle squirrel. I
> Am no more afraid to die.'
> And, not wanting to seem rude,
> I threw him a nut in gratitude.

263

What receives simple lyrical expression in this poem also underlies the reworking of myth in *Perennia*. The same tradition of thought, as I have demonstrated elsewhere,[1] is a shaping presence in the plays of the *Requiem* sequence. *Light Shadows* traces neo-Platonism's contribution to the intellectual ferment in Rome in the middle years of the first century A.D. *Moving Reflections* concerns itself with the life and work of that one of the Evangelists most fundamentally influenced by the traditions of neo-Platonic thought, St John. Given such a background it is hardly to be wondered at that Warner should next have turned his dramatic attention to one of the major episodes in the modern history of neo-Platonism—the awakening and flowering of the Florentine Renaissance.

The figure of Botticelli unites the two acts of *Living Creation*, although the play is not simply a biography of the artist, any more than *Moving Reflections* was merely a life of John. The events of *Living Creation* span the period from 1475, with the Florentine tournament won by Giuliano, to the death of Botticelli in 1510. The later years of this thirty-five-year time-span are dealt with more briefly: the death of Savonarola, in 1498, is presented in the penultimate scene of the play. Historical precision in the strict sense is not, of course, Warner's chief concern in the play. It is with the play of ideas that he is more concerned. He has taken care, though, to ensure that the text of his play faithfully reflects, not only the grander intellectual and artistic currents of the time, but also the fabric of social life. Many details of the text are based on contemporary documents. The figure of Riguardata will serve as an initial example. She appears in Act One Scene Eleven. Salvestra, Marietta and Albiera (the dramatically convenient 'stranger' from Naples) are seated at one table. Riguardata at another:

MARIETTA	Florence is dangerous to foreigners
	Who may not know our customs. See her feet?
ALBIERA	Why does she wear a bell high on her head?
SALVESTRA	Ah, Marietta, leave her innocence
	Unspoiled!
ALBIERA	Oh, no! No! Tell me, tell me all!

MARIETTA   Monna Riguardata; come and join us!
                Tell Albiera why you wear a bell.
RIGUARDATA   Oh! Are you new to Florence?
ALBIERA   Yes.
SALVESTRA   She's ours.
RIGUARDATA   You need not worry; I won't witchcraft her.
ALBIERA   We noticed your high shoes.
RIGUARDATA   Yes. Do you like them?
ALBIERA   I do.
RIGUARDATA   Then I will tell you how they feel.

In fact the gloves, bells and high-heeled slippers were the
compulsory garb of a woman declared a public prostitute.
In his volume *The Society of Renaissance Florence* Gene
Brucker translates a document relating to one Salvaza,
accused of being a prostitute and failing to wear this
costume:

This is the inquisition carried out by the excellent and honourable
doctor of law, Messer Giovanni of Montepulciano, the appellate
judge . . . of the city of Florence . . . against Salvaza, wife of
Seze, parish of S. Lucia Ogni Santi . . . It has come to the
attention of the above mentioned judge and his court . . . that this
Salvaza, wife of Seze . . . has publicly committed adultery with
several persons and has sold her body for money . . . With
respect to all of these charges, the judge intends to discover the
truth; and if she is found guilty of walking without gloves and
bells on her head or with high-heeled slippers, to punish her
according to the Communal statutes; and if innocent, to absolve
her from this accusation.[2]

(Salvaza was found guilty and required to wear the prostitute's outfit). Another document translated by Brucker lies
behind the way in which Warner develops this scene.
Francesco de' Pazzi, variously described by the girls as 'glib
. . . a practised promise-breaker . . . a suave viper',
approaches Riguardata, keen to take advantage of her
situation:

FRANCESCO   Ah! Monna Riguardata. Please believe me,
                I have great sympathy for your flushed youth
                And shivering ideals . . .

> . . . Riguardata,
> Though you are beautiful, and softly young,
> You have not married well. Meo is crippled
> In both an arm, and leg. Why! He's no man,
> You know that better than us all. Just look!
> Tawdrily dressed. You're badly shod. Your
>   home
> Has neither meat nor oil. A little bread,
> And some light wine is all. No! I have never
> Seen such a pretty girl share poverty
> With so uncouth a husband. Riguardata:
> I do have some compassion. I've decided
> From now on you will be well clothed, and lack
> Nothing your youth and beauty can require.
> This hair will be as soft as Simonetta's.
> Here; take my purse.

RIGUARDATA   I want . . . I want to stay
> With my husband.

FRANCESCO   Don't make that final. Think!
> You're poor. Your looks will soon be gone,
>   ground down
> In grief and drudgery. Don't waste your
>   bloom.
> Grow rich. Fine dresses, shoes, and a silk
>   jacket
> With belt; yes, every luxury abroad
> Is yours, with leisure, if you'll work for me.

The whole exchange is closely modelled on a legal account of
the behaviour of a certain Niccolò di Giunta—'a kidnapper
of women, violator of virgins and widows, and a panderer
who persuades honest women to lead a life of sin and
corruption'. Brucker translates the document thus:

This Niccolò went to a house owned by Landino di Martino, in the
pieve of S. Severi de Legrevallis Marine, where there lived Meo di
Venture and his wife Riguardata, an honest couple of good repu-
tation. He had several secret conversations with Riguardata, and
with cunning and deceptive words, he tried to persuade her to
commit adultery. These were his words: 'Monna Riguardata, I
have great sympathy for your youth, since you are a very beautiful
girl and you have not married well, in terms of the person and the
property of your husband. You know that Meo is crippled in one

arm and one leg so that he is not really a man. Of the things of this
world, he has none. You know this very well, for you are poorly
dressed and badly shod, and you possess nothing in this world.
You have little bread and wine, and there is neither meat nor oil in
your house. I have never seen such a pretty girl living in this
poverty and misery. I have the greatest compassion for you,
particularly since your husband is the ugliest and most wretched
man in the world, and you are so beautiful. So I have decided to
take you away from this misery and arrange matters so that you
will lack for nothing, and you will be well clothed, as your youth
and beauty require . . .' But Riguardata did not consent to these
appeals but said: 'I want to stay with my husband'. However,
Niccolò was not satisfied with this reply but said to Riguardata:
'Please don't make this your final response, but think about it. If
you will do as I ask, I will make you the happiest girl in the
world'.[3]

Albiera, to return to *Living Creation*, makes it clear that the
Riguardata of the play has previously transgressed but once
in 'some despairing moment short of cash'. Like the
Riguardata tempted by Niccolò di Giunta she finally yields,
leaving arm in arm with Francesco.

The three girls (excluding Riguardata) in this scene are
among the most purely delightful figures in the play.
Albiera's name may, perhaps, be taken from that of Albiera
di Tommaso degli Albizzi, on the occasion of whose death in
July of 1473 Poliziano wrote a series of Latin elegies and
epitaphs. The historical Albiera was the betrothed of Gismondo della Stufa and died before her sixteenth birthday.
Though Warner's Albiera is not simply a copy of this
historical prototype, it is notable that in her first speech of
the play she exclaims to her friend:

> Look, Salvestra, we
> Are both sixteen; but I'm not married yet!

Marietta perhaps owes her name to Marietta degli Strozzi.[4]
The historical prototype for Salvestra is very clearly identified in the text of Warner's play. In the opening speech of
the play Salvestra refers to 'Luca, my husband'. Later
Poliziano describes her as 'Landucci's wife' and Francesco
tells her

> I visit your apothecary's shop
> Your husband set up with your dowry at
> The Canto de' Tornaquinci.

She is identified, in short, as the wife of Luca Landucci whom we know from his diary of the years from 1450 to 1516.[5] A follower of Savonarola, Landucci's diary is a fascinating source of information both serious and trivial and has evidently attracted Warner's attention. It is Luca's wife Salvestra who tells us, in Scene Eight of the first Act, that

> Only last week, in Volterra, a boy
> Was born with a bull's head, three teeth, a horn
> Like a rhinoceros. The top of his head
> Was open like a pomegranate, bursting
> With fiery rays. Its arms and legs were hairy;
> And, bless my soul! its feet were simply claws!
> It lived three hours. The midwife died of fright.

Landucci's diary tells us (in an entry dated 25th September, 1474) that

We received a letter written by Matteo Palmieri, captain of Volterra . . . it related the following marvel, namely, that in these days there had been born in Volterra a boy (that is, a monster) which had the head of a bull, and three teeth, with a lump of skin on the head like a horn, and the top of the head was open like a pomegranate, with fiery rays coming out. Its arms were all hairy, and its feet were like a lion's with lion's claws . . . The mother died the fourth day. The midwives and the other women present half died of fright.[6]

Other anecdotes in *Living Creation* are also derived from Landucci—such as that of the spread of the plague, and of the man sentenced to life imprisonment who died of the plague, recounted by Marietta in the first scene of Act Two.[7] To Marietta's account Salvestra adds the following, later in the scene (she is speaking to Albiera):

> While you were away,
> A man was hanged here; taken down as dead,
> But woke up! So they tried to bring him round,
> Gave him the kiss of life, carted him to
> Santa Maria Nuova hospital;

> Nursed him to health two weeks. He vowed revenge,
> And criticized the staff: and so the Priors
> Decided he should hang a second time
> As soon as he was well. This time he was
> Successful, and hanged dead.

The passage is, once more, based firmly upon Landucci's account of the affair. The entry in his diary is dated 28th March, 1487:

> The following case happened: A man was hung on the gallows here in Florence, and was taken down for dead, but was later found not to be so. He was carried to Santa Maria Nuova (hospital), and remained there till the 11th April. And those in charge at Santa Maria Nuova finding him of a bad nature, and hearing him talk of taking vengeance, etc., the 'Eight' decided to have him hung a second time, and their sentence was carried out.[8]

One more such indebtedness to Landucci deserves to be noted, since it relates to an important scene in the emotional pattern of *Living Creation*, Act Two Scene Twelve, the tense moments before news of Lorenzo's final illness. Landucci's diary contains an interesting account of the omens which anticipated the death of Lorenzo:

> 1492. 5th April. At about 3 at night (11 p.m.) the lantern of the cupola of *Santa Maria del Fiore* was struck by a thunderbolt and it was split almost in half; that is, one of the marble niches and many other pieces of marble on the side towards the door leading to the *Servi*, were taken off in a miraculous way; none of us had ever in our lives seen lightning have such an effect before . . . Many pieces of marble fell outside the building . . . one piece falling on the stepping-stones in the street . . . another piece was hurled across the street, and struck the roof of the house opposite the said door, where it split the roof and many beams and vaultings, and finally buried itself in the ground under the cellar . . . A man called Luca Ranieri lived there.[9]

It is an abbreviation of this account which forms the basis for Warner's scene:

SALVESTRA   Oh, Sandro, Sandro!
SANDRO   Sit! I'll sketch you there
            Once more. Why so excited?

MARIETTA   Thunderbolts
               And lightning struck the top of the cathedral,
               And two of the marble summit balls have
                    crashed—
               One in the piazza . . .
SALVESTRA   Towards the Medici Palace!
               The other crushed Luca Ranieri's home!
ALBIERA   The city lions, docile in their cage,
               Have turned and fought each other to the
                    death.
               It's all unheard of!
SANDRO   Look up! A new comet![10]

The festivals and jousts with which the early scenes of
Warner's play are so much concerned are presented in terms
which owe much to contemporary accounts.[11] A single
example will perhaps suffice for now, since it will also serve
to show how the dramatist's use of such sources involves a
good deal more than the merely slavish transcription of
original documents. In Act One Scene Two, Giorgio
Vespucci addresses Botticelli:

> Sandro, we hoped to find you here today
> Feeding the eagles as elusive honour
> Is courted by the heavy sweat of steel.
> Prince Giuliano, twenty-one and lithe,
> Rides with a man-at-arms who lifts up high
> The banner of Alexandrian taffeta
> That you have painted. It shows swiftest thought
> Transfigured by imagination –
> A life-size lady in a suit of gold
> Down to the knee, her feet on flowers of fire;
> In her right hand a lance, and in her left
> Medusa on a shield.
> Medici olive binds god Cupid's hands
> With glistening cord, while, over all, the sun
> Shines above Pallas' hair entwined with flowers
> Lifting the wind.

A manuscript from the Strozzi Library, now in the
Biblioteca Nazionale in Florence, provides a direct source
for this description of this banner carried at the joust of 1475.

In his still invaluable study of Botticelli, Herbert P.Horne
provides both the Italian text of part of this document and an
English summary. The English summary can be quoted to
illustrate Warner's indebtedness to it:

According to this account, in the equipage of Giuliano was a
man-at-arms on horseback, who 'bore a great staff painted blue,
from which hung a standard of Alexandrine taffety, jagged and
fringed about; and in the upper part of this standard was a sun, and
in the middle a great figure in the likeness of Pallas, habited in a
tunic of fine gold, which reached to the knees; and under the tunic
was a white vestment shaded with finely ground gold, and a pair of
buskins on her legs. And the feet of this figure rested upon two
flames of fire; and from the said flames went forth other flames,
which consumed certain branches of olive that were in the standard, from the middle downwards; and from the middle upwards
were branches without fire. She had upon her head a burnished
morion of antique form; and her locks, which were all inwove,
fluttered to the wind. This same Pallas held in her right hand a
tilting-lance, and in her left hand the shield of Medusa. And near to
this figure, was a field adorned with flowers of various colours, and
from it rose the stump of an olive, to the trunk of which was bound,
by a golden cord, a God of Love, with his hands behind him. And
at his feet lay his bow, quiver, and broken arrows. There was set
upon the trunk of the olive, to which was bound the God of Love, a
legend of golden letters, in the French tongue, which read, LAS-
ANS PAR: and the aforesaid Pallas fixedly looked towards the sun,
which was above her'.[12]

Horne attributes this banner to Andrea Verrocchio, not
Botticelli (an attribution which has not gone unchallenged).
That Warner credits Botticelli with its creation is not an
error, but a concentration and adaptation of the 'facts' in
pursuit of the dramatic design. We shall encounter further
examples of the same procedure as, of course, we should
encounter them in the work of any worthwhile writer of plays
on historical subjects.

Even if he is not bound by literal fidelity, Warner does like
to allow his characters to speak words of their own wherever
dramatically helpful. So, when Ficino joins in the mourning
for Simonetta, in Act One Scene Thirteen, and offers conso-

lation to Giorgio Vespucci, he does so in words that have
been carefully adapted from the text of two of his letters. As
the bell tolls he addresses himself to Vespucci:

> She passes from our shadows into light.
> Dear Giorgio; withdraw into your soul.
> She who, so beautiful, was dear to you
> You will find there, through the Divine Creator,
> Far, far more lovely in her Maker's form
> Than ever in her own. Yield all to God.
> He alone is eternal life, and lifts
> Sorrows, in death, from his loved worshippers.

Part of this speech is drawn from the letter of consolation
which Ficino addressed to Gismondo della Stufa on that
occasion of the death of Albiera degli Albizzi in 1473 which
has already been mentioned earlier:

If each of us, essentially, is that which is greatest within us, which
always remains the same and by which we understand ourselves,
then certainly the soul is the man himself and the body but his
shadow. Whatever wretch is so deluded as to think that the shadow
of man is man, like Narcissus is dissolved in tears. You will only
cease to weep, Gismondo, when you cease looking for your Albiera
degli Albizzi in her dark shadow and begin to follow her by her own
clear light. For the further she is from that misshapen shadow the
more beautiful you will find her, past all you have ever known.

Withdraw into your soul, I beg you, where you will possess her
soul which is so beautiful and dear to you; or rather, from your soul
withdraw to God. There you will contemplate the beautiful idea
through which the Divine Creator fashioned your Albiera; and as
she is far more lovely in her Creator's form than in her own, so you
will embrace her there with far more joy.[13]

The final lines which Warner gives to Ficino in the speech
quoted above are adapted from the closing sentences of
another of Ficino's consolatory letters, this time to 'Bernardo
Bembo, the Venetian orator':

Farewell, and live in God, since He alone is eternal life. He alone
drives death and the sorrow of death far from his worshippers.[14]

Warner's synthesis of the two letters is particularly astute
and is important dramatically for the way in which it places

emphasis upon Ficino's Christianity. The Platonic ideas of the first of these two letters are absent in Warner's lines. The Christian consolation which Ficino so unambiguously offers here is one measure of the falseness of some of the charges which are to be brought against him and his influence later in the play. When, later in the play, Ficino gives Lorenzo advice of a more immediately practical nature, about his diet, Warner has once more adapted words from Ficino's own writings. Ficino advises his master that

> Honey is the best friend sick people have;
> Fresh cheese, sweet apples, betany, and figs.
> But those who eat should sit among the pines
> To inhale their scent; or lie beneath a vine:
> And rub the body with oil from those trees.
> Mix with young, carefree people who are healthy,
> And—not too much diversity of food.

All of Ficino's advice is taken from Chapter Twelve ('The diet, housing, and conversation of old people') of Book Two ('How to Prolong Your Life') of his *Liber de Vita*.[15] (It seems a shame that Lorenzo is not offered that book's advice to eat 'jujubes, hyssop, coral . . . but above all pistachios'!).

To trace every such borrowing (assuming it to be possible) would be a largely pointless activity. Other instances will, in any case, demand consideration later. For the moment let us content ourselves with just one more example. In the voluminous Latin poetry of Angelo Poliziano there can be few things more intriguing and individual than his funeral ode for Lorenzo:

> Quis dabit capiti meo
> aquam, quis oculis meis
> fontem lacrimarum dabit,
> ut nocte fleam,
> ut luce fleam?
> Sic turtur viduus solet,
> sic cycnus moriens solet,
> sic luscinia conqueri.
> Heu miser, miser!
> O dolor, dolor!

Laurus impetu fulminis
illa illa iacet subito,
laurus omnium celebris
Musarum choris,
Nympharum choris;
    sub cuius patula coma
et Phoebi lyra blandius
et vox dulcius insonat:
nunc muta omnia,
nunc surda omnia.
    Quis dabit capiti meo
aquam, quis oculis meis
fontem lacrimarum dabit,
ut nocte fleam,
ut luce fleam?[16]

John Sparrow observes that

The more one thinks about this poem—the last tribute by the greatest scholar to the greatest ruler of the day—the more remarkable it seems. Nothing like it had been written—at least by Politian—before. The opening words are taken from the Vulgate: 'Quis dabit capiti meo aquam et oculis meis fontem lacrimarum?' (Jer., IX, 1). It is unclassical in form and feeling, and it is—surely?—an artistic failure. But, set to music, it evidently took the ear of the time, and when, two years later, Politian himself died and Bembo in turn came forward as an elegist, it was this *Monodia* that he singled out for mention; and with considerable poetic licence (but in entirely conventional elegiacs) he represented Politian as dying while in the act of reciting it at Lorenzo's funeral.[17]

The influential setting of this ode was by Heinrich Isaac. Lorenzo had brought Isaac to Florence from Ferrara in 1480, to be cathedral organist and Master of the Chapel of San Giovanni. It is the music of Isaac that Warner uses in Act One Scene Fourteen at the High Mass which is the setting for the Pazzi conspiracy. There Lorenzo escapes death. In the symmetrical moment of Act Two Scene Fourteen is Lorenzo's funeral. The stage directions are for '*Slow drum. Funeral procession. Funeral music*'. From the public balcony (theatrically, at any rate, the same balcony from which Lorenzo addressed the crowd on the occasion of his escape from death, and from which Poliziano had earlier—Act One Scene Thirteen—spoken his elegy for Simonetta) Poliziano laments Lorenzo in an imitation in quatrains of the Latin poem just quoted (an imitation which radically alters the poem's conclusion):

> Come, pour water on my head,
> Give my eyes the fountain's tears
> So that I may weep the dead,
> Weeping still when morning clears.
> So the bereft turtle-dove,
> Nightingale, and dying swan,
> Mourning loss of earthly love,
> Weep as shadowed death creeps on.
> Now the laurel fallen lies
> After lightning's sudden stroke.
> Though the earthly body dies,
> And the nymphs and Muses choke
> With their sobs of broken grief,
> And his tongue's for ever mute,
> Yet our hearts must find relief,
> Though this world's left destitute
> Of the man who held us dear,
> Saved our city and our arts:
> He has nothing left to fear.
> Now he lives on in our hearts.

While the text of the play offers no explicit endorsement of Bembo's symbolic fiction, it is doubtless no accident that these should be Poliziano's final words in *Living Creation*.

The creative adaptation of such source materials, interesting as a study in the dramatist's methods, can only make artistic sense within the framework of the writer's larger conception of the play. It is from such details, however suggestive and significant, to larger questions of dramatic purpose that we must now turn.

Living Creation's epigraph throws light on one central area of Warner's concerns in the play. The title-page carries the following epigraph: '*Chloris eram quae Flora vocor: Ovid, Fasti* V.195'. The text of the play itself re-employs the same Ovidian line. In Act One Scene Seventeen, Botticelli presents his painting 'Primavera' to the court of Lorenzo. Lorenzo invites Poliziano to interpret the painting's myth:

LORENZO   Poliziano! Can you read the myth?
POLIZIANO   Yes, Ovid tells how Zephyr, the spring wind,
                    Breathed, seized on Chloris—nymph all
                        winter-bare—
                    And turned her into Spring. 'I who was Chloris
                    Now am called Flora.'
SANDRO   Yes. The year's new bride.

The legend may well be Ovid's own invention. It occurs in that section of the *Fasti*'s poetical calendar which is devoted to May, to the festival of the Floralia and its origins. The Floralia extended from April 28th to May 3rd. Ovid summons up the goddess and invites her to explain her own name and nature:

So I spoke, and the goddess answered my question thus, and while she spoke, her lips breathed vernal roses: 'I who now am called Flora was formerly Chloris: a Greek letter of my name is corrupted in the Latin speech. Chloris I was, a nymph of the happy fields where, as you have heard, dwelt fortunate men of old. Modesty shrinks from describing my figure; but it procured the hand of a god for my mother's daughter. 'Twas spring, and I was roaming; Zephyr caught sight of me; I retired; he pursued and I fled; but he was the stronger, and Boreas had given his brother full right of rape by daring to carry off the prize from the house of Erechtheus. However, he made amends for his violence by giving me the name of bride, and in my marriage-bed I have naught to complain of. I enjoy perpetual spring; most buxom is the year ever; ever the tree is clothed with leaves, the ground with pasture. In the fields that are my dower, I have a fruitful garden, fanned by the breeze and watered by a spring of running water. This garden my husband filled with noble flowers and said, "Goddess, be queen of flowers." Oft did I wish to count the colours in the beds, but could not; the number was past counting. Soon as the dewy rime is shaken from the leaves, and the varied foliage is warmed by the sunbeams, the Hours assemble, clad in dappled weeds, and cull my gifts in light baskets. Straightway, the Graces draw near, and twine garlands and wreaths to bind their heavenly hair. I was the first to scatter new seeds among the countless peoples; till then the earth had been of but one colour'.[18]

The epigraph and the episode from which it comes have a manifold relevance to *Living Creation*. Insofar as it comes from an account of the Floralia it reminds us of the central importance of festival and public ritual in Renaissance Florence, and thus in *Living Creation*. Flora, as the herald of spring, as 'queen of flowers', introduces us to some of the most centrally important images of the play: of spring, both literal and metaphorical (it ought to be noted that the play's first performance was on 21st March, 1985—the spring equinox), and flowers. The part played by Zephyr reminds us, perhaps, that in Latin *spiritus* means both 'the wind' and 'inspiration'. Ovid's legend is a tale of metamorphosis. His playful etymology need not be taken too seriously as etymology, but it does stand as an emblem of the creative adaptation by one culture of the materials of another earlier culture. As such it has an obvious relevance to the very idea of the Renaissance. It is a legend, too, of the metamorphosis of the human into the divine, of the ephemeral into the eternal. *Living Creation* is about art's capacity to perform a closely related transformation, the time-bound translated into the timeless. Above all, Ovid's story of Zephyr and Chloris/Flora is a myth of the creative and re-creative powers of love.

The extensive ceremonials of Renaissance Florence gave it a means of seeing itself as the fulfilment of its own myth, seeing itself at the point of intersection between human and eternal, seeing its own social order as reflection and articulation of a larger cosmic order. To read the extensive accounts of the city's elaborate ceremonies ('Since the city is large, it needs ceremonies'[19]) is to be reminded of Chapman's vision of the goddess Ceremony:

> The Goddesse *Ceremonie*, with a Crowne
> Of all the stars, and heaven . . . descended.
> Her flaming haire to her bright feet extended,
> By which hung all the bench of Deities;
> And in a chaine, compact of eares and eies,
> She led Religion; all her bodie was
> Cleere and transparent as the purest glasse:
> For she was all presented to the sence;
> Devotion, Order, State, and Reverence

Her shadowes were; Societie, Memorie;
All which her sight made live, her absence die.
A rich disparent Pentackle she weares,
Drawne full of circles and strange characters:
Her face was changeable to everie eie;
One way lookt ill, another graciouslie;
Which while men viewd, they cheerfull were & holy:
But looking off, vicious and melancholy:
The snakie paths to each observed law
Did *Policie* in her broad bosome draw:
One hand a Mathematique Christall swayes,
Which gathering in one line a thousand rayes
From her bright eyes, *Confusion* burnes to death,
And all estates of men distinguisheth.
By it *Morallitie* and *Comelinesse*
Themselves in all their sightly figures dresse.
Her other hand a lawrell rod applies,
To beat back *Barbarisme*, and *Avarice*,
That followd, eating earth and excrement
And humane lims; and would make proud ascent
To seates of Gods, were *Ceremonie* slaine;
The *Howrs* and *Graces* bore her glorious traine,
And all the sweets of our societie
Were Spherde, and treasurde in her bountious eie.[20]

Richard Trexler's *Public Life in Renaissance Florence* is a massive study of ceremony's 'lawrell rod' in the life of Renaissance Florence—under such headings as 'The Ritual of Celebration', 'The Ritual of Foreign Relations', 'The Ritual of Crisis' and 'The Charismatic Center: Innocence and Martyrdom'. Trexler observes that

In the chronicles of Florentine history, contemporaries recorded seemingly endless, seemingly identical descriptions of scores upon scores of formal processions involving major parts of the population.[21]

Trexler quotes Dati's description of a celebratory Florence with its streets

full of young women and girls dressed in silk and decorated with jewels and precious stones and pearls.[22]

It is to such a world that Marietta invites the newly-arrived
Albiera in the first scene of the play:

> These rusty tears that drizzle down your cheeks,
> Albiera, must be sparkled into gems;
> For here in Florence on the Baptist's day
> Trumpets, innumerable viols and flutes,
> Banners and stamping horses, sweets, and wine,
> Dresses that make the silkworm hide its head,
> And pageantry to steal the world's acclaim,
> All this is ours. We walk our silver streets
> And each shop flaunts its wealthiest merchandise,
> Jostling the next in gorgeous ostentation
> To grip the eye and shake a sudden blink.
> Our sleeves brush gold. Pearled shoes tread the far East.
> Our heads are crowned with garlands from the fields,
> While higher ladies bend in dazzling crowns,
> Their husbands' riches heavy on their necks.
> All crowd to Santa Croce's piazza
> And spread in circles. There, the highest row,
> Is for the mighty. Next, in front, for those
> No longer apt for gracefulness. Below
> Is, waiting, ours; strewn with midsummer flowers
> For us to weave, young women who will please
> The courtesy of music with our steps.

An anonymous poet describing a dance of 1459 provides us
both with a source for some parts of this speech and with an
explicit sense of the kind of significance which the Florentine
mind gave to such rituals of celebration:

> Three levels around with lovely seats,
> > The one higher than the other, so that he sees
> > Who sits down first and who later . . .
>
> And it appears that one plans an order
> > That the first row, closest to the fence,
> > Was elected for the great and worthy [male]
> > > citizens.
>
> And the next, a little lower and parallel,
> > For the women who are not apt at dancing
> > Either because of age or obesity or widowhood.

And the one in front was decorated solely
    So that the women and girls who would be making
        the *festa*
    All around [the area] would have a place to rest . . .

The whole appeared a heaven of lovely roseate circles,
    In which the count represented the sun,
    And the [Florentine] women and *garzoni* shining
        stars.[23]

It is entirely fitting, then, that much of the meaning of *Living Creation* should be carried by the contrasts it sets up between certain Florentine ceremonials. The opening scenes of the play are dominated by the joust of 1475. 'Reality', myth, ceremony and art are intricately interwoven in such an episode. In one sense, of course, such a carefully arranged event was a political demonstration, an ostentatious assertion of Medici wealth and prowess, a corollary of the sumptuary laws of 1473. At the same time this joust, like that of Lorenzo in 1469 (recalled by Warner's Lorenzo in Act One Scene Five) was obviously intended to have a meaning that went beyond the requirements of practical politics. When poets celebrated the jousts (Pulci wrote *La Giostra* as a response to the joust of 1469) they sought to elucidate and develop the mythical and symbolic significance of what had been public ceremonies. Poliziano's *Stanze Cominciate per la Giostra del Magnifico Giuliano de' Medici* find in the events of 1475 lessons about civil order and disorder, about Love and Death, about Beauty and Fortune—and, of course, about the Medici. The ceremonial tournament prompts the poem (though perhaps it might be truer to say that both grow from the same background of thought and presupposition). The poem, in its turn, prompted, or at any rate exerted a shaping influence upon, the paintings of Botticelli. All three—joust, poem, paintings—cast a fresh light on the human 'realities' which underlie them. Reality and the created artifacts all reflect and transform one another. History and myth, reality and imagination, become well-nigh inseparable. Given the theatrical impossibility of an adequate representation of the joust onstage, Warner succeeds in finding a degree of onstage stylization in its reporting that goes some way towards providing a dramatic equivalent for the procedures of the joust itself. The key scene is Act One Scene Seven, the actual report of the joust, rather than preparations for it. The scene contains nineteen speeches. They are disposed with a symmetry which mimics the encounter they describe. The first nine speeches of the scene are distributed in the following order: Lorenzo—Herald—Simonetta—Vespucci—Francesco—Albiera—Marietta—Domenico—Sandro. The tenth speech is again the Herald's:

> The flag of Florence, dear and noble city,
> Today is carried in Medici hands.
> Giuliano di Piero di Cosimo,
> Secure your helmet; raise your jousting-lance,
> And prove your knighthood on this Baptist's Day.
> *Trumpet. They charge.*

After this climactic moment the preceding sequence of speakers is precisely reversed, so that the remaining nine speeches in the scene occur in the following order: Sandro — Domenico — Marietta — Albiera — Francesco — Vespucci — Simonetta — Herald — Lorenzo. The dramatist has transmuted jousting space into theatrical time.

The joust is not, of course, the only ceremony of the first Act of the play. The Crowning of Simonetta, immediately after Giuliano has accepted the wreath as victor in the tournament, presents itself as another intersection of human and divine. The ceremony of the mourning of Simonetta in Scene Thirteen is followed by the savage disruption of ceremony in the assassination of Giuliano during High Mass. The governing ceremonies of Act Two of the play are necessarily rather different. Certainly the carnival that 'sets the devil on the fire' is in preparation in Scene Three, and Lorenzo, with his 'Company of the Star' seeks to create another ceremony that will unify Florence:

> A fresh creation to unite all parts
> Of Florence, not each neighbourhood alone;
> The young, the rich, the poor; each knot's untied
> Under the Star of Venus.

Act Two Scene Four, however, brings us Clarice and Poliziano debating the propriety of Lorenzo's latest ceremonial. It is in the consideration of ceremonial, typically, that their differences are most plainly visible:

POLIZIANO   Clarice,
       Six floats have been prepared with stage sets, built
       In image to depict the Life of Christ.
CLARICE   Yes, so they should; and always have: but now
       Beside the Bible stories, other carts
       And carriages present our family.
       It is not right. Orsini up in Rome
       Never allow the fair-ground in their home,
       Nor let crude actors strut before the crowds
       Dressed as ourselves!
POLIZIANO   Madonna; just this once,
       To praise Lorenzo, all the city votes
       To show its gratitude. You should be proud!
       The caravan of pageants shows the Roman
       Consul Aemilius Paulus coming home
       In triumph with such wealth no Roman paid
       Taxes for fifty years, thanks to his conquests.
CLARICE   Well, that was ancient Rome. Today, tomorrow,
       Taxes must still be paid—we pay too much![24]

Scarcely could there be a greater contrast between the voices of dry realism and of the creative, mythopoeic imagination. It is the last fully Laurentian ceremony of which we are to hear. The next scene records the invitation (partly under Clarice's influence) of Savonarola to take up his residence in the Dominican monastery of San Marco. Amongst his prophecies is

      a scourge to carnival
    Sweeping away the tinsel that deforms
    Great Dante's city.

Savonarola's great sermon in Scene Nine of Act Two stands in counterpoint to Simonetta's aria to spring in Scene Eight of Act One. The lamentation for Simonetta in Scene Thirteen of Act One is balanced by that for Lorenzo in Scene

Fourteen of Act Two. The 'trial' which was the joust of the play's opening scenes finds its own macabre ceremonial inversion in the trial by fire recounted in Scene Sixteen of Act Two. Doffo Spini recounts events to Ficino:

> Fra Domenico of San Marco's garden,
> Defending his mad Prior, challenged Franciscans
> To walk through fire to prove their calumny
> Of Savonarola. While you were away,
> The pent crowd waited for Domenico
> Holding a crucifix, and Savonarola
> Carrying high the Host, to test the flames.
> Each side delays. Franciscans want the other
> To strip, so fire can burn the skin; and both
> In fears innumerable find delays,
> With superstitions that each crucifix
> Is a half-mandrake diabolical,
> And such-like cowardly fatuities.[25]

There is no victor to crown after this 'trial'. Another ritual does inevitably ensue, however; one that must be performed with a proper Florentine regard for how it might be interpreted:

DOFFO SPINI See! Here he comes. Look! They erect a
               scaffold,
               And pile brushwood, all soaked in oil and resin
               To make it burn. With him there hang two
               more
               Life-haters, Fra Domenico and Silvestro.
VESPUCCI It looks so like a crucifixion scene!
DOFFO SPINI We thought of that, and what the crowd might
               say,
               So one cross-beam's been sawn.

The contrast is between the predominantly (but not exclusively) creative ceremonies of Act One and the predominantly (but again not exclusively) destructive ceremonies of Act Two. In Act One events off-stage are presided over by the joust; in Act Two the sense is of surrounding flames off-stage, in the death of Savonarola and in the bonfire of 'vanities' summoned up by his sermon.

It is to the pleasanter ceremonies of Act One that we must return. In such ceremonies the Medici sought to create effective emblematic expression of their aspirations. In the joust of 1469 Lorenzo's standard depicted laurel branches, in an obvious and oft-repeated pun on his name; the standard bore as inscription the French words *Le Tem[p]s Revient*. The phrasing was picked up and echoed more than once in Pulci's poem; the allusion is to Virgil's Fourth Eclogue. The reign of Lorenzo is to be a spring renewal. It is to be a world where

> The young must dance, the life-force be respected,
> And sprigs of energy must push beyond
> Mere branches of past opportunity
> If the great cycle of the ages is
> To bear its fruit.

In the words of the second Prologue to Act Two of *Living Creation* the first years of Lorenzo's rule were 'high spring-time'. Of those years *la Bella Simonetta* is, in Warner's play, the 'incarnation' of Spring (Vespucci describes her thus in Act One Scene Seven). Originally from Genoa, Simonetta Cattaneo first came to Florence in 1469 as the sixteen-year-old bride of Marco Vespucci. In the tournament of 1475 Giuliano wore her favours:

> He bows to Simonetta. She throws down
> Her favour. A boy page has picked it up;
> Tosses it to him. He catches it, and bows
> Once more to her, and wears it round his arm.

Simonetta was loved by both Lorenzo and Giuliano. Quite what force we should give to the word 'loved' in such a statement is problematical; are we to think simply in terms of 'elaborate . . . ceremonial compliment'?[26] That is surely to underestimate the reality of Giuliano's passion, though we need not, certainly, share the suspicions of Francesco in *Living Creation*:

> Young Simonetta may think that she's Spring,
> Marco her husband being far away,
> But Marco's brother, Piero, feels defiled
> And bears a grudge.

Translated into myth, the relationship of Simonetta and Giuliano is at the centre of Poliziano's *Stanze*. The charms of the nymph Simonetta are exquisitely delineated by the poet:

> Candida è ella, e candida la vesta,
> ma pur di rose e fior dipinta e d'erba;
> lo inanellato crin dall'aurea testa
> scende in la fronte umilmente superba.
> Rideli a torno tutta la foresta,
> e quanto può suo cure disacerba;
> nell'atto regalmente è mansuaeta,
> e pur col ciglio le tempeste acqueta.
>
> Folgoron gli occhi d'un dolce sereno,
> ove sue face tien Cupido ascose;
> l'aier d'intorno si fa tutto ameno
> ovunque gira le luce amorose.
> Di celeste letizia il volto ha pieno,
> dolce dipinto di ligustri e rose;
> ogni aura tace al suo parlar divino,
> e canta ogni augelletto in suo latino.[27]

Simonetta died on the 26th April, 1476, perhaps of consumption. Lorenzo himself records the impact of her death:

There died in our city a lady for whom all the people of Florence were moved to grief. It was no wonder that this should be so, for she was truly adorned with as much beauty and grace as any lady ever had. Among her other excellent gifts she had so sweet and attractive a manner that all the men who made her acquaintance believed themselves to be deeply loved by her. More than this, the ladies and young women of the time were not envious of this most remarkable of her qualities, but rather gave great praise to her beauty and kindness. It seemed to be hard to believe that so many men could love her without jealousy, and that so many ladies praised her without envy. Her death aroused great pity for her youth and beauty. Her beauty seemed even more radiant in death. All men desired, in verse or prose, to celebrate her beauty or to accuse death of greed and cruelty.[28]

These words are echoed in the tribute Lorenzo pays to Simonetta in Act One Scene Thirteen of *Living Creation*:

All Florence mourns, and little wonder, for
She was adorned with every human grace.
Beauty, in death's unearthly radiance,
Excels, reflected in our flashing grief.
Look! Evening's star sky-rides with a new splendour!
Her soul has climbed up high where angels dance.

The later lines here repeat the most striking image from one of the four sonnets ('O chiara stella, che co'raggi tuoi') Lorenzo wrote on the occasion of Simonetta's death. Del Lungo gives an account of the supposed circumstances of the poem's composition:

It is related that after the reception of the news, Lorenzo went out into the calm spring night to walk with a friend, and as he was speaking of the dead lady he suddenly stopped and gazed at a star which had never before seemed to him so brilliant. 'See,' he exclaimed, 'either the soul of that most gentle lady hath been transformed into that new star, or else hath it been joined together thereunto.'[29]

In *Living Creation* Simonetta is 'Giuliano's dream'. It is not only the artists who see her in terms both of mythical ideal and everyday reality. To Giorgio Vespucci she is

this girl-Venus wafted to our shore,
Our cousin Marco's wife.

At the joust—the offstage presence of which dominates Act One Scene Four—she is dressed as the Queen of Spring. She is a central figure in Lorenzo's ceremonial vision, a vision of a world full of shape and significance:

Let all rejoice in our festivity,
With dancing, singing, banquets, graceful games
Where human forms, through which bright silks and
    gems
Convert themselves to spirit, may love peace
Sent down from Heaven throughout all Italy.
Redeunt Saturnia regna. Florence herself
Is Queen, and glories in our corporate joy.

The motif of renewal is reaffirmed in Lorenzo's quotation, once more, from Virgil's Fourth Eclogue. Simonetta may, as

Vespucci has said, be an 'incarnation' of Spring. Giuliano
can say of her that her

> loveliness reflects the Supreme Good
> Beyond our transitory world, where life is born.

Yet we are never allowed to forget that she is also a vulnerable
human being. She worries for the safety of Giuliano in the
joust, though there can be no doubting that the occasion was
too well 'scripted' for him ever to have been in danger. She is
a Queen of Spring who 'dread[s] to make a speech to all this
crowd'. In Scene Ten she makes an unexplained departure
from the stage. Scene Eleven begins with Salvestra telling us
that:

> The gorgeous Giuliano sent our poet
> To summon April, Simonetta, back.

News of Simonetta's illness arrives before the end of the
scene, interwoven with the episode of Francesco's callous
exploitation of the beauty of Riguardata. Marietta reports
the news of both:

> I passed him [Francesco]. He's already sold her to
> The public brothel. Simonetta's ill.
> Lorenzo's sent Stephano, his own doctor.
> Her breathing's dusty.

Francesco's treatment of Riguardata becomes an image of
Death's seizure of Simonetta. Only the brief Scene Twelve
intervenes between Marietta's report and the mourning for
Simonetta which occupies Scene Thirteen. That scene, in
turn, ends with Lorenzo's announcement of his intention of
celebrating High Mass for Simonetta's soul—and is
immediately followed by the events of the Pazzi conspiracy.
Simonetta's human vulnerability effectively becomes a symbol of the fragility of all that Lorenzo has achieved and of all
that he aspires to achieve. In her beauty, and the moment in
which it finds ceremonial celebration, is a resonant image of
the transitory glory of all that is most human. Her beautiful
speech which closes Act One Scene Eight fittingly records a

moment of spring both literal and metaphorical, a moment of spring both inside and outside time:

> Sunrise now bathes the sleeping cheeks of all
> Creation, making fresh the blush of spring,
> Throwing a necklace of ten thousand stars
> Over new green to hide her nakedness
> With sudden showers and colours in the grass:
> Daisies that wink at night and drop the head,
> The sea-shore myrtle, mountain violet,
> Snowdrops who fight the hard, teeth-chattering frost,
> Crocus, and brave and dangerous aconite,
> While mottled skies blow clearer with mild days,
> Summon the blustering February winds
> From March, to calm them with a poet's power
> To make old young, re-shed the tears of things
> Long past, call up the dead and beautiful
> For our delight, and turn the seasons round.
> April is here with all her gift of life
> And spring runs riot now that winter dies.
> Delicate, strong, with graceful dignity
> She opens up, under the fires of heaven,
> Freshness and wonder in each pulse that hides,
> Swims, creeps or flies, bounds or parades or prowls:
> The vulnerable wren twines her slight twigs;
> From far, gust-skipping swallows have returned
> Wing-fed on bias, to speak low to eggs;
> Chaffinch, and all the company of air,
> Mate, nest, and sing, while the white dress of light
> Fills with the laughter of a grateful world,
> With bold vitality of courting men
> As women's merriment hops to and fro.
> Now, as the queen of flowers, the rose, unfolds
> The scented innocence of youth, disclosed
> In early loveliness revealed, unspoiled,
> That art, most beautiful of all our games
> On earth, begins: the timeless dance of love.

Simonetta's beauty, the splendours of Laurentian ceremonial, the achievements of Lorenzo's Florence—all may persuade us that 'spring runs riot now that winter dies'. Yet the seasonal nature of this way of thinking ought to serve,

simultaneously, to remind us of the necessary transience of
what has been achieved. We have already seen that even in
Lorenzo's Florence winter has its agents. Francesco de'
Pazzi has earlier observed that Giuliano is

> Too high too young. Not everyone who bends
> Acknowledges subordination to
> The proud Medici.

Ficino has advised Lorenzo that 'the Pazzi cannot love you'.
Simonetta's hymn to spring is her final utterance of the play.
Soon she is dead and Giuliano has no doubts that Spring has
disappeared with her:

> I have no words. Grief closes round my eyes
> And weighs my tongue, now Simonetta's dead.
> She, like a Venus, rose up through the waves
> Of Florentines, blown here from Genoa.
> Each barefoot step she pressed upon the grass
> Imprinted flowers that grew where she had passed,
> And left in every heart a sense of spring.
> *(Bending to kiss the corpse)*
> Chrysalis of eternity, goodbye.
> *(Closing her eyes)*
> Your brief hour lived, for ever close each eye.
> Winter has come too soon.

'Winter has come too soon'—what Giuliano recognizes in
Simonetta's death is later to be recognized by Botticelli, in
his penultimate speech of the play, in his sense that
'summer's breath fails with a little frost'. Yet it is essential to
the play's working out of its meaning that we should acknowledge that in art there might be ways of giving to 'spring' a
different kind of permanence. Simonetta herself speaks of
the

>   poet's power
> To make old young, re-shed the tears of things
> Long past, call up the dead and beautiful
> For our delight, and turn the seasons round.

As early as Scene Two Domenico (Ghirlandaio) had pointed
out that on the banner painted for the joust 'Pallas' face / Is

Simonetta'. After Simonetta's last words, but before news of her death, we are presented with Botticelli's 'Mars and Venus', in which Giuliano recognizes himself and Simonetta. The very details of the picture respond both to the painter's contemporary world and to the iconography of myth. Lorenzo enquires

> What are those bees that trepidate his hair?

and Ficino has a learned explanation to offer:

> Sweetness and sting united, *discordia concors*:
> Venus tames Mars, but loves her opposite,
> And from their union Harmony is born.

But as Sandro himself points out—without contradicting Ficino's gloss upon the picture—the 'bees' also have another more 'local' significance:

> Round Giuliano's head
> Are wasps from the Vespucci coat of arms.
> A pun upon their name: *Vespa*—wasp!

In all probability Botticelli's picture was not painted until 1485, well after the deaths of Simonetta and Giuliano. Certainly the picture was painted well after Poliziano had begun—and abandoned—his *Stanze*. In *Living Creation* the sequence is reversed. In Scene Ten Poliziano enters carrying the 'Mars and Venus' and promises

> Prince Giuliano, I will celebrate,
> In stanzas, as our Sandro has in paint,
> That beauty seated on the grass, your love,
> The rose-cheeked Simonetta.

We need not suppose that these are errors made in ignorance of the facts. Modern scholarship, in any case, largely dismisses the possibility that the major paintings of Botticelli contain portraits of Lorenzo's court. Horne dismisses such suggestions as a 'fantastic medley of misconceptions'.[30] Warner's purpose is not, I would suggest, to contradict such dismissals or to revive the earlier view in any literal or dogmatic sense. For the dramatist such ideas are, rather, a way of suggesting the kinds of transformation which art performs upon reality, the way in which it, too, gives a ceremonial significance to that which is finest and most beautiful in its surroundings, how it finds visions of the eternal in the world of mutability. Vision and imagination, working upon the materials of a fallen world, may apprehend an unfallen one. Ficino formulates the aspiration:

> The moving air, alive with trembling numbers,
> Bows reverently, parting for its guests
> The dancers, who embody harmony
> And lift the stillness of a summer's day
> Into sweet mathematics up to God.
> When I am in my hillside home, the house
> Cosimo gave me, and I look across
> At your great villa of Careggio,
> I often pray that the soul's harmony
> For which I've searched so long may be revealed
> To some rare painter, perhaps in our time;
> Some supreme master of the single line
> Who knows a sudden gesture, and each glance,
> Are outward music of an inner song,
> And can, holding our eyes and hands with wonder,
> Leap into vision through imagined thought.

It is in the 'Primavera', the presentation of which is the climax of Act One and brings it to a close, that Ficino's aspiration finds fullest realization. It is in such terms that Sandro introduces it. To Lorenzo's enquiry—'what painting do you bring?'—he replies

> Ficino's dream; your challenge to my brush;
> A picture for your own Academy
> On the green slopes of Montevecchio.[31]

Through the reactions of those who witness the revelation of the 'Primavera' Warner offers an interpretation of the painting. In outline this interpretation is virtually identical with that offered by Edgar Wind.[32] Botticelli himself identifies the painting's central figure:

> Calm Venus, mother of life's harmony,
> Presides, virtuous, clothed.

Its representation of the metamorphosis of Chloris, expli-
cated by Poliziano, we have considered earlier. The three
figures on the right are thus identified—as they are by
Wind—as Zephyr, Chloris and Flora. The second group of
three figures, on the left-hand side, is identified by Vespucci
and explained by Ficino as the Three Graces:

VESPUCCI   that Grace who turns her back,
                     Chastity, moves towards Voluptuousness,
                     Drawing sweet Married Love round after her.
                              . . .

FICINO   Grace in giving, accepting, returning, while
                     Placed palm to palm, and interlocked, they lift
                     The crowned knot of the dance. Once more we
                          see
                     Descent, Rapture, Return; front, back, and
                          side;
                     A metamorphosis of love unfolds
                     In Venus' garden. Fructified in time
                     By passion's breath, we grow, dance, then
                          return
                     To heaven, like Mercury, in contemplation,
                     Prayer reaching up to move aside the clouds
                     That shield us from the scorching light of God.

The interpretation offered by Warner's characters goes
beyond Professor Wind in at least one striking instance.
Ficino questions Botticelli:

FICINO   The structure of the whole's in every part,
                     Sandro; yet there's one thing I cannot see
                     Or understand. Where's the third group of
                          three?
SANDRO   Mercury points up. Where would you expect?
VESPUCCI   Above, out of the picture!
SANDRO   Yes. No man
                     Can paint the Holy Christian Trinity
                     Of which our triads in this life below
                     Are glass-stained imitations.

Sandro goes on to identify the 'models' for the figures in his
painting. The metaphorical sense in which such identifica-

tions might be understood has already been suggested. He
explains to Lorenzo:

SANDRO   Your brother, yes; and Simonetta's there—
                Scatters tight roses from her dress-held lap.
                I spend my idle hours, as well you know,
                Walking the streets, sketching the passers-by.
                Those soft, diaphanous Graces you see dance
                Are sitting by you; gentle friends of mine:
                Salvestra, Marietta, Albiera.
                Look hard; and see Clarice there presiding—
                The mother of your children and your wife.
DOMENICO   And who is Chloris? Tell, now. Please don't
                    blush!
SANDRO   Er . . . just a lady from the city square
                Called Riguardata.
FICINO   Zephyrus is you!
SANDRO   I paint self-portraits on the right-hand side
                At times; if I feel moved.
POLIZIANO   Cupid's my pupil!
                Your little son, Piero!
LORENZO   All are there!

The artist is Zephyrus. It is he who effects the metamorphosis, it is through the activity of art that she who was Chloris
can become Flora, that the mutable can become the eternal

> Glimpsed through the seasons of this passing world.

Botticelli's painting, it is widely accepted, was influenced by
the *Stanze* of Poliziano. So too was 'The Birth of Venus'
which Lorenzo, indeed, describes as

> A duet danced between two sister arts,
> Painting and Poetry

when given his first sight of it in Act Two Scene Three. Here
art's transformation of the world of mutability inescapably
has about it an almost elegiac quality. The painting is
unveiled:

LORENZO   What an unutterable sense of loss:
                It's Simonetta!
MARIETTA   From so long ago.
SALVESTRA   Oh, she brings back my teen-age youth.

High spring has gone; it can only be remembered. The 'Simonetta' of the 'Birth of Venus' had already, as it were, passed through one work of art. The gap between reality and myth is greater but all the more moving:

SANDRO   It was your Angelo
                         Who gave the theme: his verses on the joust
                         For Giuliano.
LORENZO   Say them now, my poet.
POLIZIANO   A naked woman with an angel's face
             Blown on a shell, wafted toward the shore
             By Zephyrs to where Hours with loosened pace
             Welcome her like a sister, and restore
             Her modesty with Nature's endless grace
             Of flowers. Her soft loveliness must awe
             Those who look on. Her *left* hand crossed one
                         breast;
             Her other held her long hair where was best.

Poliziano's lines here are an adaptation and abbreviation of stanzas 99-101 of Book One of the *Stanze*. The rhyme-scheme reproduces the *ottava rima* of Poliziano's poem. The poet's emphatic *left* is a more-or-less diplomatic attempt to draw attention to the fact that in his painterly transcription of the lines Botticelli has reversed the actions of Venus' hands. Consideration of Botticelli's great painting prompts from Lorenzo and Ficino a fresh clarification of their attitudes:

LORENZO   Our lives need more than self, for there must be
             A clear, still centre to intensity,
             And you have found it.
FICINO   Beauty is divine.
             We worship God in things he has created
             So we can later worship things in God.
             At one with our own innocent Idea
             We reach full life, and seem in loving God
             To love ourselves.
LORENZO   Here's a farewell to flesh:
             Carne, vale! Sing it while I leave
             To find my wife, Clarice.

The first of the Prologues to Act Two of the play has its relevance here, in its recognition of the brevity of spring and

its Platonic myth of the charioteer, as well as in triadic
patterning of thought;

> I have my hand upon the pulse of life:
> One half the thread is spun. No spring returns
> For man, or nature; and new buds begun,
> Rife in fecundity, must take their turn.
> Yes, we three Fates unfold our Mother's law—
> Necessity breeds consequence from acts—
> Even as three Graces' light timidity
> Can pour the love of Venus in our hearts.
> Each god, though one, reveals himself in three.
> Prosperity can only find fresh flower
> When Reason, our soul's charioteer, can be
> True master of both horses, black and white:
> One, Aspiration; striving for the sky,
> To balance black Desire, each held controlled.

The precarious—but rich—springtime of Laurentian Florence was created by the momentary holding in balance of a
whole series of conflicting (or seemingly conflicting) impulses.

The philosopher of this 'springtime rebirth of old learning' is Ficino. Friend and teacher of Lorenzo, Ficino's rich
diversity is amusingly described by Michael Allen:

Translator from the Greek and commentator; Christian apologist,
theologian, teacher, exegete, priest; musical theorist and notable
performer; mythologist, metaphysician, lapsed astrologer; belle-
trist, ethician, versifier, dialectician; medical theorist and prac-
titioner and love theorist; psychiatrist, Thomist, demonologist;
Hermetist, Orphic, Augustinian, Dantean, dietician; historian of
poetry, religion, philosophy, and pleasure; quietist, mystic, mage,
humanist, wit; devout son and timid sycophant; above all, Neopla-
tonist, Ficino was a highly derivative and original, conservative
and bizarre, succinctly repetitive scholar-thinker.[33]

Our first encounter with Ficino in *Living Creation* is in the
company of Lorenzo, who introduces him as a man whose
central philosophical concern is 'reconciling Plato with sweet
Christ'. Ficino found no opposition between Christian doctrine and Platonic philosophy. Rather Platonic thought
offered a kind of philosophical confirmation of Christianity.

Platonic thought is a 'pia philosophia'.[34] In a letter to Johannes Pannonius he observes that

> in these times it pleases divine Providence to confirm religion in general by philosophical authority and reason until, on a day already predestined, it will confirm the true religion, as in other times, by miracles wrought among all peoples.[35]

Kristeller's is a particularly clear statement of Ficino's position:

> The renewal of Platonic philosophy is, on the one hand, part of the general rebirth of human arts and institutions. On the other it is intended to lead men to salvation in accordance with the Christian religion and so to serve as a necessary instrument for the eternal plan of divine Providence.[36]

The reconciliation of apparent contraries is a recurrent feature of Ficino's thought—sense and spirit, wisdom and pleasure, for example. A masterpiece such as his commentary on the *Philebus* originated as lectures given in a church, and is centrally concerned with the reconciliation of pleasure and wisdom.[37] The Ficino of Warner's play affirms that

> Man's end, here on earth,
> Is to make pleasure one with wisdom.

'But how?' enquires Sandro. Ficino's reply adapts the maxim which was inscribed upon the walls of his Academy:

> With three angels:
> Beauty, Truth, Proportion. Flee excess!
> Be happy in the present.[38]

The senses are a possible means for the perception of the divine. A letter to Peregrino Agli contains one of many relevant passages in Ficino's writings:

> We do indeed perceive the reflection of divine beauty with our eyes and mark the resonance of divine harmony with our ears—those bodily senses which Plato considers the most perceptive of all. Thus when the soul has received through the physical senses those images which are within material objects, we remember what we knew before when we existed outside the prison of the body. The

soul is fired by this memory and, shaking its wings, by degrees
purges itself from contact with the body and its filth and becomes
wholly possessed by divine frenzy. From the two senses I have just
mentioned two kinds of frenzy are aroused. Regaining the memory
of the true and divine beauty by the appearance of beauty that the
eyes perceive, we desire the former with a secret and unutterable
ardour of the mind. This Plato calls 'divine love', which he defines
as the desire to return again to the contemplation of divine beauty;
a desire arising from the sight of its physical likeness.[39]

Such passages lie behind Ficino's words to Lorenzo in Act
One Scene Seventeen:

> sense-impressions reach the soul through doors
> And windows of the body, our fine senses,
> Stamp our imagination with their image
> Which we compare with our innate ideas,
> And judge, for better or for worse, to be
> Beautiful, true, or wise; veiled in birth-dreams,
> Dawning self-wakening finds what we know.

They also inform his ringing affirmation in Act Two Scene
Eight (also addressed to Lorenzo):

> Respect vitality.
> We know our Saviour joins himself to man
> Directly; what must follow then is man
> Can reach for God through his God-given senses.

It is surely to Ficino's influence (though not, of course,
exclusively so) that we should attribute Lorenzo's aspirations for the education of his son:

> Teach him to reach up high to worthy aims,
> To have compassion on the small, the frail,
> And to love life, living creation through
> His soul, his mind, his body, and each dusk
> Rip away darkness from the twinkling sky
> With faith in a new dawn, with enterprise
> The child of mastery's delighted strength.

The central reconciliation of Laurentian Florence is of
Christian and classical. For Lorenzo the ceremonies of Florence are created from these two influences:

Look! The Greek gods enhance the Baptist's Day!

The 'Primavera' is the quintessential articulation of Lorenzo's springtime world, and it is in terms of this same reconciliation that Lorenzo describes the picture:

> Classical beauty, Christian harmony,
> The Old World and the New, join, blessed by Love.

Love, though, has its enemies, reconciliation its opponents. Savonarola is only the most dramatic of these, and we will consider him later. There are several anticipations of his entry. Where Ficino and Lorenzo find a creative and harmonious reconciliation, others discover a conflict and a betrayal. At the death of Simonetta, Vespucci feels that a choice must be made:

> Here, today,
> Upon her corpse I vow myself to God.
> From this hour on I yield my classic mind
> Up, to be priest, to Christ.

Clarice, one suspects, always felt out of place in Florence. Though she had her qualities she was lacking in some of the ones most desirable in the environment in which she now found herself. As Horsburgh puts it:

Intellectually Clarice was not distinguished. She gives the impression of a certain prim sourness of disposition which must at times have been depressing to Lorenzo's mercurial soul. She was lacking in that supreme gift of the Gods—imagination.[40]

Inevitably there was much in the Florence created and shaped by her husband that Clarice found objectionable. The appointment of Poliziano—a humanist drenched in classical learning—as tutor to her son must have seemed to Clarice a symbol of all in Florence that she disliked and mistrusted. Act Two Scene Four of *Living Creation* records something of their well-documented quarrel:

POLIZIANO   This city, now so unified by war
             And sudden peace, could split in two without
             The benediction of your husband's touch.
             Thank all the gods on high!

CLARICE   Now, that's what's wrong!
                    You, an ecclesiastic, think much more
                    Of Virgil, Plato, and God knows what pagans
                    Else, when you should teach my son of Christ!
                    Oh, what this city needs is a new spirit
                    Far from the nakedness and revelry,
                    The painted harlots, and the monks with lutes,
                    Lascivious wives and daughters out in search
                    Of eyes that flatter, and the tickling tongue,
                    To turn us back to sanctity and God.
                    Isn't cold Aphrodite on your mind
                    Far more than ever is our Virgin Mary?
POLIZIANO   I teach Piero both the word of God
                    And style of Cicero.

The very structure of *Living Creation* reproduces this interaction of classical and Christian.

The first word of the play's first scene is God. The last
word of the play's last scene is God. The Christian singular
noun is not one to which Clarice could object. This main
body of the play exists, however, within another enfolding
frame—a frame of Prologue and Epilogue. These relate the
events and ideas of the scenes in Florence both backwards in
time to earlier cultures and forwards to our own times. These
Prologues and Epilogues are spoken by the three fates. The
world of pre-Christian mythology to which art, ceremony
and thought make constant allusion in Renaissance Florence
is here presented in more direct fashion. In the dramatic
scheme of things Platonism stands before and after the
Christian neo-Platonism of Lorenzo's Florence, for the three
Fates are derived from Book X of the *Republic*. There they
are an important feature of the myth of Er, a passage which
has frequently exerted its influence upon Warner's work.
Singing to the music of the Sirens, dressed in white robes and
with garlands upon their heads are the three Fates, Lachesis
the past, Clotho the present, and Atropos the future. They
are part of the mechanism by which each soul chooses its
destiny. The souls are addressed by Lachesis:

Souls of a day, here shall begin a new round of earthly life, to end in
death. No guardian spirit will cast lots for you, but you shall choose

your own destiny. Let him to whom the first lot falls choose first a life to which he shall be bound of necessity. But Virtue owns no master: as a man honours or dishonours her, so shall he have more of her or less. The blame is his who chooses; Heaven is blameless.[41]

It is in such terms that the first Prologue to Act One speaks:

> We, robed in white with garlands on our heads,
> Are the three daughters of Necessity,
> Our Mother. Married domesticity
> Cannot be ours. I spin the present threads
> Of each and every one of you alive.
> Yes, it was I, Clotho, the youngest, whom
> You cried to when you first sparked in the womb:
> To the bee-hive of birth made you survive.
> *(Indicating Lachesis)*
> Look to your past! Lachesis on her throne
> Allotted all your chances; in her lap
> Are sample lives for you to choose. The map
> Of life is hers, the voyage is your own.
>   The future lies with Atropos, who hears
>   No plea. She cuts each life's thread with her shears.

Lachesis and Atropos, in the two sonnets that follow, introduce the first statement of one of the play's central themes. We, they know, live under the shadow of impending destruction. To be overawed by that shadow, to accept its inevitability fatalistically is a tempting luxury. In the temptation lies the abandonment of all human aspiration. The message of Lachesis and Atropos is that these are not dangers and temptations that man has not faced—and overcome—before. Using a traditional version of the entry of the Black Death into Europe[42] these two sonnets locate the flowering of the Renaissance against an earlier threat of 'mankind's destruction':

LACHESIS

> Look to your past! For in it you will find
> Mankind's destruction has been faced before.
> We need not always weep. To overawe
> Is easy. To reply, shake off, unbind
> Is the great challenge. Listen, now; and learn.
> In thirteen forty-seven, in the Crimea,

A trading-post of Genoese, in fear,
Besieged by Kipchak soldiers, would not turn
Its loyalty. The Kipchaks took the town
By catapulting plague-blown corpses in.
Sick galleys fled to Sicily: and down
To Egypt, up through France, Austria, Spain,
England, the Baltics, Sweden, to the snow
That Black Death cut one third of Europe's skein.

ATROPOS

One in three humans putrefied, to burn,
For that one act of evil. Persevere!
This time we know the consequence. I shear
According to your acts. From that dark urn,
In spite of all, some beauty rose, refined
To rarest life-enhancing wonder, for
(*Coming downstage, and laying aside her shears*)
Our Chaucer's laughing, ever-open door
Of love, and lust, and ladies was defined
By that extermination, and the glow
Learned from a golden city's impish brain—
The plague-racked Florence of Boccaccio.
Tonight we leave behind this origin
Some hundred years. Florence's dome, red-brown,
Crowns young Lorenzo's city here. Begin!

Here is human achievement and creativity 'defined'—not destroyed—by the threat of destruction. The challenge has been accepted and overcome. The responsibility is ours— 'fate' is the consequence of our own acts. Act Two is introduced by two further Prologues. They are spoken, this time, by Clotho and Lachesis. Atropos remains silent. The mid-point of the play offers us past and present. Our choice of our future—Atropos represents what is to come—must await the end of the play. Clotho's Prologue, with its invocation of another of Plato's myths (the chariot of the soul) has been considered earlier. The choice for man is not of return—'no spring returns / For man or nature', since 'Necessity breeds consequence from acts'. It is on human responsibility, upon the enduring human capacity for choice, that Lachesis places her stress—both in what has happened and is about to happen in the play and, by implication, in the decisions that we must make. Her opening lines are an

expansion of Plato's beautiful words in the *Republic*—αἰτία
ἑλομένου· θεὸς ἀναίτιος:[43]

> Store this: the gods are not responsible
> For free choice man makes in stupidity.
> Lucidity is all. If there is fault,
> The chooser bears that freedom evermore.
> Strife alternates with harmony. Lorenzo
> Was three when Rome's long empire, overrun
> Under the dome of Constantinople, fell
> To the young Máhomet the Second's knife.
> High springtime yields to summer, then to age.
> Our second act follows the story through
> Dying Lorenzo's life-work thrown to waste,
> Squandered by Savonarola's piety.
> She who allots now takes her leave of you,
> And begs you think of your posterity.

When Atropos closes the play—and completes the Platonic
frame which encloses its Christian central panels—her language returns us directly to the myth of Er, in a conclusion
which is reminiscent (as regards tone and metre) of that of
Goethe's *Faust*. The Chorus Mysticus closes *Faust*:

> Alles Vergängliche
> Ist nur ein Gleichnis;
> Das Unzulängliche,
> Hier wird's Ereignis;
> Das Unbeschreibliche,
> Hier ist's getan.[44]

At the close of *Living Creation* we are faced with the need to
choose, to take or not to take the kind of path that will lead us
to the kind of conclusion towards which Goethe's great play
has moved:

> Horror intransigent,
> Laughter and youth,
> All that is transient
> Teaches some truth.
> Lost in life's meadow
> Searching for love
> Each one's a shadow
> Thrown from above.

> Find when, invisible,
> I cut your fear,
> Incomprehensible
> Thought is made clear.
> Atropos severs
> Your threads, one by one:
> All your endeavours
> Are judged by the sun.
> Here you have seen extremes;
> All now's complete.
> May you choose wisdom's dreams
> Till next we meet.

Destruction and death are recurrent presences in the main body of the play, as well as in its 'frame'. They are the context in which the characters of the play must make their choices.

Warner is careful not to present Laurentian Florence as any kind of idyll. It exists and creates itself in an environment that is threatening and difficult. The plague is a contemporary reality as well as part of the city's historical background. Within the city, from the very first scene of the play, are voices of dissent and rebellion. The first half of the play focuses these in the person of Francesco de' Pazzi. Poliziano's *Coniurationis Commentarium* provides a fascinating contemporary account of Francesco and his part in the conspiracy—from, naturally, a thoroughly pro-Medici standpoint.[45] We need not, here, trace all the political ramifications, internal and external, of the Medici's consolidation of their power. *Living Creation* places great stress on the constant difficulties faced by Lorenzo—his creativity exists as 'defined' by such difficulties. The deaths of Simonetta—from natural causes, and of Giuliano—at the hands of the conspirators, are fierce reminders of mortality. Lorenzo's response to the conspiracy is ruthless. The conspirators are executed and the very name of Pazzi is abolished, their property confiscated ('palaces, stables all / Down to the poultry and the household pans'). It need not surprise us that art and ceremonial have their part to play too. Lorenzo instructs Sandro:

> Forty gold florins
> Are yours. Paint each of the conspirators
> In portrait frescoes on the public walls
> Of Prison and Grand Brothel; and beneath
> Lines, epitaphs, that I shall write on them
> For all to see.

His proclamation, having announced the punishments, is that

> Now
> A medal shall be struck, given free to all
> Who stood by us in our calamity.

The spring cannot, indeed, return. 'Strife alternates with harmony'. Lorenzo's achievements spring, not from any attempted avoidance of the world's threats, but from a committed willingness to take up the challenges that they pose.

Lorenzo's world is a world of both beauty and energy—a world, in the terms of two of the play's most frequent images, of both flowers and horses. At its centre is a capacity to respond to the energies of creation itself—'of life / And pleasure, arts, air, music, and the young'—without losing sight of the creator they speak of (the recurrent motif of spectacles in the play is a semi-comic affirmation of the importance of 'vision'). The response to creation is the desire for further creation. The arts are an obvious example. Creative energy, we are reminded, found expression in other ways too. Vespucci is a name whose associations do not end with the paintings of Botticelli. It is to Botticelli that Giorgio Vespucci offers some 'advice':

> Well; you could sail, perhaps, and find the Indies
> Like my dear nephew, Amerigo; paint
> The monsters and the naked human folk
> Who carve existence from strange innocence:
> The men with shaved heads cut like a cock's comb,
> Walking with always folded arms. The girls,
> Bare-breasted, carry their hands dangling down;
> Paint foreheads, cheeks, and legs; and, humming, sway
> Under exotic plants that speak and weave.[46]

More than one 'new world' is being created in this springtime of Florence. Lorenzo's 'vision of all-creating life' is, he says, quickened by Botticelli's art; Ficino affirms that 'Art nurtures faith'. We might, almost as readily, invert both propositions on the evidence of what we see in the first act of *Living Creation*. At the very centre of the play lies an emblem of the quintessential energy of creation itself. The two Prologues before Act Two are sonnets of an unorthodox but telling kind. They employ both initial and terminal rhyme as follows (they also continue the inter-rhymed technique of the second and third Prologues to Act One):

CLOTHO: life / One / begun / Rife / law / Necessity /
            timidity / pour / three / Prosperity / be / True /
            sky / To.
LACHESIS: Store / stupidity / Lucidity / more / Strife /
            overrun / Under / knife / High / through / Dying
            / piety / who / posterity.

The pattern is a double helix. The very structure of creation finds its emblem at the centre of the play. Creative renewal is further affirmed in the languages and forms of both art and science.

The second half of *Living Creation* is acted out beneath the considerable shadow of Savonarola. It is a misleading simplification to think of Savonarola as simply a crude antithesis to Lorenzo and his circle. Of course he detested much that Lorenzo represented, or that he believed Lorenzo to represent. Savonarola was, to put it mildly, a force that disturbed the necessarily precarious equilibrium that the Laurentian reconciliations had achieved. Ficino's vision of Platonic thought as an adjunct of Christianity was anathema to Savonarola. Too much of Lorenzo's ceremonial seemed to him to be designed to glorify the people and things of this world. Savonarola's interest was in a different kind of renewal. Yet in that very interest was a kind of affinity, odd as it may seem, with Lorenzo and his circle. Both belonged in the long tradition of those who believed Florence's destiny to be as a centre of renewal and rebirth.[47] Lorenzo, indeed, had originally invited Savonarola to Florence. His power base at the

convent of San Marco was a Medici foundation too. Though
their visions were radically different, they shared the sense
that Florence was no ordinary city, that its responsibilities
were not ordinary ones. For Lorenzo renewal was inseparably bound up with love. For Savonarola it could only come
through repentance and atonement. His first appearance in
Living Creation, in Act Two Scene Seven, finds Savonarola
denying Lorenzo's influence in bringing him to Florence ('I
have come called by the word of Christ / As Prior to San
Marco; not by man'), and being questioned by Albiera.
Salvestra wrongly takes the question to be idle curiosity:

ALBIERA   They say you are austere; but have you been
                 In love?
SALVESTRA   Oh, Albiera! What a question!
SAVONAROLA   I played the lute; and still I love its sounds
                 For holy words. Yes, daughter. Long ago,
                 Facing my parents' home across the street
                 In old Ferrara, came a family
                 Exiled from Florence for opposing your
                 Medici: yes, you've guessed: the Strozzi clan.
                 Roberto Strozzi's daughter with dark eyes
                 Stared at me from the window opposite
                 As I was shaving—those winding streets are
                     narrow—
                 And there she was, so close we nearly touched.
                 I fell in love. We walked. A servant whispered
                 To me that she was illegitimate.
                 Imagine my disgust! I fought it down,
                 Obsessively in love: forgave her all!
                 Even the fact her mother was not hers!
                 Two months I wrote a letter every day;
                 Composed her songs: Laudomia's silken hair!
                 She never wrote back, but we now linked hands
                 And laughed, held buttercups under our chins
                 To find each other's tastes. I bought new
                     clothes
                 Gorgeous as those St. Francis shrugged before
                 He ran to God. One day, high on Ferrara's
                 Ramparts, the air was soft. I played her song.
                 Laudomia smiled, and looked so beautiful
                 I asked her to marry me. She froze in pride;

And said the noble Strozzi could not think
Of marriage with the lower Savonarolas,
Grandchildren of a doctor! From that day
I've never looked upon a woman's face
With joy.[48]

It is in the absence of love and joy from his vision that
Savonarola is most fundamentally at odds with Lorenzo and
his circle. For him there can be no possibility that our sense
perceptions of this world might be a channel to the apprehension of the divine. For Savonarola this world is no more
attractive

> In its sucked sweetmeat decadence and sin
> Than a dead horse strawed in a stable yard.

Savonarola's impassioned sermon in Act Two Scene Nine is a
whirlwind of loveless moral invective. He can envisage love
only in perverted or squalid forms, can understand only
desire and never aspiration. All balance has gone. His world
is a world of all-surrounding sexual traps:

> Look, mothers! how you trick up your fresh girls
> As nymphs brought out to parade this Cathedral
> And taunt men's eyes on cattle-market day . . .
> I call a curse on nudity today,
> Whatever form or shape—statue, or glass,
> Goldwork or ceiling—it may contaminate.
> Lascivious pictures lead to amorous thoughts,
> Thoughts on to actions, actions toss to Hell! . . .
> Great ladies beg the brothels should be closed.
> What? Are you jealous? But I say to you
> Fat kine of Bashan who oppress the poor,
> First take the jewelled beam out of your eye!
> Your wanton, proud extravagance of clothes,
> Your faces rubbed with paint, your charcoaled eyes,
> Your dyed hairs, opened arms, seek to ensnare
> Priests and young monks in love-nests, poisoned,
>   perfumed
> Houses of sin . . .
>   Lust contaminates
> All things.

His orgy of 'purification' seeks to make of Florence 'the New Jerusalem, / Destined inheritor of mighty Rome!'. Florence is to be 'the city ruled by Christ' and the 'vanities' must be burnt to make her ready. To such as Doffo Spini Savonarola is a man without 'civilizing taste / Or style'. He and his followers are

> Grey hypocrites who bleat eternal Lent,
> And forget Christ was once a wedding-guest.

He lacks, that is, the proper understanding of ceremony that would make him a fitting citizen of the Laurentian Florence in which Doffo Spini has grown up.

In *Living Creation* Lorenzo and Savonarola meet only once—at Lorenzo's death-bed in Act Two Scene Thirteen. We have two conflicting accounts of the encounter between the two just prior to Lorenzo's death. One is in a letter from Poliziano to his friend Jacopo Antiquario of Perugia. According to Poliziano, Savonarola came to offer moral counsel to Lorenzo. He exhorted him to hold fast to his Christian faith, to resolve upon a good life if he recovered, and to resign himself to death if that were God's will. Lorenzo responded as a good Christian to all three exhortations, and asked Savonarola for a parting blessing. Savonarola recited the prayers for the dying, and Lorenzo devoutly joined in the responses. Poliziano's letter contains some interesting human details. Given a potion of pulverized diamonds and pearls by the physician Lazaro of Pavia, and asked how it tasted, Lorenzo replied 'as things usually taste to a dying man'. Poliziano also records Lorenzo's expression of regret that he had not lived long enough to complete the libraries he had begun to assemble. According, however, to two early biographers of Savonarola, Cinozzi and Burlamacchi,[49] the encounter between Lorenzo and Savonarola was somewhat different in tone and outcome. They suggest that the dying Lorenzo was full of remorse—especially for his part in the sack of Volterra, the alterations he had made in the Dower Fund, and for the fierceness with which he had punished the participants in the Pazzi conspiracy. Lorenzo demanded Savonarola's presence to hear his confession, say these accounts, because he was the only 'true' religious he

knew. Savonarola declared three conditions which Lorenzo
must fulfil before Savonarola would grant him absolution.
Lorenzo must declare his faith in God, must make restitution
of all goods and property that he had wrongly appropriated,
and must restore to the people of Florence the liberty of
which he had deprived them. At the third of these demands
Lorenzo silently turned his back upon Savonarola, who left
the room without giving Lorenzo absolution. A few hours
later, says this account, Lorenzo died tortured by his unfor-
given sins and by the prospect of Hell. There seems little
reason to regard most of this as anything more than the
distortions of propaganda (though it is hard to see that
Savonarola would emerge from the episode with much credit
even if this account were true). Warner, though, has found it
useful to conflate elements from both accounts in his version
of Lorenzo's death. He has also borrowed from the chronicle
of Bartolommeo Cerretani (and transferred to Ficino) an
incident in which a Camaldulensian friar took off his spectacles and placed them to the lips of Lorenzo to confirm that he
was still alive.[50] In *Living Creation* (as in Poliziano's account
of proceedings) Lorenzo had already been confessed, by his
own confessor, before Savonarola's arrival:

SAVONAROLA Lorenzo.
LORENZO   Prior.
SAVONAROLA   Have you confessed? Been shriven?
                         Received the Host, God's Body? How did it
                              taste?
LORENZO   As all things do inside a dying mouth,
                     Even the latch-key to eternity.

Of Lorenzo's supposed causes for remorse we hear of only
one, the sack of Volterra. Savonarola is perhaps more sympathetic than one might have expected in his observations:

SAVONAROLA You say the sack of Volterra still haunts
                     Your conscience.
LORENZO   So it does! Oh God.
SAVONAROLA   It was
                     Milanese mercenaries, not yourself,
                     Whose bloodlust burst and could not be
                         controlled.

Savonarola's 'three questions' are here. Lorenzo affirms his faith in God and recognizes that his handling of the Dower Fund has been unsatisfactory—especially so insofar as his behaviour has opposed that very spirit of love so central to his own philosophy:

> My pain
> Has been so great I have neglected, passed
> Without full opposition, those sad laws
> That snatch young wedding from the lips of love
> And force her into poverty and vice.

His response to Savonarola's third question departs from the 'evidence' offered by Cinozzi and Burlamacchi:

SAVONAROLA   Will you restore the city's liberties?
LORENZO   Like Cicero, there are two things I wish:
                   That I may leave all Florentines in peace
                   And liberty, when I discard this corpse;
                   And that each citizen may hold the chance
                   To help our common good in self-respecting
                   Trade or occupation.
                   POLIZIANO *and* FICINO *enter*.
                                   Come, my friends.
                   Yes; there's a third: I wish that creeping death
                   Had spared me to complete your libraries.
                   My star is setting. No tears. Will you read
                   The Last Words of our Lord and Christ to me?

Savonarola does so, and Warner's account thus ends with nothing of the fierce divisiveness that characterizes the narratives of Savonarola's biographers. We should notice that Warner's Lorenzo dies with the worlds of classical thought and Christian faith still reconciled in his mind. He alludes to Cicero, but his final action is to kiss the crucifix.

With Lorenzo's death an era comes to an end, the springtime is unmistakably succeeded by winter. Botticelli observes with pain that

> Now begin the troubles of Italy.[51]

Vasari described the days of Lorenzo as 'a veritable golden age for men of genius'.[52] The two years following Lorenzo's death saw an extraordinary series of deaths amongst men of influence and genius. Botticelli, in the final scene of *Living Creation*, communicates something of the period's horror:

> Now a vast sense of loss
> Crowds in between my ears, plentiful being
> Rotting away in grossest negligence.
> A Florentine is like a crucifix
> Thrown among devils, also Florentines.
> Domenico my friend dies of the plague.
> Angelo Poliziano's dead;
> With Pico, poisoned. All my world has passed.

In a fascinating article, 'Death and Politian', Juliana Hill catalogues some 21 deaths in this period—Lorenzo himself, Innocent VIII, Domenico Ghirlandaio, Ferrante I of Naples, Politian, Gian Galeazzo Sforza, Pico della Mirandola, Matteo Maria Boiardo and many others. Of the 13 deaths for which she can suggest a cause, she attributes some five to poisoning and another three to plague. It is hardly surprising that she should write that

> Vendetta, conspiracy, murder, pestilence, fanaticism, war, invasion and sudden, unexpected death—these were the circumstances of Politian's life, and the violent background against which the normal generation of his contemporaries struggled to survive.
>
> Death is indeed the symbol of this violent age which is said to have inaugurated the Renaissance and which culminated in 1494, 'the horrible year of the French invasion' when the sermons of Savonarola vociferated the doom not only of Florence but of all Italy.[53]

It has been the burden of *Living Creation* that human creativity can—must—assert itself in the face of such circumstances. The central statement of the play has an obvious relevance some five hundred years after the death of Lorenzo.

Botticelli had been a leading spirit of the springtime of Lorenzo's Florence. Paintings such as the 'Birth of Venus' and the 'Primavera' speak eloquently of the very essence of that time of vitality and beauty, and its delicate balance of sense and spirit. His 'Mars and Venus' effects a magical union of human and mythical, his 'Pallas and the Centaur' translates political reality into the highest art. Now, in his 'vast sense of loss', he turns elsewhere for a vision that might sustain him. To what extent Botticelli ever became a fully committed follower of Savonarola must remain a matter of some debate. Ronald M. Steinberg has offered arguments for doubting the certainty with which many earlier accounts concluded that the painter was an enthusiastic and whole-hearted follower, that he was 'openly an ardent *piagnone* or ultra-religious supporter of Savonarola'.[54] Steinberg believes that the evidence allows us to go no further than the suggestion that

Botticelli obviously knew of Savonarola (which certainly is to be expected), and for an unknown length of time, to an unknown degree, and for unknown reasons, he may even have been interested in Savonarola (which is also to be expected).[55]

Warner's Botticelli is too open and receptive a spirit to make any dogmatic rejection of Savonarola. Act Two Scene Nine opens with an exchange between Botticelli and Ghirlandaio:

DOMENICO   All right! We disagree. That man is evil:
              An enemy to beauty and to God!
SANDRO   But say he's right?
              Enter SAVONAROLA.
SAVONAROLA   Look steadily at life!
              You two have power to lead the eye astray,
              Domenico and Sandro—image makers.

In the following scene Sandro discusses the friar with the hot-headed Doffo Spini but refuses to be swept up in the heat of his passion:

You know . . . I am slow to take up sides,
Though loyal once I have. Please give me time
To learn more of this man.

These conversations take place before the deaths of Lorenzo and Savonarola. We next see Botticelli talking to Doffo Spini after the execution of Savonarola:

SANDRO	Why did you do it—you and your companions?
DOFFO SPINI	Ah, Sandro. Do you know, if I had been

Closer acquainted with the burning friar,
I might have been a greater devotee
Than you! Because we are old friends, I'll say
What happened—but you keep it to yourself!
Benozzo Federighi was the cause,
Not I; and if we had released the friar—
Sent him back to San Marco (for the truth
Is, we could find no fault at all in him)—
The predatory mob would soon have sacked
The city, and—God knows!—we should have been,
Each of us, cut in pieces!

This short scene (Act Two Scene Seventeen) is not Warner's invention. Horne's study of Botticelli includes a passage from the 'Chronicle' of Simone Filipepi (brother of the painter):

I will here below copy out a record which I made on the 2nd November, 1499. Alessandro di Mariano Filipepi, my brother, one of the good painters which our city has had in these times, related in my presence, being at home, by the fire, about the third hour of the night, [*i.e.*, about eight o'clock in the evening,] how on that day, in his workshop, in the house of Sandro, he had been discoursing with Doffo Spini, about the case of Fra Girolamo. And in effect, upon Sandro questioning him, (because he knew that the said Doffo had been one of the chief persons who had always been chosen to examine him,) that he should tell him the plain truth as to what faults they found in Fra Girolamo, by which he deserved to die so infamous a death; whereat Doffo then replied to him: 'Sandro, have I to tell you the truth? Not only did we never find in him mortal sin; but, moreover, neither was venial sin found in him.' Then Sandro said to him: 'Wherefore did you cause him to die in so infamous a fashion?' He replied: 'Not I, but Benozzo Federighi was the cause of it. And if this prophet and his companions had not been put to death, and had they been sent back to San Marco, the people would have put us to sack, and we should all have been cut to pieces. The matter had so far gone forward, that thus we determined for our safety, that they should die'.[56]

Another passage from the same 'Chronicle' records Doffo as
saying that

he never had any intercourse with Fra Girolamo until he was put in
prison . . . and that had he heard Fra Girolamo before that time,
and been acquainted with him, as Simone here (turning to me) I
should have been a greater partisan of his than Simone; because
nothing except good was then seen of him until his death; but his
case had gone forward in such sort, that it needs must have been
done to him, as was done to Christ.[57]

In *Living Creation* the exchange with Doffo Spini perhaps
matters, not so much for what it tells us about the degree of
Botticelli's adherence to Savonarola's views, as for the way it
forces upon the painter the realization that this is no longer
the Florence he had known. It is a Florence imbued with
neither the vision of Lorenzo nor of Savonarola; it is a
Florence of timorous expediency. That is the note upon
which the final scene of the play begins.

Earlier scenes of the play have shown us a Botticelli whose
imagination spoke the language of Ficino's, Poliziano's and
Lorenzo's vision of the world. Now it is Savonarola's vision
which informs his creative imagination. Amongst the paintings of Botticelli there are two which seem to be most
thoroughly influenced by the iconography of Savonarola's
thought. These are the 'Crucifixion', sometimes referred to
as the 'Mystic Crucifixion' or 'Magdalen at the Foot of the
Cross' (in the Fogg Museum of Art, Harvard University) and
the so-called 'Mystic Nativity' (in the National Gallery,
London). In *Living Creation* Botticelli's speeches in the final
scene of the play are accompanied by on-stage projections of
these two paintings. The 'Magdalen at the Foot of the Cross'
may well be, as Horne suggests, the work of Botticelli's
studio rather than of Botticelli himself. The composition is
simple and striking, its full significance enigmatic. At its
centre is Christ upon the cross. In the left foreground,
embracing the foot of the cross, is Mary Magdalen; to the
right is a standing angel who is holding an animal in the air,
by a hind leg, which he appears to be striking with a rod.

Behind the angel are dark clouds and flames. On the left of
the picture is a view of Florence; immediately above it is a
clear, light sky and above that a circle of light in which is
seated God offering his blessing, an open book in front of
him. Just below the figure of God white shields bearing red
crosses appear to fall through the sky. The painting evidently
relates to one or more passages in the writings and sermons of
Savonarola. One parallel, suggested by Horne, is with Savonarola's vision of the *Crux irae Dei*, a vision described in his
Compendio delle Rivelazioni:

While preaching in San Lorenzo during Lent of 1492, I saw, on the
night of Holy Friday, two crosses. The first was black and in the
middle of Rome; its top touched the heavens and its arms extended
over all the land, and above it was written these words: CRUX
IRAE DEI. Immediately that this appeared the weather became
disturbed; clouds came flying through the air bringing winds, and
hurling lightning and arrows, and it rained hail, fire and swords,
and killed a great number of people so that few remained on earth.
After this came a time of serenity and clear skys and another cross
was seen. This was golden, as high as the first, and was above
Jerusalem. It was so resplendent that it lit all the world, and above
it was written: CRUX MISERICORDIAE DEI, and all the generations of men and women from all parts of the world came and
adored it and embraced it.[58]

Horne interprets the painting as a representation of the first
of these two crosses, with Florence replacing Rome. The
Magdalen is an image of the repentant soul, embracing the
crucifix for protection against God's wrath. The animal
Horne identifies as a fox, an emblem of vice, relating it to the
fox in the Song of Solomon (2.15) which destroys the vine-
yard. Some later interpreters have added to and amended
Horne's views.[59] The prostrate figure has been identified as
not only the Magdalen, but Florence itself. It has been
pointed out that white shields emblazoned with crosses were
the standard symbol of the Guelfs. The angel's beating of the
animal has been taken to represent the castigation of Florence for its sins. From the robe of the 'Magdalen' there can
be seen emerging a small, fierce-looking animal with its teeth

bared. Is this perhaps a wolf, symbol of those who persecute the church? Other passages in Savonarola's sermons, while not explaining every detail of the picture, make it clear that the painting is a visual re-statement of Savonarola's frequently repeated prophecy of that renovation of the church which would be preceded by the castigation of Florence and Italy. Botticelli has found in the prophecies of Savonarola a 'myth' which will give meaning and shape to his 'sense of loss', to the death and destruction which has replaced the creative energy of Lorenzo's Florence:

> All my world has passed.
> (*Slide of 'Magdalen at the Foot of the Cross'*)
> And falling shields red-blazoned with a cross
> Show the Divine wrath striking down Florence.
> An angry angel holds the fox, Deceit,
> That spoils all vines of peace, and devils hurl
> Brands burning to the earth. Ah, Christ! Look on
> Our utter waste of all your loveliness,
> And, prostrate, let us cling beneath your feet
> With Magdalen.

A vivacious Albiera had opened the play. It is a subdued Albiera who closes the play with Sandro, reporting that

> Death is rife.
> Officers went into the hospitals
> This morning, and drove out all those with plague.
> They put a pulley on a rope outside
> The Arte de Corazzai, just to hang
> Any who might return into the city.
> It is a brutal and harsh remedy.

Against a background of such events, in the context of the French invasion of Italy, and under the influence of Savonarola's prophecies, it is hardly surprising that Botticelli's imagination should have become increasingly apocalyptical in his later years. The 'Mystic Nativity', for example, clearly interprets the events of the Nativity and the Adoration of the Shepherds in the terms of Fra Girolamo's prophetic interpretation of Italian history. The painting bears, across its head, an inscription in uncial Greek. Horne translates it as follows:

This picture, at the end of the year 1500, in the troubles of Italy, I, Alessandro, painted in the half-time after the time, at the time of the fulfilment of the 11th of St.John, in the second war of the Apocalypse, in the loosing of the devil for three and a half years: then he shall be chained according to the twelfth, and we shall see him trodden down as in this picture.[60]

We need not set about the elucidation of the inscription's (and the painting's) enigmas. In general terms it is probably sufficient to say that Botticelli's painting is intended as an image of the new birth of Christ, that renovation of the Church prophesied by Savonarola. Horne describes it, with much justice, as 'the most spiritual, perhaps, and certainly one of the most lovely and imaginative of all Botticelli's works'.[61] As the slide-projection of this picture overlooks the last moments of Botticelli's life, in *Living Creation*, the painter explains the human significance its subject has for him:

> For me the stable child at Bethlehem,
> Hope of the homeless, outcast, and the cold,
> Rejected, and the afraid, blows through my thoughts,
> Stirring my dying brush across the paint.

Though he has found another 'vision', he has lost his earlier capacity to find in this world those images of the divine that Ficino had earlier spoken of in reflecting upon 'The Birth of Venus':

> Beauty is divine.
> We worship God in things he has created
> So we can later worship things in God.
> At one with our own innocent Idea
> We reach full life, and seem in loving God
> To love ourselves.

Now Botticelli can see nothing save the dreadful transience of things:

When the trees' tousled hair rustles with dawn,
And rough ship's rigging's whispered through by
    ghosts
Who whistle in key-holes, moan down chimney-breasts,
When the high morning star has banished night,
Unveiling all the brightness of new day,
The East wind falls, and streaked clouds hint of rain,
And shells, those varied footprints of the waves,
Scatter across the sprawled and beaten sand,
See, there is nothing left unshakeable,
Solid, or lasting. Burn all I have sketched!
The iron bar of conscience bends to gold;
Hard gold relaxes when seduced by heat;
Slight gunpowder can turn a king to dust,
And summer's breath fails with a little frost.
My whole life has been wasted.
(Destroys sketchbook)
                    All my paintings
Burn, that are not Christ's: for what is art,
And innate taste that cannot be acquired,
When man, the triumph of creation, turns
Into a jackal?

Botticelli, in his grief, can only reject this world. In Act One
Lorenzo found comfort for, and some relief from, his grief
through the surrounding images of mutability. Retaining his
power to look upon and discover meaning in this world he
felt, finally, no need to reject it. In Act One Scene Sixteen
ceremony again clarifies experience and asserts meaning.
Albiera, Salvestra, and Marietta—the three 'graces' of
Botticelli's painting—are brought, by Domenico, to Lorenzo as he mourns his brother and considers the aftermath of
the Pazzi conspiracy:

DOMENICO   Three girls outside, with life picked from the
                 fields,
             Ask leave to lay their pity at your feet.
LORENZO   *(Looking out of the window at mob)*
             We must restrain, hold back our active friends.
             Forgiveness, too, is tragic, as it springs
             From heartbreak; we are men, not gods: but
                 thanks,
             To you, and all. Yes! Let kind beauty in.

Enter MARIETTA, ALBIERA, SALVES-
TRA; FICINO *behind.*

MARIETTA	Lilies, blossom of Medici oranges;
ALBIERA	Anemones for short-lived happiness;
SALVESTRA	And violets, the tears of Lent, for grief;
MARIETTA	These April gifts increasing day exchanges
ALBIERA	For Winter's dark and seeming endlessness.
SALVESTRA	Brief was the cornflower crown in laurel leaf.
LORENZO	All things that grow upon the the fruitful earth

Must die. The uncontainable's enclosed.
Those aspirations are confined, foreclosed,
That brighten and idealize our birth.
The furthest reaches naked thought, in mirth,
Explores round circling heaven, or hell
    exposed,
Creation's joy, all that we had supposed
Possible, lies in soil—one sunflower's worth.

Lorenzo's grief is contained—it finds expression in a sonnet (inverted because Lorenzo's emotional world has been turned upside-down, but a sonnet nevertheless) spontaneously shared between four speakers (the first rhyme of the sonnet is 'oranges', the last 'worth'). Warner had made earlier use of the same technique of inversion in the sixth poem of *Morning Vespers*. The artistic form survives and consoles, art's ceremonies implicitly affirm the enduring presence of meaning and order in this world, however immediately powerful the sense of grief and loss. Botticelli, on the other hand, destroys his sketchbooks and wants all his paintings burnt that 'are not Christ's'. Now Botticelli experiences this world only in terms of 'life's chains' from which he seeks release in death. He has lost the capacity to find in the mutable world a language that speaks articulately of human significance. He can find meaning in God alone. Again, the contrast can be pointed up by comparison with the sonnet we have just considered. The language of the flower-bearing girls is the symbolic language of Botticelli's own 'Primavera', deeply rooted in the traditions of symbolic thought, a means both of joying in and transcending this world.[62] Unable any longer to share such a vision, having lost the capacity to 'see' in the sense that Ficino had earlier elaborated, the dying

Botticelli can only elect to turn away from living creation and towards his creator. The great painter chooses to close his eyes:

> See how the hawk towers the highest sky,
> Views the vast earth, while somewhere, far below,
> One speck, its trainer, waits; decides, in joy,
> To leave limitless freedom and return
> Down to the wrist from which it flew? A girl,
> Grown into woman, of her own free will,
> Visits her grandfather? So let me choose
> To close my eyes, released from all life's chains,
> And walk into the outstretched hands of God.

Like so many of the other works discussed earlier in this study, *Living Creation's* concern is with the survival or otherwise—personal or historical—of a way of seeing and knowing, perhaps, finally, of loving, which so much in the world seems to threaten and darken. The work of Francis Warner lies outside the mainstream of contemporary poetry. It is more deeply and fully traditional than most contemporary work. Its roots are in the Bible and Plato, in Renaissance forms of thought and expression; it is not, though, the work of a writer ignorant of the difficulties and dangers of the contemporary world. In the face of those dangers, in full awareness of their horror, it seeks still to assert with Shelley that

> The One remains, the many change and pass;
> Heaven's light forever shines, Earth's shadows fly;
> Life, like a dome of many-coloured glass,
> Stains the white radiance of Eternity.[63]

Notes

LYRICS

1 *Acumen*, 3, (1986), pp.73-4.
2 *Collected Poems of Sir Thomas Wyatt*, ed.K. Muir, 1949, p.92.
3 *Ibid.*, pp.49-51. The repetition is less complete in 'Suffryng in sorrow in hope to attayn'.
4 *Ibid.*, p.3.
5 *Ibid.*, p.21.
6 *Ibid.*, p.174.
7 Many of Davenport's best essays are collected in his volume *The Geography of the Imagination*, 1984.
8 *Ibid.*, pp.21-22, 334.
9 *Early Poems*, 1964, p.5.
10 Faerie Queene, III, VI, 47, 5.
11 'Sonnet', *Collected Poems*, p.105.
12 'Song', *Collected Poems*, p.28.
13 'A Definition', *Collected Poems*, p.105.
14 'Sonnet', *Collected Poems*, p.123.
15 'Impromptu', *Collected Poems*, p.104.
16 'For Penny and Robin Hodgkinson', *Collected Poems*, p.209.
17 Donne, *The Elegies and the Songs and Sonnets*, ed.H.Gardner, 1965, p.61.
18 Quoted from *English Madrigal Verse, 1588-1632* ed. E.H.Fellowes, revised and enlarged by F.W.Sternfeld and D.Greer, 1967, p.490. Warner quotes this lyric in his essay 'The Poetry of James Joyce', in *James Joyce: An International Perspective*, ed. S.Bushrui and B.Benstock, 1982.
19 See R.T.Davies, ed., *Medieval English Lyrics*, 1963, p.204. See also Davies' appendix of Types and Titles of the Virgin Mary, pp.371-8.
20 *The Song of Songs* IV.12.

PASTORAL, ELEGY AND EPITHALAMIUM

1 See Suheil Bushrui, 'The Poetry' in *Francis Warner. Poet and Dramatist*, ed. T. Prentki, 1977, pp.110-11.
2 See, for example, J.H. Hanford, 'The Pastoral Elegy and Milton's *Lycidas*', *PMLA*, XXV, 1910; T.P. Harrison, Jr., *The Pastoral Elegy*, 1939.
3 Mary Strickland, 'A true experience', *Cambridge Town Crier*, Feb. 1st, 1986, p.9.

4 Quoted from *The Idylls of Theocritus and the Eclogues of Virgil*, translated by C.S. Calverley, 1908, p.7, and from *Lycidas*, lines 50-1, p.167. Quotations from Milton are from *The Poetical Works of John Milton*, ed. H. Darbishire, 1958.

5 There seems here to be an echo of Coleridge's lines 'On Donne's Poetry':

> With Donne, whose muse on dromedary trots,
> Wreathe Iron pokers into true-love knots;
> Rhyme's sturdy cripple, fancy's maze and clue,
> Wit's forge and fire-blast, meaning's press and screw.

Certainly Coleridge's is an important presence in other areas of the poem.

6 *Lycidas*, 25-38.

7 The text of *Plainsong* in *Collected Poems* reads 'A cart-truck runs'; this is presumably a printer's error. In *Early Poems* and *Poetry of Francis Warner* the line reads 'A cart-track runs' which clearly makes better sense.

8 Josephine Miles, 'The Primary Language of *Lycidas*', in *Milton's Lycidas. The Tradition and the Poem*, ed. C.A. Patrides, 1961, p.97.

9 In their excellent *London Book of English Verse* (2nd revised edition, 1952), Read and Dobrée devote one section to what they call the 'symphonic poem'—poems marked by 'the complexity of the emotions or ideas to be expressed, and the imperative need of comprehending a diversity of emotional responses within a single artistic form', p.xii.

10 Suheil Bushrui has previously pointed to the influence of this poem upon the tenth of Warner's *Experimental Sonnets*. See Chapter Four.

11 Coleridge, 'Dejection: An Ode', 47-49, 67-69.

12 *Matthew 24, Mark 13*.

13 *Cambridge Town Crier*, Feb.1st, 1986, p.9.

14 e.g., *Job* 37.9, 38.1, 40.6; *Isaiah* 40.24; *Jeremiah* 23.19; *Zechariah* 7.14.

15 *Op.cit.*, pp.115-16.

16 D. O'Brien, *Empedocles' Cosmic Cycle. A Reconstruction from the Fragments and Secondary Sources*, 1969.

17 *Ibid.*, p.1.

18 Fragment 8, translated by C.M. Bakewell, *Source Book in Ancient Philosophy*, 1907, p.43.

19 Fragments 11 and 12, translated by G.S.Kirk and J.E.Raven, *The PreSocratic Philosophers*, 1957, p.323.

20 Fragment 17.

21 K.Freeman, *The Pre-Socratic Philosophers*, 1946, p.184.

22 See my *Francis Warner and Tradition*, 1981, pp.23-5.

23 The same poem is echoed in *Meeting Ends*. See my *Francis Warner and Tradition*, p.179 (note 21).

24 *Englands Helicon*, ed. H. Macdonald, 1949, p.192.

25 *Ibid.*, p.194.

26 *The Poetical Works of Robert Herrick*, ed. F.W. Moorman, 1921, pp.190-1.
27 *Poems of Charles Cotton*, ed. J.Buxton, 1958, pp.41-3.
28 *Poems of John Clare's Madness*, ed. G.Grigson, 1949, p.130. (Only the first two stanzas are quoted.) (A happier variation on the same original is to be found in 'The Invitation', Grigson, p.163.).
29 *Collected Poems*, 1954, pp.139-40. The poem (of which I have omitted the final stanza) appeared in *A Time to Dance* (1935).
30 Herrick, *ed.cit.*, p.35.
31 *Amanda* (1653). Quoted from *A Treasury of Seventeenth Century English Verse*, ed. H.J. Massingham, 1919, p.144.
32 Kathleen Raine, 'Poetry in relation to Traditional Wisdom', The Guild of Pastoral Psychology, 1958, p.17.
33 *Poetry of Francis Warner*, 1970, p.10.
34 *e.g.*, A.K.Hieatt, *Short Time's Endless Monument*, 1960; 'The Daughters of Horus: Order in the Stanzas of *Epithalamion*' in *Form and Convention in the Poetry of Edmund Spenser*, ed. W. Nelson, 1961; E.Welsford, ed., *Spenser: Fowre Hymnes and Epithalamion*, 1967; A.Fowler, *Triumphal Forms*, 1970.
35 *Triumphal Forms*, ed.cit., p.148.
36 *Opera Omnia*, Basel, 1573, I, 10.
37 Douglas Brooks, *Number and Pattern in the Eighteenth-Century Novel*, 1973, p.169. See also Pietro Bongo, *Numerorum mysteria*, 1599, p.501.
38 J.C.Cooper, *An Illustrated Encyclopaedia of Traditional Symbols*, 1978, p.120.
39 *Triumphal Forms*, ed.cit., pp.151-4.
40 *Ibid.*, p.159. Though he makes no appearance, Pico is an important off-stage presence in *Living Creation* (e.g. Act II, Scenes 13 and 18).
41 Cooper, *op.cit.*p.118.
42 *Martianus Capella and the Seven Liberal Arts.Vol.II: The Marriage of Philology and Mercury*, translated by W.H. Stahl, R. Johnson, E.L. Burge, 1977, p.284.
43 *Living Creation*, 1985, p.38.
44 Spenser, *Epithalamion*, 433.

PERENNIA

1 On the debate about this term see, *inter alia*, W.Allen, Jr., 'The Epyllion: A Chapter in the History of Literary Criticism', *Transactions and Proceedings of the American Philological Association*, LXXI, 1940; J.F. Reilly, 'Origins of the Word "Epyllion"', *Classical Journal*, XLIX, 1953-4; V.d'Agostino, 'Considerazioni sull' epillio', *Rivista si studi classici*, 4, 1956; P.Miller.'The Elizabethan Minor Epic', *Studies in Philology*, LV, 1958; W.Allen, Jr., 'The Non-Existent Classical Epyllion', Studies in Philology, LV, 1958.
2 M.M.Crump, *The Epyllion from Theocritus to Ovid*, 1931.

3   E.S.Donno's *Elizabethan Minor Epics*, 1963, is a very useful collection of such Elizabethan (and seventeenth-century) epyllia.

4   See J.Swahn, *The Tale of Cupid and Psyche*, Lund, 1955; G.Megas, *Das Märchen von Amor und Psyche in der griechischen Volksüberlieferung*, Athens, 1971; J.Wright, 'Folk-tale and literary Technique in Cupid and Psyche', *Classical Quarterly*, 21, 1971; D.Fehling, *Amor und Psyche*, Mainz, 1977; A.Scobie, *Apuleius and Folklore*, 1983.

5   See, for example, Andrew Lang, *Custom and Myth*, revised edition, 1885, pp.64-86.

6   Carl C. Schlam, *Cupid and Psyche. Apuleius and the Monuments*, Pennsylvania, 1976.

7   Robert Southey and S.T. Coleridge, *Omniana, or Horae Otiosores*, ed. R. Gittings, 1969, p.83.

8   See E.J.Brzenk, 'Pater and Apuleius', *Comparative Literature*, 10, 1958; P.Turner, 'Pater and Apuleius', *Victorian Studies*, 3, 1960.

9   See E.Visser, 'Louis Couperus and Apuleius', in *Aspects of Apuleius' Golden Ass*, ed. B.L.Hijmans, Jr., and R.Th. van der Paardt, 1978.

10 Many other versions are discussed in E.H. Haight, *Apuleius and His Influence*, 1927.

11 *Faerie Queene*, III.VI.50.

12 Conveniently available in Volume 2 of George Saintsbury's *Minor Poets of the Caroline Period*, 1906.

13 Edited by R.Helm, 1898. Fulgentius' discussion of Cupid and Psyche begins on page 66.

14 *ed.cit.*, p.9.

15 I have quoted from the version printed in *Thomas Taylor the Platonist*, edited by Kathleen Raine and George Mills Harper, 1969, pp.427-35. The preface to this volume explains that 'the book is an offspring of the Yeats International Summer School'—of which Warner was, for many years, the Assistant Director. See 'Candlesmoke' (*Collected Poems*, p.32).

16 Lucius Apuleius, *The Golden Asse*, Adlington's translation (1566), 1933, p.89.

17 *Ibid.*, p.93.

18 *Ibid.*, p.94.

19 In the first edition of *Perennia* (1962), and in the texts of the poem contained in *Early Poems* (1964) and *The Poetry of Francis Warner* (1970), this oak is described as 'ivy-covered'. The 'ivy-coloured' of the *Collected Poems* is presumably a printer's error. In stanza LV the 'Give' of the text in the *Collected Poems* is likewise a corruption of 'Gave' in earlier texts of the poem.

20 Apuleius, *ed cit.*, p.95.

21 *Ibid.*, p.95.

22 Longus, *Daphnis and Chloe*, Thornley's translation (1657), Introduction by George Saintsbury, 1933, pp.42-3.

23 Apuleius, *ed.cit.*, p.91.

24 The influence of Apuleius upon Blake's own work is discussed in Chapter 7, 'Blake's Cupid and Psyche' of Volume 1 of Kathleen Raine's *Blake and Tradition*, 1969.

25 Though there are no direct verbal echoes, these verses are reminiscent of *Isaiah* 11.6-8.

26 Apuleius, *ed.cit.*, p.102.

27 Raine and Harper, *op.cit.*, p.431.

28 Apuleius, *ed.cit.*, p.107.

29 *Ibid.*, p.107.

30 See *Light Shadows*, 1980, p.53; *Living Creation*, 1985, p.41.

31 See Michael J.B. Allen, *Marsilio Ficino and the Phaedran Charioteer*, 1981.

32 *Phaedrus*, translated by J.Wright. Quoted from *Five Dialogues of Plato bearing on Poetic Inspiration*, ed. A.D.Lindsay, 1910, p.231.

33 *Ibid.*, p.241.

34 *Ibid.*, p.241.

35 Warner's lines on the plunging and rearing of the black horse are based on Socrates' account. Apuleius himself may well have been influenced by the same passage. See Gertrude C. Drake, 'Candidus, A Unifying Theme in Apuleius' Metamorphoses', *Classical Journal*, 64, 1968.

36 Salacia's dream seems not to be *Perennia's* only debt to the *Phaedrus*. The prophetic oak-tree of stanza XXIII may well be indebted to *Phaedrus* 275B. Bearing in mind the setting of *Perennia*, it is also interesting to note the following passage: 'This is a glorious resting-place.For the plane-tree I find is thick and spreading . . . how delicious too is this spring trickling under the plane-tree . . . it would seem . . . that the place is sacred to some nymphs and river-god . . . summer-like and clear there rings an answer to the choir of the cicadas', translated by Wright, *ed.cit.*, p.209.

37 Apuleius, *ed.cit.*, p.115.

38 *Ibid.*

39 *Ibid.*

40 *Ibid.*

41 *Ibid.*, p.117.

42 *Ibid.*

43 Chaucer, *The Second Nun's Tale*, 515. All of Perennia's tasks have models in folklore. See Stith Thompson, *Motif-Index of Folk Literature*, revised edition, 1956, Vol.III, H.1118, 1333, 1511.

44 Apuleius, *ed.cit.*, pp.119-20.

45 *Ibid.*, p.121.

46 *Ed.cit.*, pp.59-60.

47 *Comus*, 1002-1011. Quoted from *The Poetical Works of John Milton*, ed. H. Darbishire, 1948, p.485.

48 Raine and Harper, *op.cit.*, p.433.

49 *Il Penseroso*, 139-54. Quoted from Darbishire, *op.cit.*, pp.427-8.

50 Kathleen Raine, *Collected Poems 1935-1980*, p.37. Originally published in *The Year One*, 1952.

51 Versions of the Three Graces are a feature of Warner's plays. Agappy, Wrasse and Callisterne in *Meeting Ends* are one version of the motif; Albiera, Salvestra and Marietta are another in *Living Creation*. Ficino himself is, of course, an important character in the same play.

52 Edgar Wind, *Pagan Mysteries in the Renaissance*, revised edition, 1967, pp.46-7.

53 *Ibid.*, pp.47-8.

BEYOND THE CLASSICAL

1 *The Life and Letters of William Cowper*, ed. William Hayley, 1835, p.172-3. Cowper was writing in 1783.

2 Thomas Fuller, *The History of the Worthies of England*, ed.J.Nicholls, 1811, Vol.I, p.177.

3 F.M. Prestcott, *Mary Tudor*, revised edition, 1952, p.165 ff.

4 *The Victoria History of the Counties of England. A History of the County of Cambridge and the Isle of Ely*, ed. A.P.M. Wright, Vol.VI, 1978, p.251.

5 Biography by D.F.Corcos, in *The History of Parliament. The House of Commons*, 1509-1558, ed. S.T. Bindoff, Vol.II, 1982, pp.401-3.

6 The stanzas are quoted in *The Chronicle of Queen Jane, And of Two Years of Queen Mary*, ed. J.G. Nichols, 1850, p.2.

7 See, for example, G.D. Zimmermann, *Irish Political Street Ballads and Rebel Songs*, Geneva, 1966.

8 Both are included in *The Common Muse*, ed. V. de Sola Pinto and A.E.Rodway, 1957.

9 *Ibid.*, p.187.

10 A.J.Peacock, *Bread or Blood. A Study of the Agrarian Riots in East Anglia in 1816*, 1965. A lively narrative of events can be found in C.Johnson's *The Ely and Littleport Riots, With an Account of the Trials and Executions in 1816*, Littleport, 1893.

11 Peacock, *op.cit.*, p.14.

12 *Ibid.*, pp.37-8, 52-4.

13 See E.J.Hobsbawm and G.Rudé, *Captain Swing*, 1969.

14 'The Song that is Christmas', *Western Mail Literary Review*, December 4, 1965.

15 'The Poetry', in *Francis Warner. Poet and Dramatist*, ed. T. Prentki, 1977, p.111.

16 R.L. Greene, *The Early English Carols*, revised edition, 1977, pp.xxxii-xxxiii.

17 *Ibid.*, p.clx.

18 See, for example, nos. 150-4.

19 Examples in Greene include nos. 142-4, 147-55.

20 Greene, *op.cit.*, p.clxix.

21 See, for example, Greene nos. 6 and 263.

22 See *Francis Warner. Poet and Dramatist*, ed. T. Prentki, 1977, p.2.
23 *Ibid.*
24 Alexander Montgomerie, *The Cherrie and the Slae*, ed. H. Harvey Wood, 1937, p.24.
25 C.S.Lewis, *English Literature in the Sixteenth Century Excluding Drama*, 1954, p.111.
26 H.P. l'Orange, *Studies on the Iconography of Cosmic Kingship*, Oslo, 1953.
27 *Genesis* 3.3.
28 *Exodus* 8.22.
29 'The Poetry of James Joyce', in *James Joyce. An International Perspective*, ed. S.B. Bushrui and B. Benstock, 1982, pp.122-3.
30 See Chapters Five and Seven.
31 Gloss to 'Maye', line 54.
32 Plutarch, *The Philosophy, Commonly Called The Morals*, translated by Philemon Holland, 1657, p.1083.
33 A useful summary is provided by C.A.Patrides, 'The Cessation of the Oracles: The History of a Legend, *Modern Language Review*, 60, 1965, pp.500-7.
34 Giles Fletcher, *Christs Victorie, and Triumph*, Part One, Stanza 28. Quoted from W.B. Hunter, Jr., *The English Spenserians*, 1977, p.46.
35 Lesley Burnett and Robert Burchfield, 'The Language of Francis Warner', in *Francis Warner. Poet and Dramatist*, ed. T. Prentki, 1977, p.2.
36 Quoted from Paul Oliver, *The Story of the Blues*, 1972, p.101.
37 In *Francis Warner. Poet and Dramatist*, ed. T. Prentki, 1977, p.121.
38 Paula Burnett, ed., *The Penguin Book of Caribbean Verse in English*, 1986, p.xli.
39 John Heath-Stubbs, *Selected Poems*, 1965, pp.87-8; Dick Davis, *The Covenant*, 1984, pp.34-7.
40 These stanza numbers refer to the Fourth Edition of 1879.
41 T.W.H. Crosland, *The English Sonnet*, 1917, p.37.
42 John Fuller, *The Sonnet*, 1972, p.48.
43 Ingrid Melander, *The Transcendent Flame.Thematic/Structural Complexity in Francis Warner's Experimental Sonnets*, Umea, 1987, pp.42-7.
44 On pages 139, 140, 181, 213, 214 (twice), 215 (twice), and 216.

EXPERIMENTAL SONNETS

1 Samuel Daniel, *A Defence of Rhyme* (?1603). Quoted from *Elizabethan Critical Essays*, ed. G. Gregory Smith, 1904, Vol.2, p.366.
2 *Romeo and Juliet*, I.v.92-110.
3 George Puttenham, *The Arte of English Poesie* (1589). Quoted from *Elizabethan Critical Essays*, ed. G. Gregory Smith, 1904, Vol.2, pp.62-3.

4 I am very grateful to Dr. Ingrid Melander for allowing me to see her study of the *Experimental Sonnets*, prior to its publication as *The Transcendent Flame. Thematic/Structural Complexity in Francis Warner's Experimental Sonnets*, Umea, 1987. The present chapter is much indebted to her work.

5 The Oxford English Dictionary, in its entry on 'vivisecting', quotes J.J.G. Wilkinson writing, in 1876, that 'the vivisecting scalpel is all human cruelty'—a sentiment and an image echoed many times in the language of Warner's plays and poems.

6 See E.R.Curtius, *European Literature and the Latin Middle Ages*, translated by W.R. Trask, 1953, pp.83-5. The modesty need not, of course, be wholly affected.

7 All quoted from *Elizabethan Sonnets*, ed. S. Lee, 1904, Vol.2, pp.115, 357, 157.

8 *Francis Warner and Tradition*, 1981, p.34.

9 *As You Like It*, II.vii.137.

10 *Macbeth*, V.v.23-6.

11 Book Two, Chapter VIII, Rule 23.

12 John Webster, *The Duchess of Malfi*, V.iv.53-4.

13 *The Countess of Pembroke's Arcadia*, Book 5, Chapter 5.

14 Ingrid Melander, *The Transcendent Flame*, 1987, p.7.

15 *Delia*, 1592, Sonnet V.

16 The pairing is not uncommon. It occurs, for example, in the second sonnet of Sidney's *Astrophil and Stella* (again in the final couplet); in Sonnet 86 of Spenser's *Amoretti*. It also occurs in another Shakespearian final couplet, that of no. 58—another poem about 'emotional slavery' (to borrow a phrase of John Kerrigan in his edition of Shakespeare's *Sonnets and A Lover's Complaint*, 1986, p.8).

17 *Othello*, V.ii.345.

18 *Astrophil and Stella*, 1, 1-4.

19 *e.g.* 'sweet analytics' (I.i.6); 'sweet Valdes and Cornelius' (I.i.98); 'sweet pleasure' (II.ii.25); 'sweet Mephostophilis' (III.i.58; III.i.196; III.ii.11; V.i.76); 'sweet embracings' (V.i.92); 'sweet Helen' (V.i.99). All references are to the text of the play in *The Plays of Christopher Marlowe*, ed. R. Gill, 1971.

20 Shakespeare's *Sonnets* nos. 35 and 18; Browning 'The Patriot'.

21 *Western Mail Literary Review*, August 7th, 1965.

22 *Amoretti*, no.34. Other interesting variations include no.XI of Lodge's *Phillis* and no.XXV of Smith's *Chloris*.

23 Seamus Heaney, 'Valediction', *Death of a Naturalist*, 1966, p.46.

24 *Volpone*, I.i.8-10.

25 Compare the use of 'chaosses' in Donne's 'Nocturnall upon S. Lucies Day'.

26 Gerard Manley Hopkins, 'God's Grandeur', line 6.

27 Donne, 'The Sunne Rising', line 10.

28 Shelley, *Adonais*, LV.9.

29 Suheil Bushrui, 'The Poetry', in *Francis Warner. Poet and Dramatist*, ed. T. Prentki, 1977, pp.110-30; Ingrid Melander, *The Transcendent Flame*, 1987, pp.18-20.
30 Bushrui, *loc.cit.*, p.123.
31 Lines 47-8.
32 *The Tempest*, IV.i.155; Dryden, 'A Song for St. Cecilia's Day', 60.
33 Melander, *op.cit.*, p.21.
34 *Coriolanus*, I.iii.64-9.
35 The first edition of the *Experimental Sonnets* placed sonnet I on the first right-hand page. Thereafter each opening contained one sonnet on each page. The resulting pairs of sonnets frequently set up striking contrasts. In the *Collected Poems* the pattern is approximated by the presentation of the sonnets two per page, but the effects of contrast are diluted when these pairs are no longer isolated on a single opening.
36 *The Rime of the Ancient Mariner*, line 193.
37 Sonnet 73, line 8.
38 'The Anniversarie', lines 6-7.
39 *The Broken Heart*, V.iii.70 & 75.
40 *Collected Poems*, p.159.
41 *The Republic of Plato*, translated by F.M.Cornford, 1941, p.344.
42 *Lying Figures*, 1972, p.46; *Requiem*, 1980, pp.120.
43 Hardy, *Tess of the d'Urbervilles*, Chapter 59.
44 *Dantis Alagherii Epistolae*, ed. P.Toynbee, 1920, p.177.
45 *Francis Warner and Tradition*, 1981, p.7.
46 Melander, *op.cit.*, p.37.
47 *Thyestes*, II.380. Seneca was later to be an important character in Warner's play *Light Shadows*.
48 Florence Emily Hardy, *The Later Years of Thomas Hardy, 1892-1928*, 1930, pp.13-14.
49 Shakespeare, *Sonnets*, no. 60, line 8.
50 *Ibid.*, no. 63, line 2.
51 Henry King, 'The Dirge', *The Poems of Bishop Henry King*, ed. M. Crum, 1965, pp. 177-8.
52 'Love's Alchymie', lines 11-12.
53 *Faerie Queene*, VII.VI.1.1-6.

LUCCA QUARTET

1 Edward Malins, *'Lucca Quartet'* in *Francis Warner. Poet and Dramatist*, ed. T. Prentki, Knotting, 1977, pp.148-55. Quotation from p.153.
2 *Ibid.*, p.148.
3 *Ibid.*, p.148.
4 *Ibid.*, p.1.

5 See *Defensio Secunda, Works of John Milton*, ed. F.A. Patterson, *et al.*, (Columbia Edition), 1931-40, Vol.8, pp.126-7.
6 Byron, *Letters and Journals*, ed. L.A. Marchand, 1973-82, Vol.IX, p.79.
7 Jakob Korg, *Browning and Italy*, 1983, p.88.
8 *Ibid.*, p.94.
9 *Ibid.*, p.124. Browning actually names the location as Pella in the Alps, but the poem relates to Prato Fiorito.
10 *Ibid.*, p.125.
11 *The Works of John Ruskin*, ed. E.T. Cook and A. Wedderburn, 1903-12, Vol.IV, p.347.
12 *The Diaries of John Ruskin*, ed. J. Evans and J.H. Whitehouse, 1956-, Vol.3, p.801.
13 *Works*, 1903.Vol.XXXIII, pp.xl-xlii.
14 Malins, *op.cit.*, p.151.
15 Similar, and similarly appropriate, traditions of imagery lie behind Lorenzo's tribute to Simonetta which closes Act One Scene Thirteen of *Living Creation*.
16 'Essays on the Minor Poems of Spenser', quoted from *The Works of Edmund Spenser: A Variorum Edition*, ed. E. Greenlaw, C.G. Osgood, F.M. Padelford, 1932-49, *The Minor Poems*, Vol.2, p.654.
17 *De Vulgaria Eloquentia*, translated as *Literature in the Vernacular* by Sally Purcell, Manchester, 1981, p.56.
18 Malins, *op.cit.*, p.151.
19 Donald Posner, *Annibale Carracci. A Study in the reform of Italian painting around 1590*, 2 Vols., 1971.
20 See, for example, Harold E. Wethey, *The paintings of Titian*, Vol.III: *The Mythological and Historical Paintings*, 1975. pp.203-4.
21 Definitions from the *Oxford English Dictionary*. The second incorporates Dr Johnson's definition.
22 E.H. Fellowes, *English Madrigal Verse, 1588-1632*. Revised and enlarged by F.W. Sternfeld and D. Greer, 1967.
23 *Spring Harvest*, II.
24 Quarles' *Emblems* have their part to play in Warner's dramatic works. See my *Francis Warner and Tradition*, 1981, pp.49-63.

MORNING VESPERS

1 *The New Catholic Encyclopaedia*, 1967, Vol.14, p.631. This is no longer strictly true, but the parallel remains valid in general terms.
2 *Lying Figures*, 1972, p.43; *Requiem*, 1980, p.117.
3 *Francis Warner and Tradition*, 1981, p.25.
4 See Chapter II of my *Francis Warner and Tradition*.
5 Charles Williams, *He Came Down From Heaven*, 1984 (Orig. publ.1938), pp.93-4.

6   This poem was later to provide a model of stanza-form for another of Warner's poems, 'Beirut, April 1983'. See Chapter 9.
7   Warner's play *Moving Reflections* was later to take the composition of this Epistle as one of its subjects.
8   See *He Came Down From Heaven*, 1938; *The Figure of Beatrice*, 1943.
9   See Desmond Graham, *Keith Douglas 1920-1944*, 1974, p.220.
10 Keith Douglas, *Complete Poems*, ed. D.Graham, 1978, p.112.
11 'I am like the centre of a circle, to which the parts of the circumference are all related in a similar manner; you, however, are not'. There is a clear, and purposeful, echo of the aphorism associated with St. Bonaventura (it occurs in his *Itinerarius Mentis in Deum*, but may originate much earlier): 'The nature of God is a circle of which the centre is everywhere and the circumference is nowhere'.
12 See Chapter 4 for further instances of Warner's interest in the use of such central emphases.
13   Midway life's journey I was made aware
            That I had strayed into a dark forest,
            And the right path appeared not anywhere.

        Ah, tongue cannot describe how it oppressed,
            This wood, so harsh, dismal and wild, that fear
            At thought of it strikes now into my breast.
    (Translated by Laurence Binyon, 1979).
14 'It is hard to say where the highest point of this arch [of life] is . . . but in the majority I take it to be somewhere between the thirtieth and fortieth year. And I believe that in those of perfect nature it would be the thirty-fifth year'. *Convivio*, IV, xxiii.9. Both text and translation are quoted from Dante, *The Divine Comedy* translated with a commentary by Charles S.Singleton, 1970, *Inferno*, Vol.2, p.3.
15 Williams, *He Came Down From Heaven*, ed.cit. p.96.
16 Lines 39-40.
17 *The Works of Geoffrey Chaucer*, ed.F.N.Robinson, 2nd edition, 1961, p.774.
18 From *Works and Days*, translated by H.G. Evelyn-White (Loeb). Quoted thus in A.B.Giamatti, *The Earthly Paradise and the Renaissance Epic*, 1969 (Orig. publ. 1966), pp.17-18.
19 *Odyssey*, VII, translated by Robert Fitzgerald, 1962, p.102.
20 *Poetical Works*, ed. G. Keynes, 1974 (Orig.publ.1946), p.89.
21 The final couplet of Shakespeare's sonnet 54 is also very relevant here.
22 That the Colin Clout of Spenser's *Shepheardes Calender* was the poet-lover of another Rosalind is a precedent that so allusive a poet as Warner is unlikely to have overlooked.
23 W.B.Yeats, *The Wind Among the Reeds*, 1899, p.74.
24 Barbara Seward, *The Symbolic Rose*, 1960, p.122.
25 Ernst Robert Curtius, *European Literature and the Latin Middle Ages*, translated by W.R.Trask, 1953, pp.94-98.
26 *Ibid.*, p.97.
27 See *Francis Warner and Tradition*, 1981, p.175.

28 III.iii.91-3.
29 From Henry Lichfield, *The First Set of Madrigals of 5 Parts*, 1613. Quoted from *English Madrigal Verse 1588-1632*, ed. E.H. Fellowes, Revised F.W. Sternfeld and D. Greer, 1967, p.130.
30 'The Triple Fool'. Text from John Donne, *The Elegies and The Songs and Sonnets*, ed.H.Gardner, 1965, p.52.

SPRING HARVEST

1 *Spring Harvest*, Martin Booth, Drayton, 1981.
2 There are evident echoes here of the manner of Herrick and his 'cleanly-Wantonnesse' ('The Argument of his Book').
3 *Francis Warner. Poet and Dramatist*, ed. T. Prentki, Knotting, 1977, p.119.
4 W.B. Yeats, *Essays and Introductions*, 1961, pp.366, 370, 383.
5 *Luke* I.76-79; *c.f.* also Milton's *Samson Agonistes*, line 11.
6 Dante, *The Convivio*, quoted thus by Charles Williams, *He Came Down From Heaven*, (Orig.Publ.1938), Grand Rapids, 1984, p.96.
7 *Ephesians*, 5.11.
8 *Ephesians*, 5.8-9.
9 *I John*, 1.5.
10 Act I Scene 6.
11 P. Bonnard, in *The Vocabulary of the Bible*, ed. J.J. von Allman, 1958, p.247.
12 The closing words of *Lying Figures*.
13 *Experimental Sonnets*, XI.

PERSONS AND PLACES

1 See Edmund Blunden *Christ's Hospital. A Retrospect*, 1923.
2 L.A. Marchand, *Byron. A Biography*, 1957, Vol.1, pp.104-5.
3 *The Scotsman*, May 25, 1985, p.5.
4 e.g. *Western Mail Literary Review*, March 13 and April 10 1965.
5 See *Modern Poetry of the Arab World*, translated and edited by Abdullah al-Udhari, 1986.
6 'Two Fragments on Love', II.2.
7 'For Bisharri', in *Gibran of Lebanon*, ed.S.B.Bushrui and P. Gotch, Beirut, 1975, p.1. This poem is not included in Warner's *Collected Poems*.
8 *Eleven Poems* by Edmund Blunden, Cambridge, Golden Head Press, 1965, p.7.
9 The title 'Bells' has a particular significance insofar as it was Blunden's nickname as a schoolboy; see his 'Country Childhood' in

Edwardian England, ed. S. Nowell-Smith, 1964, p.567. See also Warner's 'Inscription: In a copy of Edmund Blunden's *Near and Far*, presented to Robert and Elizabeth Burchfield' (*Collected Poems*, p.182).

10 The poem is dated 'Sligo, 1961', and was presumably written on the occasion of one of the Yeats International Summer Schools.

11 See the acknowledgements in Kathleen Raine's *Blake and Tradition*, 1968, Vol.1. p.x.

12 *Acumen*, 5, p.39.

13 Yeats, 'A Prayer for My Daughter'.

14 *Orlando Furioso*, VII, 11. Quoted from *Ariosto's Orlando Furioso*, Selections from the Translation of Sir John Harington, ed. R. Gottfried, Bloomington, 1963, p.154.

15 *Poetical Works*, ed. J.C. Smith and E. de Selincourt, 1965, (Orig. publ. 1912) p.568.

16 'On my First Son'.

17 *Elizabethan Critical Essays*, ed. G. Gregory Smith, 1967. (Orig. publ. 1904), Vol.2, p.3.

18 *Romeo and Juliet*, III, 5.138; *Macbeth*, I.3.25. (Warner had earlier used the same phrase in the final couplet of the last poem in his *Morning Vespers*).

19 *Pericles*, III.1.27-34.

20 *Pericles*, ed. F.D. Hoeniger, 1969. (Orig. publ. 1963), p.lxxii.

21 Andrew Motion, *Dangerous Play. Poems 1974-1984*, 1985, p.41.

22 See Anthony Bailey's excellent *Rembrandt's House*, 1978.

23 *Ibid.*, p.224.

24 See my *Francis Warner and Tradition*, 1981, p.152.

25 *Africa*, IX, 453-7; as quoted in E. Panofsky, *Renaissance and Renascences in Western Art*, 1960, p.10. 'If your life should—as my soul hopes and wishes—go on long beyond mine, better times are in store for you; this Lethean sleep will not last forever. After the darkness has broken, future generations may be able to return to the clear brightness of the past.' (My translation)

26 Peter Burke, *The Renaissance*, 1964, p.2.

27 E. Panofsky, *op.cit.*, 1960, pp.10-11, 37.

28 Giorgio Vasari, *The Lives of the Painters. Sculptors and Architects*, translated by A.B. Hinds, Revised edition, 1963, Vol.1, p.290.

29 *Acumen*, 5, 1987, p.39. (One small misprint has been corrected in the text quoted here.)

30 The sun-dial is an important emblem in Warner's *Requiem* plays. See my *Francis Warner and Tradition*, 1981, pp.30-32.

31 These examples are taken from *A Book of Sundial Mottoes*, compiled by Alfred H. Hyatt, 1903, pp.13, 15 and 42.

MOVING REFLECTIONS

1 *Francis Warner and Tradition*, 1981, p.204.
2 *Ibid.*
3 *Light Shadows*, 1980, p.iv.
4 *Moving Reflections*, 1983, p.iv.
5 *De Sacra Poesi Hebræorum* (1753), English translation by G. Gregory, *Lectures on Hebrew Poetry*, 1793.
6 *Ecclesiastes* 3.1-8.
7 *Psalms* 102.4-7.
8 *Eclogue* IV, 11.7-10, 13-14, 18-23.
9 G.B. Kerford, 'Logos', *The Encyclopaedia of Philosophy*, ed. P. Edwards, 1967, Vol.5, p.83.
10 See Eusebius, *Praeparatio Evangelica*, 13: 12.
11 D.E. Gershon, 'Logos', *Encyclopaedia Judaica*, 1971, Vol.11, col. 461-2.
12 *Matthew* 27.45 and 51.
13 *The Digby Plays*, ed. F.J. Furnivall, (Early English Text Society), 1896, p.55.
14 'On the Virtues and Offices of Ambassadors', *The Works of Philo Judaeus*, translated by C.D. Yonge, 1855, Vol.4, p.107.
15 *The Oxford History of the Classical World*, ed. J. Boardman, J. Griffin, O. Murray, 1986, p.549.
16 Albino Garzetti, *From Tiberius to the Antonines*, translated by J.R. Foster, 1976, p.72. When, in the Prologue to Act Two of *Moving Reflections*, Warner describes Tiberius as 'torn apart / By bursts of frenzied inactivity' his indebtedness to this passage is clear.
17 Tacitus, *The Annals of Imperial Rome*, translated by Michael Grant, 1979, pp.202-3.
18 *Ibid.*, p.227.
19 See L.R. Taylor, 'Tiberius' Refusals of Divine Honors', *Transactions of the American Philological Association*, 60, 1929, pp.87-101.
20 Tacitus, *op.cit.*, pp.175-6.
21 Quoted from M.R. James, *The Apocryphal New Testament*, 1980 (Orig. publ. 1924), pp.156-7.
22 e.g. The *Report of Pilate* and *The Vengeance or Avenging of the Saviour*. Both texts are included in James.
23 'Pannag is a millet, and has a head heavy with vast numbers of edible seeds. The related Latin word *panis* means bread. Since pannag seeds are hard and very white, they make good flour', Winifred Walker, *All the Plants of the Bible*, 1958, p.162.
24 *Moving Reflections*, p.15.
25 St. Augustine, *Confessions*, translated by C. Bigg, 1900, pp.232-3.
26 This passage may owe something to William Temple's commentary on the relevant verses of the Gospel. See William Temple, *Readings in St. John's Gospel*, 1959 (orig. publ. 1945), p.367. William Temple

baptized Warner, and his wife, Frances Temple (after whom Warner was named) was the poet's Godmother.
27 *The Mishnah*, translated from the Hebrew with Introduction and Brief Explanatory Notes by Herbert Danby, 1977 (orig. publ. 1945), p.323.
28 *Ibid.*, p.250.
29 *Ibid.*, p.323.
30 Though its chronology is far from unambiguous, the Apocryphal *Gospel of the Nativity of Mary* seems to say nothing which would make such an interpretation untenable; see *The Ante-Nicene Fathers*, ed. Rev. A. Roberts, J. Donaldson, 1886, Vol.8, pp.384-7.
31 H.B. Workman, *Persecution in the Early Church*, 1980 (Orig. Publ. 1906), p.9.
32 'Apology', in *The Ante-Nicene Fathers, ed.cit.*, Vol.3, p.22.
33 Warner's chronological foreshortening is evident if one bears in mind the dates of, say, the martyrdom of Ignatius (c.107 A.D.), the correspondence of Pliny and Trajan (c.112 A.D.) and the martyrdom of Polycarp (c.155 A.D.). A plausible date for the death of John would be 100 A.D.
34 J.B. Lightfoot, *The Apostolic Fathers*, 1889, Part II, Vol. II, p.35.
35 *Ibid.*, p.359.
36 D.W. Bauer, *Die Briefe des Ignatius von Antiochia und der Polykarpbrief*, 1920, p.189.
37 *The Oxford Dictionary of the Christian Church*, ed. F.L. Cross, 1957, p.676.
38 W.H.C. Frend, *Martyrdom and Persecution in the Early Church*, 1965, p.197.
39 Lightfoot, *op.cit.*, pp.560-61
40 *Ibid.*
41 *Letters*, 5.19.
42 *Ibid.*, 6.16.
43 *The Letters of the Younger Pliny*, translated by B. Radice, 1974 (orig. publ.1963), pp.293-4.(10.96).
44 *Ibid.*, p.294.
45 *Ibid.*, p.295.(10.97).
46 Lightfoot, *op.cit.*, Part II, Vol III, pp.480-81.
47 *Ibid.*, p.483.
48 Eusebius, *Church History*, III.23, in *A Select Library of the Nicene and Post-Nicene Fathers*, ed. P. Schaff, H. Wace, (Reprinted 1976), Vol.1, p.150.
49 Quoted thus in E. Hennecke, *New Testament Apocrypha*, ed. W. Schneemelcher, 1975, Vol.2, p.78.
50 *Ibid.*, pp.256-8.
51 *The Oxford Dictionary of the Christian Church*, 1957, p.1331.

LIVING CREATION

1 See my *Francis Warner and Tradition*, 1981, especially pp.153-5, 162-3.
2 Gene Brucker, *The Society of Renaissance Florence. A Documentary Study*, 1971, p.192.
3 *Ibid.*, p.196-7.
4 See the account of her in Isidoro del Lungo, *Women of Florence*, Translated by Mary C. Steegmann, 1907, p.201.
5 *A Florentine Diary from 1450 to 1516, By Luca Landucci, Continued by an anonymous writer till 1542*, With Notes by Iodoco del Badia, translated by Alice De Rosen Jervis, 1927.
6 *Ibid.*, p.12.
7 *Ibid.*, pp.23-4.
8 *Ibid.*, p.43.
9 *Ibid.*, pp.52-3.
10 See Judith Hook, *Lorenzo de' Medici*, 1984, p.185.
11 See, for example, P.Kristeller, ed., 'Un Documento Sconosciuto sulla Giostra di Giuliano de' Medici', *La Bibliofilia*, XLI, 1939, pp. 405-17; A. Rochon, *La Jeunesse de Laurent de Médicis (1449-1478)*, Paris, 1963.
12 See Herbert P.Horne, *Botticelli, Painter of Florence*, With Introduction by John Pope-Hennessy, Princeton, 1980 (Orig. publ. in 1908 as *Alessandro Filipepi, Commonly Called Sandro Botticelli, Painter of Florence*). See pp.156 and 354 for the translation and original of this document.
13 *The Letters of Marsilio Ficino*, translated from the Latin by members of the Language Department of the School of Economic Science, London, Vol.I, 1975, pp.54-55.
14 *Ibid.*, p.150.
15 Marsilio Ficino, *The Book of Life*, A Translation by Charles Boer of *Liber de Vita* (Or *De Vita Triplici*), Irving (Texas), 1980, Book Two, Chapter 12.
16 Quoted from *Renaissance Latin Verse*, edited by Alessandro Perosa and John Sparrow, 1979, pp.140-1.
17 *Italian Renaissance Studies*, edited by E.F. Jacob, 1960, p.405.
18 Ovid, *Fasti*, translated by J.G.Frazer, (Loeb), 1951, pp.275-7.
19 Richard C.Trexler, *Public Life in Renaissance Florence*, 1980, p.xvii.
20 From Chapman's completion of Marlowe's *Hero and Leander* (1598). Text from *Elizabethan Minor Epics*, edited by E.S.Donno, 1963, pp.88-89.
21 Trexler, *op.cit.*, p.213.
22 *Ibid.*, p.249.
23 *Ibid.*, pp.238-9.
24 The passage relates to the Feast of San Giovanni in 1491. See Trexler, *op.cit.*, pp.451-2.

25　Contemporary accounts of this episode are numerous. See H.Lucas, *Fra Girolamo Savonarola*, 1906, Chapter XIX, 'The Ordeal by Fire'.

26　Horne, *op.cit.*, p.53.

27　Quoted from *The 'Stanze' of Angelo Poliziano*, translated by David Quint, Amherst, 1979, Book I, Stanzas XLIII-IV. Quint translates as follows (p.23):

> She is fair-skinned, unblemished white, and white is her garment, though ornamented with roses, flowers, and grass; the ringlets of her golden hair descend on a forehead humbly proud. The whole forest smiles about her, and, as it may, lightens her cares; in her movement she is regally mild, her glance alone could quiet a tempest.
>
> From her eyes there flashes a honeyed calm in which Cupid hides his torch; wherever she turns those amorous eyes, the air about her becomes serene. Her face, sweetly painted with privet and roses, is filled with heavenly joy; every breeze is hushed before her divine speech, and every little bird sings out in its own language.

28　*Comento ad alcuni sonetti d'amore*, in Lorenzo de' Medici, *Scritti Scelti*, ed. E. Bigi, 1955, pp.315-6. My translation.

29　Del Lungo, *op.cit.*, p.173.

30　Horne, *op.cit.*, p.53.

31　The 'Primavera' was, in all probability, painted for Lorenzo di Pierfrancesco, rather than for Lorenzo the Magnificent. See Horne, *op.cit.*, p.50. The 'inaccuracy' serves obvious dramatic purposes.

32　See Chapter VII, 'Botticelli's Primavera', in Edgar Wind, *Pagan Mysteries in the Renaissance*, Revised edition, 1967.

33　Michael J.B. Allen, *Marsilio Ficino and the Phaedran Charioteer*, 1981, p.2.

34　See P.O. Kristeller, *The Philosophy of Marsilio Ficino*, translated by V.Conant, 1943, p.27.

35　*Ibid.*, p.29.

36　*Ibid.*

37　See Marsilio Ficino, *The 'Philebus' Commentary*, ed. Michael J.B. Allen, 1975.

38　See *Letters, ed.cit.*, Vol.I, p.40.

39　*Ibid.*, p.44.

40　E.L.S. Horsburgh, *Lorenzo the Magnificent*, 1908, p.320.

41　*The Republic of Plato*, translated by F.M. Cornford, 1941, p.344.

42　See Robert S. Gottfried, *The Black Death. Natural and Human Disaster in Medieval Europe*, 1985 (Orig.publ.1983), pp.36-7.

43　'The blame is his who chooses: God is blameless', Plato, *The Republic*, With an English translation by Paul Shorey, (Loeb), 1942, Vol.2, pp.506-7.

44　*Goethes Werke*, (Bibliothek Deutscher Klassiker), 1966, Vol.4, p.525. Translated as follows by Philip Wayne (*Goethe, Faust. Part Two*, 1959, p.288.):

All things corruptible
Are but a parable;
Earth's insufficiency
Here finds fulfilment;
Here the ineffable
Wins life through love.

45 See the translation by Elizabeth B. Welles, included in *The Earthly Republic. Italian Humanists on Government and Society*, ed. B.G. Kohl and R.G. Witt, 1978, pp.291-322. A good modern account can be found in Sir Harold Acton's *The Pazzi conspiracy: the plot against the Medici*, 1979.

46 The speech has its sources in the American drawings of John White and the prose accounts which accompanied them on first publication. See *America 1585. The Complete Drawings of John White*, ed. P. Hulton, 1984, especially pp. 109, 110 and 113.

47 See Chapter I, 'The Myth of Florence', in Donald Weinstein, *Savonarola and Florence. Prophecy and patriotism in the Renaissance*, 1970.

48 The source for this story of disappointed love is the early biography of Savonarola by Fra Benedetto, *Vulnera Diligenti*. Relevant extracts are printed in Alessandro Gherardi, *Nuovi Documenti e Studi intorno a Girolamo Savonarola*, 1887.

49 Fra Placido Cinozzi, *Estratto d'una epistola fratris Placidi de Cinozis Ordinis Praedicatorum S.Marci de Florentia*, [n.d.]; Pacifico Burlamacchi, *Vita del P.F. Girolamo Savonarola*, 1761.

50 Bartolommeo Cerretano, *Storia Fiorentina*, [n.d.]; see Horsburgh, *op.cit.*, p.352.

51 See Horne, *op.cit.*, pp.184 and 295.

52 Giorgio Vasari, *The Lives of the Painters, Sculptors and Architects*, translated by A.B.Hind. Revised edition, 1963, Vol.II, p.84.

53 Juliana Hill née Cotton.'Death and Politian', reprinted from the *Durham University Journal, June 1954*, With corrections, four appendices, and two illustrations, [n.d.], p.5.

54 Charles Seymour, *Michelangelo's David*, Pittsburgh, 1967, p.61.

55 Ronald M.Steinberg, *Fra Girolamo Savonarola, Florentine Art, and Renaissance Historiography*, Athens (Ohio), 1977, pp.24-25.

56 Horne, *op.cit.*, p.292.

57 Horne, *op.cit.*, p.293.

58 Quoted thus in Steinberg, *op.cit.*, p.71.

59 A useful survey of such interpretations can be found in Steinberg, *op.cit.*, pp.66-77.

60 Horne, *op.cit.*, p.295.

61 *Ibid*, p.300.

62 For this tradition and its relevance to the work of Botticelli, see the two volumes by Mirella Levi D'Ancona, *The Garden of the Renaissance*, Florence, 1977 and *Botticelli's Primavera. A Botanical Interpretation*, Florence, 1983.

63 *Adonais*, lines 460-4.

Index of Works by Francis Warner

General Index